CW01333515

Praise for
Our Dear Friends in Moscow

"*Our Dear Friends in Moscow* is a work of powerfully intimate reportage which tracks the spiritual and emotional journey of a cadre of young reporters who came of age between the fall of the Berlin Wall and the rise of Putin; between those brief years of journalistic freedom and the return of nationalistic censorship in which, for a writer, the choice was to become either a government flack or be hounded into exile or worse. What each of these friends opted to do, resist or submit, and the cost of these decisions on all aspects of their lives yield a portrait of a talented generation who aged into a future that none of them saw coming." —Richard Price, novelist and screenwriter for *The Wire*

"*Our Dear Friends in Moscow* is an illuminating, engrossing, and ultimately heartbreaking portrait of Putin's Russia, told through the eyes of a small group of friends now divided by war, politics, and a vision for the future. Soldatov and Borogan have given us a raw, unsparing, and intimate look at a Russian generation that began in great hope but ended in perpetual conflict. If you're looking for a book that explains how the West fell out with Moscow, you've found it."
—David McCloskey, former CIA analyst and internationally bestselling author of *The Seventh Floor*

"This is a book that lifts the lid on how Putin has not only bludgeoned Russian liberals but also corrupted so many of them. Soldatov and Borogan have written a profound account of the emasculation of Russia's once-vibrant media."

—Robert Service, author of
A History of Modern Russia

"Poignant and illuminating, Soldatov and Borogan tell the story of modern-day Russia through the overlapping lives of a group of journalist friends. *Our Dear Friends in Moscow* is a tale of inspiring courage and wrenching compromise, written with intimacy, affection, and a heavy heart."

—Clarissa Ward, chief international correspondent, CNN, and author of *On All Fronts*

OUR DEAR FRIENDS IN MOSCOW

OUR DEAR FRIENDS IN MOSCOW

THE INSIDE STORY OF A BROKEN GENERATION

ANDREI SOLDATOV | IRINA BOROGAN

PublicAffairs
New York

Copyright © 2025 by Andrei Soldatov and Irina Borogan
Cover design by Ann Kirchner
Cover images © Aleksandr Zubkov via Getty Images;
© Prostock-Studio / Shutterstock.com
Cover copyright © 2025 by Hachette Book Group, Inc.

Hachette Book Group supports the right to free expression and the value of copyright. The purpose of copyright is to encourage writers and artists to produce the creative works that enrich our culture.

The scanning, uploading, and distribution of this book without permission is a theft of the author's intellectual property. If you would like permission to use material from the book (other than for review purposes), please contact permissions@hbgusa.com. Thank you for your support of the author's rights.

PublicAffairs
Hachette Book Group
1290 Avenue of the Americas, New York, NY 10104
www.publicaffairsbooks.com
@Public_Affairs

Printed in Canada

First Edition: June 2025

Published by PublicAffairs, an imprint of Hachette Book Group, Inc. The PublicAffairs name and logo is a registered trademark of the Hachette Book Group.

The Hachette Speakers Bureau provides a wide range of authors for speaking events. To find out more, go to hachettespeakersbureau.com or email HachetteSpeakers@hbgusa.com.

PublicAffairs books may be purchased in bulk for business, educational, or promotional use. For more information, please contact your local bookseller or the Hachette Book Group Special Markets Department at special.markets@hbgusa.com.

The publisher is not responsible for websites (or their content) that are not owned by the publisher.

Print book interior design by Bart Dawson.

Library of Congress Cataloging-in-Publication Data

Names: Soldatov, Andreï author | Borogan, I. (Irina) author
Title: Our dear friends in Moscow : the inside story of a broken generation / Andrei Soldatov and Irina Borogan.
Description: First edition. | New York : PublicAffairs, 2025. | Includes bibliographical references and index.
Identifiers: LCCN 2024044779 | ISBN 9781541704459 hardcover | ISBN 9781541704473 ebook
Subjects: LCSH: Soldatov, Andreï | Borogan, I. (Irina) | Journalists—Russia (Federation)—Biography | Journalism—Political aspects—Russia (Federation) | Russia (Federation)—Politics and government—1991–
Classification: LCC PN5276.S575 A6 2025 | DDC 070.4/3092 [B]—dc20250227
LC record available at https://lccn.loc.gov/2024044779

ISBNs: 9781541704459 (hardcover), 9781541704473 (ebook)

MRQ-T

1 2025

CONTENTS

Preface vii

PART I

Chapter 1: Welcome to *Izvestia* 3

Chapter 2: The Apartment on Gogolevsky Boulevard 15

Chapter 3: Ring of Spies 25

Chapter 4: That's the St. Petersburg Way 36

Chapter 5: Cast Out 44

PART II

Chapter 6: Languishing in Limbo 57

Chapter 7: Playing with the Spies 63

Chapter 8: When the Cold War Was Over 73

Chapter 9: New Beginnings 84

Chapter 10: Comrades in Arms 92

Chapter 11: Beslan 104

Chapter 12: Old Flame 117

Chapter 13: Baranov on the Edge 126

Chapter 14: The Arrangement 138

CONTENTS

Chapter 15: To the Streets — 146

Chapter 16: The Game of Succession — 152

PART III

Chapter 17: Return of the Empire — 165

Chapter 18: The Urinals in Ostankino — 174

Chapter 19: Losing One's Soul — 186

Chapter 20: The End of Old Times — 200

Chapter 21: Dreams of Russia — 207

PART IV

Chapter 22: Ukraine — 221

Chapter 23: Farewell Party — 238

Chapter 24: Foreboding — 248

Chapter 25: The War — 257

Epilogue — 273
Acknowledgments — 291
Notes — 293
Index — 305

PREFACE

Russia has always been on the outskirts of Europe, desperate to be inside. The political history of the country is one of constant battle between isolation and modernization through reconnection with the West. Russia's way of connecting, isolating, and then reconnecting to the world has often been through war: Peter the Great's wars, the wars with Napoleon, and World War II, when soldiers returned from battle with a new taste for Western material culture, and some with Western ideas.

The war that started in February 2022 in Ukraine was part of the same pattern. But this time, Russia was fighting against a former part of the Soviet Union, a war in which contact with the West was minimal. There were no Russian soldiers on the streets of Paris, no British or American soldiers in Russian villages, as there had been German soldiers during World War II.

The result of the war, no matter how it ends on the battlefield, will be Russia's further isolation. The Western world is now tired of Vladimir Putin, and its sanctions against Russia will entrench the country's isolation from Western Europe and the United States.

The re-isolation of Russia is not, however, just a consequence of the war in Ukraine. It is, rather, a deliberate strategy intended to reverse a trend that began in 1991, when Russia became more and more globalized. It came closest to the West in around 2011–2012—the moment when Putin decided to reassert his power. He understood that globalization—through ideas and technologies—was the biggest threat to him. What we've experienced since 2011 is a series of actions and maneuvers intended to detach Russia from the West. After two years of isolation conveniently imposed by COVID-19, Putin made the drastic move of severing the country completely from the West by attacking Ukraine.

This book is the story of Putin's campaign to wall off Russia from the West, told through a group of friends who were on the front line of the ideological battle over Russia's future following Putin's ascent to power. Many of them ended up as key players on the Putin side.

It is a personal story, since they were our friends at a time when we could never have imagined that our lives, our perceptions of truth, and our hopes for our country could diverge so profoundly.

In the spring of 2000, a group of journalists met at *Izvestia*, a Russian daily newspaper. Putin had just been elected president and the country was in the middle of the Second Chechen War.

In the years that followed, we kept each other, and our significant others, in sight: Evgeny Krutikov, a deeply traumatized scion of an elite Soviet family whose ties with military intelligence mystified everybody; Sveta Babayeva, a reporter in Putin's press pool; Petya Akopov, an intellectual with a soft spot for North Korean postage stamps and the North Korean regime; and Zhenya Baranov, a war correspondent with deep ties to Serbia. Later, they were joined by Baranov's wife Olga Lyubimova, a TV host with close family ties to Nikita Mikhalkov, a film director who had a significant ideological influence on Putin.

By 2022, some of our dear friends in Moscow were serving Putin in one way or another. Meanwhile, we were in London, in exile, separated from our families and wanted by Russian authorities.

What happened? How could we have ended up on such violently opposed sides?

PREFACE

To answer that question, we decided to reconnect with our former friends in Moscow. Thanks to the internet, that was possible even from exile. To our surprise, some of them responded and agreed to talk to us.

This book is our attempt to follow this group, and a few other people who would become significant to us, throughout the optimistic first years of the 2000s—a period that included the relative liberalism of Dmitry Medvedev's brief reign, the annexation of Crimea and the repressions that followed in 2016–2021, and the current attack on Ukraine—to show the journey that Russia has made during these years from a highly globalized and aspirational society to a dismal walled-in fortress.

PART I

CHAPTER 1

WELCOME TO *IZVESTIA*

Moscow is at its best in spring. The sunny days and balmy nights arrive after the long and exhausting winter, and every Muscovite tries not to miss the opportunity for long walks along the boulevards and embankments, and the pleasurable, almost euphoric feeling of warm air on bare skin.

On one Saturday in late May, though, the city felt abandoned. Many had already headed out to their suburban dachas—their weekend routine from May to August. There were almost no people on the tree-lined boulevards or in the broad squares. There was barely any traffic on Tverskaya, the ordinarily bustling main city street that heads north from the Kremlin. Even Pushkin Square, the traditional social meeting point, was empty. The greenish figure of Russian poet Alexander Pushkin loomed almost alone over the square atop his monument. He seemed to have turned away in disgust from the dark gray brutalist building to his right, adorned with the logo of the once mighty Soviet newspaper *Izvestia* (The News).

Although we were also on our way toward one of the commuter trains to dacha country, we were not in a holiday mood. We were in our mid-twenties with a problem to solve: we both worked for a newspaper that was dying. It was called *Segodnya* (Today), and its owner, Vladimir Gusinsky, was in trouble. A highly emotional man, a stage director by training who had made his money in banking but dreamt of becoming a Russian Ted Turner, Gusinsky had used his television channel NTV to attack the Kremlin in an election year. He had backed the loser. Once Vladimir Putin was confirmed as Russia's president, Gusinsky was doomed; everybody knew it. His newspaper was doomed, too. Its sources in the government dried up, nobody wanted to talk to its journalists, and its circulation had fallen precipitously. The days when *Segodnya* had proudly imitated the *New York Times* were gone.

We knew we needed to do something. But we didn't want to just move to another newspaper. After three years of covering crimes and terrorist bombings together, we wanted to move to a new level—to do political journalism. And not just any old political journalism. We wanted to write about Russia's security services: the FSB, or Federal Security Service, the main descendant of the KGB, and the intelligence agencies—the SVR (political intelligence) and the GRU (military intelligence). Given that the new president had roots in the KGB and that the ongoing war in Chechnya had officially been designated "a counterterrorism operation," making it the responsibility of the security services, we believed the topic would stay hot for a long time. But it was also a sensitive topic, and we wanted to work for a newspaper that was strong enough that our reporting would not be censored.

We thought we had identified the right place. The daily newspaper *Izvestia* was an old Soviet broadsheet. That spring it was going through a full-scale resurrection—with new management, a new team of journalists, and a new design. Every journalist in town was talking about the resources being pumped into the paper by the two ambitious oligarchs who shared its ownership. *Izvestia*'s editorial office probably had better access to the Kremlin and its agencies than any other news operation in the country. Many of its stories were obviously deeply sourced and insightful.

A former colleague of ours at *Segodnya*, Evgeny Krutikov, had just moved to *Izvestia* to head the political department. We knew he had extensive contacts in Russia's national security world—that was clear from his articles—and he'd been recruiting journalists. Andrei had called him to let him know that Irina was available, and Krutikov had immediately hired her. Krutikov had then invited both of us to a gathering of journalists from *Izvestia*'s political department at a dacha one of them owned—a sign that he might also hire Andrei as well.

The commuter train set off from the Yaroslavl railway station and headed slowly northeast, passing the woods of Losiny Ostrov—Moose Island, in Russian—the biggest national park within Moscow. A half hour later, we got off at the station that served the large elite holiday village of Zagoryanka, just a few miles outside the city. The village, founded as a summer resort for well-off Muscovites in the beginning of the twentieth century, was a typical dacha settlement. Kids rode bicycles on wide paths under century-old trees, their moms walking behind them. The Klyazma River was close by, ideal for swimming on hot summer days.

The standard Moscow dacha is a modest wooden house with a fruit and vegetable garden behind a wooden fence. The dacha Krutikov had invited us to was on a different scale. Behind its fence was a grand house of a dozen rooms on two floors filled with expensive-looking furniture, including an elegant chess table. There was also a huge sauna, with several showers. The host, a journalist named Dima, showed us around. We walked through a library, a stylish living room, and a spacious card room.

"Is this Madonna's villa?" Irina murmured.

Dima smiled and explained cryptically, "My father works in hydrocarbons."

Krutikov later explained that Dima's father was a big shot in the Soviet oil and gas ministry who had made real money in the 1990s.

On a table in the library was a stack of old Soviet newspapers from the late 1940s and 1950s, including issues of *Izvestia*. We all spent some time between drinks dutifully flipping through the yellowed pages.

It turned out that it was not the entire political department that had gathered at the dacha, only the new blood—the journalists Krutikov had recently hired. We did not know them very well, since they were all six or seven years older, which made a big difference. When the Soviet Union collapsed, we were still in our mid-teens. They had already graduated from university, and they had clear memories of Soviet times.

Krutikov was of the same generation, but in his old-fashioned heavy glasses and 1970s haircut he looked much older. His slouch, dry sense of humor, and quiet manner of speaking aged him as well. He was very ambitious for his department, and it soon became apparent that this ambition was part of a larger power struggle at *Izvestia*. The two oligarchs who owned the paper didn't share the asset; they fiercely competed for control, each trying to fill key editorial positions with his own appointees brought in from the outside. Krutikov was one such appointee, part of a bigger group determined to take the reins.

It was unclear whether we had a role in the tussle, but at the very least the weekend was an opportunity to explore Krutikov's contacts in the spy world to expand our own. Andrei had begun writing about the secret services a year before, but it was not easy to develop sources in that world, especially if you hadn't served in the military (we had not) and didn't have family connections in the services (we did not).

As evening descended, a barbecue was duly eaten, vodka and whiskey were in abundant supply, and we found ourselves sharing a porch swing with Krutikov, enjoying the night.

But Krutikov was not in the mood to listen to a pitch from us. Instead, he wanted to talk, and he was good at it. He seemed to have read everything ever written about spies, real or fictitious. It soon became clear that his 1970s appearance was not completely accidental: Krutikov's big hero was John le Carré's fictional British Cold War spy George Smiley. And he was not just a fan of fictional spies.

Though he was a historian by training, he hinted, here and there, at connections to Russian military intelligence, and even at some assignments in the hot spots—the Balkans, the North Caucasus. And yes, he acknowledged, connections had played a part. Soon, sipping whiskey, Krutikov was talking about his family and its tragic fate.

Krutikov's grandfather had been Joseph Stalin's deputy minister of external trade, and briefly deputy prime minister. Krutikov's father, Felix, had been surrounded by the crème de la crème of the Soviet elite from childhood. After the war, at the age of twenty-six, Felix had been sent to Paris to work for Soviet intelligence. With such a pedigree and connections, he was set to enjoy life in Paris in the early 1950s. But when Stalin died in 1953, a vicious power struggle ensued. The young intelligence officer was recalled to Moscow, promptly arrested and tortured, and finally sent to the Gulag.

Evgeny Krutikov believed his father had fallen victim to a conspiracy after Stalin's death, and it seemed he had never entirely come to terms with his family's loss of status.

"So, your family were servants of the regime?" Irina asked, only half-joking, as Krutikov finished this part of his family saga.

Irina's family had suffered a lot under Stalin. Her relatives on her mother's side were well-off farmers and Orthodox Old Believers, a sect that had opposed the official Church for centuries, a sort of Russian version of the Quakers, well self-organized and wealthy—and indeed her family had owned a beautiful, spacious house with a big garden on the high bank of the Volga until 1930. It was around that time that Stalin consolidated his power and began his attack on the peasantry. Her family was thrown onto the street, and several family members were killed. Her father had come from a region of Bessarabia bordered by Romania, Ukraine, and Moldova that would be occupied by Soviet troops in 1940 and again in 1944. The head of the family at that time, Irina's granddad, was sent to work in the labor army in Siberia. Many in his village died of famine resulting from forced collectivization.

Krutikov looked at us sharply. "Of course not. We *were* the regime," he said, with what we assumed was bitter irony.

Krutikov was a natural storyteller. It felt as though Stalin's bloody and omnipotent ministers and spies were next door, plotting their schemes under a green lamp in the Moscow woods. He was charming, mysterious, and intriguing. And once it was established that both Krutikov and Andrei were fans of the *Lethal Weapon* movies, Andrei's employment at *Izvestia* was settled.

It seemed like the beginning of another beautiful friendship.

We quickly got used to commuting every morning to the dark gray six-story asymmetrical cube on Pushkin Square where *Izvestia* had been headquartered since the 1920s. The building had become an internationally known symbol of early Soviet constructivism. The newspaper itself had been founded in 1917 as the media outlet of the revolutionary council of workers and soldiers. It presented itself as a very influential paper, and indeed, in our first weeks there, in early June 2000, we sensed we'd joined a media outfit with real access to the Kremlin. Government officials were happy to answer calls from *Izvestia*'s reporters, and the reporters were welcome at the Kremlin and the White House, the seat of the Russian government.

The paper had always been proud of its elite status. When Nikita Khrushchev became the leader of the Soviet Union after Stalin's death, he made his son-in-law the editor of *Izvestia*—an indication of how intimately connected the paper was to the center of power.

Izvestia's links to the Kremlin survived the turbulent reforms of the 1990s, but things got more complicated in the new capitalist Russia.

In the summer of 2000, when we arrived, the Administration of the President owned the dark gray building, but the newspaper was funded by two Russian oligarchs. One of them was Vagit Alekperov, the Soviet deputy minister of the Oil and Gas Industry, who in 1991 had taken three large ministry-controlled oil fields and two oil refinery factories and set up Lukoil, which became Russia's largest private oil company.[1] The other was Vladimir Potanin, the former Russian first deputy prime minister, who had benefited from participating in the murky "loans for shares" scheme in 1995, in which powerful banks lent money to the Russian government in exchange for shares of some of the country's most valuable assets. Potanin and his business partner's bank had ended up owning 51 percent of Norilsk Nickel, the world's largest manufacturer of palladium and refined nickel.[2] For Alekperov and Potanin, *Izvestia* was clearly a political asset rather than a media company. They had both created huge business empires thanks to their political connections, and they wanted to maintain their access to and influence with the Kremlin.

Izvestia's journalists, we soon discovered, were a peculiar mix of three groups. Two of them consisted of the people recently hired by representatives of each of the oligarchs; the third contained remnants of the Soviet generation, who had proved to exhibit surprisingly good survival skills.

Inside, the building showed its age. The wood-paneled corridors were of a type that was omnipresent in the Soviet government offices of the 1980s, and the large correspondents' rooms featured a pneumatic tube system for dispatch delivery, rumored to still be operational. The bosses, just like in Soviet times, had huge offices on a separate floor—the second—complete with reception rooms with red carpets. Back in Soviet times, those red carpets clearly signified that the occupant belonged in the top echelons of Soviet bureaucracy, as they could be found only in the offices of Communist bosses.

Our political department on the third floor was thriving—phones rang all day, and the floor was abuzz with reporters coming and going. The windows of our spacious office, where four reporters had their desks, faced Tverskaya Street. In the summer the windows were open, and we soon got used to the smell of Mongolian barbecue from a restaurant below.

After submitting our stories, we would inevitably hang out in Krutikov's office. Krutikov appeared to know an awful lot about the murky and fascinating world of spies, and the war zones where the intelligence wars were fought after the end of the Cold War: the Balkans and the North Caucasus. He would mention in passing names of warlords and leaders of militants we had only just started to learn about. We believed we could learn a lot from Krutikov, and he seemed to enjoy our attention.

On one particular day, every correspondent but one was in the third-floor office. The missing reporter was Sveta Babayeva, a fierce, miniature blonde who was part of Putin's press pool, assigned to cover the day-to-day activities of the new Russian president. She was in the Kremlin, as usual. She adored Putin, and he seemed to like her too, enough for her to have a photo of the two of them standing side by side that helped with the traffic police when she was stopped for speeding, which she frequently was.

It was late afternoon, and Krutikov had already sent his two Ossetian friends—Alan Kachmazov and Dmitry Medoyev, who always hung out in his office—out for a bottle of cheap and probably fake Bushmills. It was a daily ritual he'd developed since becoming head of the department to celebrate the first deadline of the day. *Izvestia* was different from all the other papers in Moscow because it had two deadlines—the first at 3:00 p.m., for proofs to be sent to the Far East edition, and then the second one in the evening, for the Moscow edition.

By the time the bottle arrived, Krutikov had returned from the afternoon editorial meeting, looking as if he'd survived a storm. Helping himself liberally to the whiskey, he told us what was going on. The bosses on the second floor were in a fierce dispute—over a cartoonist.

In a few months, Boris Yefimov, a Soviet cartoonist, would turn one hundred. Yefimov had been contributing to *Izvestia* since the 1930s, so the bosses needed to decide whether to celebrate his big day.

Yefimov's long career had started when he was sixteen years old and drew cartoons of the members of the first Russian Duma—back then he had lived in Ukraine, part of the Russian Empire. After the Russian Revolution of 1917, he had moved to Moscow, becoming one of the main cartoonists attacking the political enemies of the Communist regime. He was also the creator of the most famous poster glorifying Stalin's secret services during the Great Purge. Yefimov was beloved by Stalin—not because the Soviet dictator valued his skills: Stalin preferred dealing with broken people, and Yefimov was scarred for life when his brother Mikhail Koltsov (the brothers were Jews, well aware of Russia's tradition of antisemitism, so they'd taken Russian pseudonyms)—a prominent Soviet journalist, editor-in-chief of the major Soviet satiric magazine *Krokodil*, and one of Stalin's top war correspondents, who had covered the civil war in Spain—had been arrested and killed on Stalin's orders, accused of being a Trotskyite. Yefimov, who had published a book of cartoons with a foreword by Leon Trotsky, knew how close he came to being shot as well. And so he loyally served as chief cartoonist of *Izvestia*, taking his orders directly from Stalin.

Yefimov had survived under all the political regimes of the Soviet Union and remained active even after its collapse. His survival method was never to ask himself any difficult questions about his own role in supporting the regime and attacking the regime's enemies—whoever they were.

By 2000, his great age lent Yefimov some respectability—he was now seen as an integral part of *Izvestia*'s glorious past. He'd gotten a bit of international recognition after he'd sent a card to Britain's Queen Mother on her one-hundredth birthday and received a response—and her congratulations on his ninety-ninth birthday.

Krutikov told us that the editor-in-chief of *Izvestia*, Mikhail Kozhokin, felt uneasy about the Yefimov issue. Kozhokin was not an outsider to the system; his brother led the Russian intelligence agency's leading think tank. But he was from a new generation: a smooth and suave manager with the look of a Western banker, brought to the newspaper by the oligarch Potanin. He saw no reason to celebrate the living embodiment of Stalin's vicious propaganda.

But the editor-in-chief faced fierce resistance from the old guard. The battle lasted for weeks. No one on the junior staff was ever consulted; the struggle was fought exclusively on the second floor, and we had no access to it other than what Krutikov told us.

After a month of deliberating and arguing, the newspaper quietly canceled the Yefimov celebrations—not because of his reputation as Stalin's attack dog, but because a deputy editor, also a relic of the Soviet-era *Izvestia*, had had an argument with Yefimov in the 1960s and couldn't let it go.

At *Izvestia*, Stalinism still cast a very long shadow, as we would regularly be reminded.

On June 13, the Russian wire agencies broke the news that the security services had arrested Vladimir Gusinsky, the once powerful media mogul and owner of *Segodnya*, where we'd worked, and the NTV channel. He was brought to the Butyrka—a medieval prison in the center of Moscow—and placed in a tiny cell with six other inmates. When he was allowed to see his lawyer, Gusinsky wrote a message on a copy of his arrest warrant: "It is a political intrigue, organized by high-placed officials for whom freedom of speech poses a danger and an obstacle to their plans."[3]

The Kremlin wanted to force him to give up his media assets. An arrest of such a prominent media mogul had never happened before, and we thought it couldn't last for more than a few days. And it didn't. Gusinsky was released in three days as part of a deal in which, in exchange for his freedom, he promised to give up NTV. When he left prison, he went directly to the offices of his media company and recorded a video statement declaring that he had agreed to sell the company under duress.

We were surprised that Putin had gone so far. But what truly shocked us was that some of our former colleagues at *Segodnya*, who had also moved to *Izvestia*, were quick to rationalize the arrest. The first to do so was a leading arts critic, ostensibly a person with liberal views. The arts critic attacked the NTV channel, accusing it of bias, and hinted that a liberal satirist named Viktor Shenderovich, who had a show on NTV called *Kukly* (Puppets), regularly sought advance approval of the themes for the show from his bosses, contrary to what Shenderovich claimed. *Kukly*, a show featuring puppet characters portraying Russian politicians, was the most watched show in the country, but everyone in Moscow knew Putin hated his puppet. Shenderovich, indignant, responded with an open letter to the arts critic. The two then talked, and *Izvestia* published their conversation.[4]

It was a conversation between two very polite and intelligent people who had completely ceased to understand each other. Shenderovich, prophetically, warned that 2000 could be a second 1929, the last year of relative freedom before Stalin's terror: "We, settling our old inter-group scores today, are risking ending our discussion in the same place where the right and left 'deviationists' [the term used by Stalin to attack his political opponents] ended it in their time."

History proved Shenderovich right: soon, Gusinsky was forced into exile, and NTV was cleansed of troublemakers and turned into a strident Kremlin propaganda outlet.

In the summer of 2000, the Russian journalist community did not act as a united front against the Kremlin's attack on Gusinsky. Krutikov, who rarely wrote under his own name, made an exception that time—and also came out in support of the Kremlin's attack. Krutikov held a grudge against journalists working for Gusinsky's media companies—he considered them elitist and aloof. Many journalists in Moscow felt that way about Gusinsky's media. Gusinsky generously financed his journalists—his funding went to their ambitious reporting projects as well as their salaries, always the highest in Moscow—but the argument used by those who supported the attack was that Gusinsky had become too ambitious politically and had used his media, and his journalists, as his foot soldiers.

We knew that Gusinsky was an oligarch, and a very ambitious one, but we believed that a competition among oligarch-funded media was still better than Kremlin control.

Irina wrote a story criticizing Gusinsky's detention as a politically motivated attack on the media, and Krutikov allowed it to be published. It was possible then to have different opinions even on such a sensitive topic at *Izvestia*, but on the inside, the newspaper felt like a very shaky construction. There were passionate arguments about the oligarch owners, fueled by fake Irish whiskey. It was not entirely clear how the newspaper would survive if and when it encountered a real crisis.

CHAPTER 2

THE APARTMENT ON GOGOLEVSKY BOULEVARD

Gogolevsky Boulevard, named after the writer Nikolai Gogol, starts in the small square in front of the massive golden-domed Cathedral of Christ the Saviour and ends in the shadow of the white rectangular monstrosity that houses the General Staff of the Armed Forces in the very center of Moscow. Lined with prerevolutionary four- and five-story apartment buildings featuring big windows and decorations on the front, the boulevard is probably the prettiest in the city. The traffic on each side of the boulevard is noisy, but between them, on an unpaved walkway protected by centuries-old lindens and maples and lined with benches, young mothers walk with their kids.

In summer, in the evening, groups of young people gather on the benches. In July 2000, almost every night, a bench close to the cathedral was inevitably occupied by a cheerful, seemingly carefree group of men and women in their early thirties.

They were a diverse lot—journalists, a dentist, a lawyer, a couple of young female socialites. Bottles of wine and vodka were passed around and poured into glasses. The glasses had been brought out from the apartment building across the boulevard, where three rooms were occupied by Petya Akopov, chief correspondent in the political department of *Izvestia,* and his wife, Marina. We became part of that group, having bonded quickly with Petya after we met him at the dacha in Zagoryanka.

Soft-spoken, bespectacled, thin, with dark Mediterranean features that betrayed his Armenian and Italian ancestors and an easy smile, Petya always let his wife dominate the conversation until it got to politics.

Petya appeared to us a true scion of the Moscow intelligentsia. In their apartment full of books, he had a painting that looked like one from Vincent van Gogh's *Sunflowers* series on the wall—but his father had painted it: painting, Petya explained, was his father's hobby. A historian by training, Petya had started working as a journalist in 1991. He had gone to South Ossetia when the war broke out with Georgia and sent a few dispatches from there that became his ticket into a journalism career. Krutikov, who had studied with Petya at university, got him his first newspaper job.

Petya was always very critical of the West and didn't want to work for any form of media that promoted liberal values. He found himself at *Izvestia* thanks to Krutikov again and chose to overlook *Izvestia*'s pro-Western stance. He told us he'd gone into "internal emigration." He seemed like an eccentric, with a retro set of opinions softly spoken even if they were deeply held, and therefore no great threat to anyone.

Somehow, Petya managed to bring a carefree style to the editorial office. He often walked to work without a bag of any kind, carrying only a small notebook, a pencil, and a mobile phone.

The conversation among the group that gathered at the bench on the median strip of Gogolevsky sooner or later turned to politics. This usually happened later in the evening, after we had safely relocated to the Akopovs' apartment. Despite his charming manners, Petya's strong political views might not be appreciated by people on other benches on Gogolevsky.

Petya insisted on seeing everything in terms of an epic historical context, of empires and superpowers fighting centuries-old battles. He believed, for instance, that Russia was a much more spiritual civilization than the West, thanks to the many Russian monasteries in the north, and that, to him, explained the nature of the eternal conflict between Russia and the West. He also entertained an idea that the large number of disabled people he saw on European streets was a sign of Western Europe's inevitable decline. Apparently, it never occurred to Petya that the disabled in Russia were nowhere to be seen because they were unable to leave their apartments in many provincial towns owing to the lack of basic infrastructure—elevators and ramps with appropriate slopes. Petya also believed that Russia should turn east—to China—instead of to Europe. Once he proclaimed himself "a Russian fascist." But he would make all these shocking claims in a shy, faltering voice, with no hint of aggression.

Most of the group found his views amusing, but hardly more.

Promoting such ideas in our circles was usually taken as some form of playful provocation or a daring intellectual game. Petya's views matched those of a marginal National Bolshevik Party led by the provocative bohemian writer Eduard Limonov. The party was famous mostly for conducting spectacular street actions in Moscow, such as marches with the slogans "End the reform this way: Stalin—Beria—Gulag," and its radical aesthetics—the party's newspaper used a hand grenade as an insignia and was called *Limonka*, which means "hand grenade" in Russian but is also wordplay with the name of the party leader, Limonov. Petya, of course, was a big fan.

In the previous decade, these kinds of views had been popular among people with whom we had little contact, such as pensioners and veterans of the Soviet army, dozens of whom often gathered near the Lenin Museum building, down from Red Square, where they sold small-circulation newspapers calling for the restitution of the Soviet Union and condemning democratic reforms as a Western conspiracy. There were people with similar views at the State Duma, but they were either old Soviet Communists or marginal nationalists dreaming of the Russian empire. In the 2000 State Duma, the Communist Party held just 88 seats out of 450.[1] They had some marginal influence on Russian politics, but no presence in the government.

It was Vladimir Putin who now called all the shots. His cabinet was full of economists who touted liberal ideas, and who seemed at that moment to be promoting the rule of law, despite Vladimir Gusinsky's controversial detention. That same month, Putin granted a big interview to *Izvestia* under the front-page headline "Russia Should Not Be and Will Not Be a Police State." Accompanying the article was a photograph of Putin standing alongside editor-in-chief Mikhail Kozhokin and Sveta Babayeva in Putin's study in the Kremlin. When asked whether there was a need for a new Russian ideology, Putin said he believed that would be completely meaningless. "It cannot be invented on purpose," Putin had responded. "The moral and ethical values of the people have been developing over centuries. In Russia, as in any self-respecting state, there is a base on which we can build our own, so to speak, moral building. But for this we need to strengthen the state, the economy, and democratic institutions. Including the free press."[2]

It was a nice interview, full of high-minded promises, including ones to restrain bureaucrats, and a show of humbleness—though Babayeva admitted to us afterward that Putin had kept her and Kozhokin waiting for four hours before letting them into his Kremlin study to speak with them. This was the traditional Russian bureaucratic way of letting people know that you are almost too busy to talk to them, and way more important than they are. Putin was letting *Izvestia* know who was boss, whatever emollient comments he made for the interview.

On a warm evening in July 2000, we were sitting at the bench, talking and laughing, when a figure walked toward us, a tall, thin man with laughing eyes and a loping stride that might have belonged to Don Quixote.

"Baranov!" Petya Akopov exclaimed.

Zhenya Baranov, an intrepid war correspondent for a Russian TV channel, had just returned from a reporting trip to Chechnya. He was Petya's closest friend. Among journalists it was known that because Baranov's small TV channel lacked necessary connections in the Russian military, his way of getting close to the events was to jump with his cameraman into a passing vehicle and use his charm (and some rubles) to convince the driver to get them as close as possible to the front line.

Baranov and Petya's friendship dated to their childhood. They'd met through their parents and gone to the same university. Krutikov had hung out with them back then too, but had fallen out with Baranov many years before when, he claimed, Baranov stole his girlfriend. He never set foot in Petya's apartment on Gogolevsky for fear that Baranov might show up.

The relationships among this group of friends were intricate and complex.

Cheerful and energetic, with the kind of perfect veneer that only TV presenters have, Baranov immediately hijacked the conversation. He was fresh from a war zone and full of news. Although the Kremlin had proclaimed the end of the military stage of the war that spring after the army successfully invaded and occupied Chechnya, the war was far from over. It was, in fact, getting more brutal. Earlier that month, Chechen militants had hit several Russian military bases in Chechnya using five trucks filled with explosives driven by suicide bombers. The assaults left more than fifty soldiers dead. It was just a preview of the many terrorist attacks to hit cities across Russia in the years to come. Nobody on our bench was under any illusion that the war was likely to end soon.

As darkness fell, we all moved as usual to Petya and Marina's apartment.

The five-story structure where the Akopovs lived had been built early in the nineteenth century as an apartment building for the well-off. The architect, inspired by an Italian palazzo, had designed a fancy rusticated mezzanine featuring arched windows. The apartment at the mezzanine level, essentially the first floor, where the Akopovs resided, had been owned before the revolution by the family of a wealthy doctor. In Soviet times, it had been turned into "a communal," and several families had shared it for decades. Some years before, Petya had bought out two rooms in the apartment, where he and Marina now lived.

It was a spacious apartment by Moscow standards: four rooms, with high ceilings and windows facing the boulevard to the right of the entrance; a long, narrow room with a window facing the courtyard on the left side, which Petya had turned into his library; a big kitchen; and a bathroom with a clawfoot bathtub—all that remained of the doctor's time. Two rooms were occupied by Natalia Alexandrovna, a tiny Crimean Greek woman in her seventies who often emerged into the common kitchen to have a coffee and cigarette with the Akopovs' late-night guests. The last two rooms—a bedroom and a living room with an arched window where the couple entertained their guests—were the Akopovs'. There, it was Marina's realm.

She was certainly not the type of wife we expected of Petya. From the look of him, Petya spent more time with books than with human beings. But Marina was no librarian. An attractive blonde with a loud voice who chain-smoked, she loved imitating Marilyn Monroe's makeup style, with glossy red lipstick and a distinct eyeline. Marina adored Paris. The city matched her temperament, she believed—and she had in mind the bohemian Paris of the 1920s, the Paris of Pablo Picasso and Ernest Hemingway. She brought a little of the Left Bank to Gogolevsky Boulevard.

Marina hosted her bohemian parties in the spacious living room with its large sofa, a table with two chairs under a shiny chandelier dangling from the high ceiling, and a couch at the arched window. With a glass of wine or vodka or champagne always in hand, she treated her guests to stories of her eventful past in the late 1980s in Leningrad, now St. Petersburg. She had grown up in a working-class family but had not the slightest intention of following in her parents' footsteps. She loved parties, and she hated both getting up early and going to work.

There were plenty of opportunities to have this kind of life in the late 1980s in her hometown. Marina, a pretty girl, missed none of them. She and her girlfriends made friends with artists, musicians, and foreigners who came to the seaport to make easy money in the collapsing Soviet Union, then moving fast toward capitalism. She moved to Moscow in search of a bright future and ended up marrying Petya, which surprised his mother. Marina didn't much care. The girlfriends with whom she had shared her youth in St. Petersburg also moved to Moscow, and they would drop by often. Those resourceful girlfriends kept partying in Moscow, now moving in the circles of oligarchs and restaurateurs, and sometimes they brought their suitors with them.

At a certain point during Marina's parties on Gogolevsky, the time would inevitably come to send Petya out for more vodka. Petya would obediently comply and head out for the nearest all-night shop on the corner. Sometimes, on an evening when his interest in partying flagged, he would withdraw into his library, filled with books and stamps. He had a lifelong obsession for Chinese and North Korean stamps, which he collected and pored over in his numerous albums—probably the main reason for his horrible eyesight. His library numbered more than 2,000 books, mostly about China and North Korea.

On the July night when Baranov joined us, Marina stepped back, at least for a while, to let him hold forth. But Baranov didn't want to talk about the war. Instead, he wanted to learn more about us, the two newcomers in attendance, fresh faces in a group where relationships had been defined years ago. Irina tried to find common ground by identifying potential mutual acquaintances. At *Segodnya* we had known a young woman named Anna Pavlova,* a bright brunette with a big personality who worked in the fact-checking department. We knew she had gone to university with Petya, so Irina thought Baranov might know her as well.

It turned out that four of our friends had graduated from the same university—Petya Akopov, Baranov, Krutikov, and Anna. All of them were trained as historians, not journalists, though the Soviet Union, and then Russia, had a well-established system of journalism training, led by the journalism faculty at Moscow State University (MSU).

Studying journalism at the university was a highly prestigious endeavor. In Soviet times, it was difficult to get into the program without the right family connections, and journalist dynasties were quietly but firmly encouraged by the regime. But being a journalist in the Soviet Union was prestigious only up to a point. Soviet society was pretty strict: the ruling elites were mostly bureaucrats who were educated as engineers, then trained at a Communist Party school. Journalists had a significant role in the hierarchy—to be well-paid propagandists—but very rarely did they make it to the level where decisions were made, to become "the regime" themselves, as Krutikov had put it.

In the 1990s, after the collapse of the Soviet Union, Boris Yeltsin had changed that. He appointed a journalist, Valentin Yumashev, a ghostwriter of Yeltsin's memoirs who had married his daughter, as chief of the presidential administration. Several prominent journalists, including the editor of *Pravda*, made it to the Duma as deputies. One journalist—Yuri Shchekochikhin, a popular and universally

---

* "Anna Pavlova," just "Anna" later in the book, is a pseudonym for a reporter whose real identity we feel the need to protect at this time.

respected reporter who was very critical of the Russian security services and the war in Chechnya—became deputy chairman of the Duma security committee, in charge of overseeing legislation and funding for the security services, while retaining his position as head of investigations at *Novaya Gazeta* (New Newspaper).

Neither of us had graduated from the MSU journalism program. Irina had studied at the Academy of Printing Arts; Andrei graduated with a degree in journalism, but from a smaller and less prestigious university. Sveta Babayeva did go to MSU but had studied law.

Many of our colleagues and friends at other newspapers had no training in journalism at all. In the early and mid-1990s, new Russian media didn't care much about their reporters' education. What mattered to the editors most was that you were active and eager to work, and some new newspapers, such as the daily *Kommersant*, went as far as making a point to not hire journalists with Soviet experience at all, focusing instead on people with an education in economics. The *Kommersant* editors believed that Soviet journalism, even of Mikhail Gorbachev's pro-democracy *perestroika* sort, was a combination of propaganda and moralizing, and hardly appropriate to the new capitalist era of the 1990s. The new Russian media wanted to break the Soviet tradition, and to a great extent they succeeded—there were not many journalists in their forties and fifties still around.

Irina asked Baranov about Anna.

"She is not Anna Pavlova to me; she is Anna Borisova!" exclaimed Baranov, using her patronymic.

He grew visibly agitated. Obviously, Irina had been right. He knew her and made a point to use her maiden name. Anna was married to a very well-known TV presenter and had taken his name. This had happened years before, but apparently, it was not old news for Baranov. "We were like *this!*" he said, making a gesture to suggest an electric discharge. It was all a bit sudden and a bit embarrassing:

we hadn't expected Baranov to open up about his love life quite so quickly.

Andrei quickly changed the subject to work, a more comfortable topic. But the work we were most excited about at that moment was still secret. For two months we had been working frantically on our personal project, independent from *Izvestia*: the launch of a new website focused on the Russian security and intelligence services.

CHAPTER 3

RING OF SPIES

We'd gotten new jobs, we'd made new friends, and we were about to launch a new project of our own. The winter depression that had hit us several months earlier, after the old and disoriented president, Boris Yeltsin, had appointed a former KGB colonel, Vladimir Putin, to be his successor, had retreated, and we were full of hope.

Moreover, even though the Kremlin had launched a crusade against the independent media in the country—with Gusinsky's NTV as the first casualty—a game-changing new technology had emerged. The internet was booming, and dozens of new websites were appearing every day. Putin did not yet grasp its potential and was not paying much attention to what was going on there.

We believed this new medium was a great opportunity for us and might level the playing field that was otherwise tilted against us because of our relative youth. With only four years of experience in journalism, we were competing with the generation of journalists whose careers had started in the late 1980s and the early 1990s, a time when a new Russian elite was forming. In that tumultuous atmosphere of brutal political infighting, when the Soviet state was withering away and it was not yet clear what would take its place, our older and more fortunate colleagues had gotten to know many officials and politicians before they took up top-level positions in the new Russian government. Those officials and politicians had kept talking with them, not only because they had grown to trust them, but also because the political situation was not getting any more predictable. Even the top-level officials needed an early warning system, a service that insightful journalists could provide to their sources.

We looked at them with admiration. Unlike us, they were on a first-name basis with ministers, could call them, and walked with ease through the corridors of the government and the presidential administration. None of this access was available to us, and we understood we needed to find our own way in. We hoped that the internet might be our entry point.

In our small apartment in a nondescript Moscow high-rise, we had been talking for hours about what our own website could be. We had many ideas, some of them quite impractical. Launching a website cost money. And when we tried to persuade some businessmen to invest in one of our projects—promising them a profit from online advertising, which few people, including us, had any idea how to make happen—we failed to impress anyone enough for them to invest.

Finally, we decided to do what we really wanted to do: build a website about the Russian security services. Even though the security services had interfered in the lives of everybody in the country for decades, there was no publicly available source where one could get even basic information about them.

In the 1990s, the successor agencies of the KGB were in retreat, losing prestige and power, but for some reason no one had bothered to collect information about them and put it somewhere everyone could find it. Here was our chance to make something unique. Putin had come from the KGB, after all, and the security services were destined to play an increasing role in Russian society.

The idea was inspired by two sources. For several years, Andrei had loved browsing a website called the Project on Government Secrecy of the Federation of American Scientists (FAS). The long-term director of the project, Steven Aftergood, had created an impressive online collection of open-source data on the US intelligence community by digging into congressional reports and previously undisclosed or hard-to-find government documents and by bombarding the US intelligence community with Freedom of Information Act requests. It had become a crusade to reduce the scope of national security secrecy and promote public access to government information.[1]

The second inspiration came from a community of amateur radio enthusiasts who called themselves "Spooks." Dispersed around the world, they had been listening for decades to radio stations that they believed were operated by intelligence agencies, embassies, and the military. Although they could not decipher encrypted messages, they meticulously monitored changes in stations' activities, and sometimes this could lead to fascinating discoveries. When a group of Cuban spies was arrested in Miami in 1998, for example, for trying to penetrate a US military facility in South Florida, one radio amateur had noticed that a particular radio station changed its activity level from a weekly to a daily basis. The station was nicknamed "(S7) Russian man," because, years back, a male voice had read numbers in Russian on a frequency used by that radio transmitter. The observation about the changes gave the amateurs a lot to think about. Were these Cuban agents acting on behalf of Havana, or Moscow? It appeared that they could be acting on orders coming from Russia.

The Spooks maintained a mailing list available to everyone, and because its archive was online, and the radio enthusiasts could contribute to it from any country in the world, it became a sort of global civic operation of keeping spy stations under close watch. It also provided one answer to Juvenal's challenge: "Quis custodiet ipsos custodes?" (Who's going to guard the guards themselves?).[2]

Andrei had been fascinated by that community for years and stayed in touch with Ary Boender, the editor of the mailing list, who was based in the Netherlands. The Spooks were a dramatic example of what ordinary people with no access to secrets could do to monitor the most secret organizations in the world if they could unite their efforts online.

Andrei talked incessantly about launching something that would resemble a combination of the FAS Project on Government Secrecy and Spooks—a website that would collect and store documents about Russia's security agencies, but would also have information contributed by journalists, activists, and basically anyone interested in the topic from across the country, and maybe from other countries as well.

It took two months to finalize the idea. Russian newspapers were now routinely running stories about Russian intelligence and security services, and the stories were full of revelatory details. But it was very difficult to understand from them how the far-reaching post-KGB system, with its numerous departments and directorates, both in Moscow and spread across the country, was designed and how it worked. The security services themselves remained ultrasecretive. When they reported on their own operations, they went to great lengths to disclose as little information as possible. Every once in a while they'd produce an innocuous press release reading something like, "Our operatives arrested five poachers in the Volga region," which said almost nothing.

The site was designed to be an online watchdog of Russia's security and intelligence services. We wanted it to include dossiers on all the secret services in Russia, including organizational histories and bios of the generals and colonels involved in them—whoever we could find through open sources. To attract users, we asked our close friend and film critic Marina Latysheva to create a popular culture section that would cover espionage-related fare, from James Bond movies to John le Carré novels. The only thing left undecided was the name of the site, until Irina came up with "Agentura," a word that in Russian means "a ring of spies."

The title had a double meaning for us, because we also hoped to create a community of journalists writing about security services for different newspapers. In the 1990s, criminal reporters, including us, also covered terrorist attacks, and we relied on the feeling of camaraderie one developed standing together for hours at crime scenes cordoned off by the police: around the dead body of a contract-killed businessman, or the rubbled crater where a bomb had exploded. We had talked to some of our colleagues, and we knew that many of them were interested in sharing information. We wanted information about security agencies and their personnel to be centralized on the web, not subject to the traditional journalistic competition.

We still needed technical and financial backing. After some deliberation, we decided to approach Andrei's father. Alexey Soldatov was a Russian internet pioneer. In the late 1980s, as a head of the computation center at the Kurchatov Institute, the major nuclear research facility in the country, he had set up a team of programmers to build a computer network inside the institute. He had dreamed of such a network ever since his first and only fellowship abroad, at the Niels Bohr Institute in Copenhagen. After his team built a network at Kurchatov, they connected it to other research centers—in Dubna, Novosibirsk, Leningrad, and later to other cities in the Soviet Union. They needed a name for this network, so they had run a random word-selection program in English. The program came up with Relcom—which stood for Reliable Communications.

In August 1990, his team made a first exchange of emails with Helsinki. It was the Soviet Union's first connection to the global computer network. It was essentially a very anti-Soviet idea—to connect people instantly in a country where any act required obligatory pre-authorization.

The first political test for Relcom came when the KGB organized a putsch in August 1991. The KGB blocked and banned traditional media, but they didn't pay attention to the nascent internet. Relcom remained operational, disseminating news about resistance in Moscow and other cities to Europe and the United States.

In the 1990s, Andrei's father and his team built a major part of the national internet infrastructure. In 2000, he was an owner of the first internet service provider in the country, called, predictably, RELCOM, but the relationship between father and son was not an easy one.

Andrei's parents had gone through a dramatic divorce when Andrei was eight years old. His father now had a new family, including a new daughter, and maintained rather sporadic communication with his son. Sometimes they saw each other as little as once a year. Sometimes they found common ground and got closer.

In 2000, Andrei and his dad were getting along rather well. Soldatov Sr. agreed to lend the facilities and services of his company for the project, including a web designer, under one condition.

Alexey Soldatov was a very shrewd businessman, and he also had some experience with the government and secrecy. In his pre-internet life, he had been a prominent nuclear physicist at the Kurchatov Institute, which had been the main Soviet research facility involved in the development of the atomic bomb. His RELCOM office was on a street very near the Kurchatov Institute's massive campus on the north side of the city. RELCOM also had an ongoing project with the country's electronic intelligence agency, FAPSI, to build a nationwide network for secure financial transactions and the exchange of other sensitive information. RELCOM would contribute its network capabilities to that project, and FAPSI would provide the cryptology technologies necessary to make the communications safe.

Soldatov Sr. knew what it was like to work with government secrets and how to calculate the risks. His condition was that our website would only publish information that was open source—that had already been published. He believed it would eliminate the risk of being accused of disclosing state secrets. We agreed. We didn't plan to abandon *Izvestia*. We thought we would keep writing investigative stories—with new information—for the paper, and later republish the information on Agentura, and everybody would be happy.

As the launch date approached, Andrei spent several hours each day in our office at *Izvestia* uploading text files to the website, which lived on his Sony laptop, and drafting dossiers on the intelligence and security agencies. Most of our colleagues didn't understand why we were putting so much effort into such an obscure and potentially dangerous project. Evgeny Krutikov and Petya Akopov were supportive, though Petya didn't see the point of such a website at all.

Soon, we faced our first big problem, and the model provided by the FAS Project on Government Secrecy in America couldn't help us solve it. There was simply not enough basic publicly available information to provide an adequate outline of how the Russian secret services were structured. There was no Freedom of Information Act in Russia, and no parliamentary oversight over the secret services.

We uploaded hundreds of press clippings, but we understood that if we wanted to present organizational charts of the Russian security services to the public, such open-source data was not completely reliable. In the 1990s, Russian government agencies had undergone constant reforms and bureaucratic changes. Agencies changed names, departments became directorates, they merged and got disbanded. The security services had been through even more upheaval—the name of the main successor agency to the KGB changed six times before it became the Federal Security Service, or Federalnaya Sluzhba Bezopasnosti (FSB).

We hoped that our position at *Izvestia*, a newspaper with access to powerful Russian figures, would help us verify the information with the agencies. And we got off to a good start when the most secretive agency in the Russian intelligence community, FAPSI, agreed to see Andrei—a visit arranged with the help of Soldatov Sr.

One morning Andrei went to the FAPSI press office and laid out on the table in front of a press officer an "org chart" of the agency that we had reconstructed based on press clippings.

The officer smiled and made some corrections, adding elements to our chart. He also provided insignias for FAPSI's major departments—it turned out that each one had a separate symbol, though all featured the inevitable double-headed eagle. That was very helpful.

Every day, as we uploaded more data on the website, we grew more confident.

In early August, Krutikov called Andrei to his office.

"Look, the FSB is launching some sort of unofficial press center, which they want to make more reasonable than the official one," he said.

We both knew that the official press office, the Center of Public Communications of the FSB, was the most unresponsive of all the Russian agencies. A journalist calling the office for a comment would commonly be asked to send a written request signed by their editor and then have to wait for days or weeks for a response. It took months to secure an interview.

Krutikov shrugged his shoulders: "Apparently, they believe such a center could improve their public image, and they hired one Olga Kostina to run it. She wants to talk to you."

Andrei recognized the name. Kostina was known among journalists as a public relations officer who had once worked for a bank owned by the very powerful oligarch Mikhail Khodorkovsky, who ran the most ruthless, efficient, and tech-savvy business operation in the country—Yukos, the largest Russian oil company at the time, a combination of the extraction facilities in West Siberia and oil refineries in Central Russia.

Andrei dutifully called Kostina, and they arranged a meeting. There, Kostina explained that the unofficial press office would be more open and friendly. She also said that there was a high-level commission being formed within the FSB to oversee the new approach. Kostina, thirty years old, wearing a short haircut and an expensive-looking suit, sounded professional and suave and obviously knew a thing or two about public relations. And she hadn't come to the meeting empty-handed. She had an offer for Andrei—an interview with the newly appointed head of the Moscow department of the FSB, General Viktor Zakharov.

That sounded interesting. The Moscow department of the FSB had a unique political position within the FSB because of its location in Russia's capital. Under Yeltsin, the head of the department was also deputy head of the entire FSB. Traditionally, the department had supplied officers to the highest positions in the agency, but now its status was being challenged by outsiders. Vladimir Putin had come from St. Petersburg and had brought with him to Moscow hordes of officers from that city. But Zakharov was born in Moscow, studied in Moscow, and spent his career in the Moscow KGB. He was actually the first Muscovite inside the FSB that Putin had promoted in two years. What made him so special? Why had the president chosen him? Exploring those questions would make a good story.

Andrei had never interviewed an FSB general before, and he was excited at the prospect. The next morning at 10:00, Andrei was waiting on Bolshaya Lubyanka Street, at the entrance to the huge rectangular concrete early-1980s monstrosity that housed the Moscow FSB. An officer emerged and showed him in. They crossed a big hall with two gigantic, ugly paintings on the walls depicting Chekists, Lenin's secret police, in leather jackets holding red banners. The officer smiled proudly. "In the 1980s we wanted to help a young painter and commissioned him to make those paintings," he said. When he gave the name of the painter, Andrei was surprised—he had become very successful, famous for his flattering portraits of high-level officials and celebrities.

One floor up, Andrei was shown into a large conference room with an extended table and seated at the far end of it. Nine men in gray business suits walked in and sat on both sides. They didn't give their names; they just said they were "consultants" to the general.

Then General Zakharov arrived in full dress uniform and sat down at the far end of the table, all his consultants strategically placed between him and the journalist. He had inexpressive eyes and a round, plump face with drooping cheeks. He held a few sheets of paper in his hands.

Andrei tried to say something, but the general started to read aloud from the sheets in front of him. The sheets contained Andrei's questions, which the FSB had requested in advance. The sheets also contained the answers, which the general was now reading.

Frustrated, Andrei tried to ask something personal, something about the general's career, but Zakharov was unmoved. "There is nothing special about my career," he said. "I was born into a family of workers, and I graduated from the Moscow Institute of Railway Engineers. Two years later I entered the KGB." The nine consultants remained silent. It was a complete disaster.

At the end of the meeting Zakharov gave Andrei an audiotape. He said it contained songs about the FSB, written by the agency's press officer.

On the tape, a hoarse male voice sang to upbeat music on a synthesizer:

> Always at the front, always at one's post,
> Don't touch Russia—
> A Chekist is always vigilant.

Andrei wrote up the interview. The next day, one of *Izvestia*'s editors, an imposing, bearded man known for his encyclopedic knowledge of Russian literature, approached him. "Andrei, I know it might sound rude, and you know I love your writing, but . . . this interview, it might have some bits of information, but it's completely unreadable." Andrei could only agree; he felt exactly the same way.

The following week, Kostina called to say how happy the FSB was with the interview. The agency reposted it on its website, where it is still available to this day.[3] Kostina also had a new offer—an invitation for Andrei to join the pool of journalists attached to the FSB.

She explained that the FSB wanted to have five trusted journalists on call from the main newspapers, so that if something happened, the security service could summon them to the Lubyanka headquarters and share the information with them. They would publish essentially the same story in their five newspapers simultaneously.

Being an approved mouthpiece of the security services was a far cry from the idealistic notions we had for our new venture. The FSB had openly set its sights on building a full-scale propaganda and disinformation machine with the help of the newspapers—but we didn't want to be part of it.

CHAPTER 4

THAT'S THE ST. PETERSBURG WAY

On August 8, 2000, at around 6:00 p.m., Moscow's rush hour, the political department gathered in Evgeny Krutikov's office at *Izvestia*. There weren't enough chairs, so those without sat on the wide windowsill. It was another sunny and warm summer evening, and, as always at this hour, there was a bottle of Bushmills on Krutikov's desk. All the reporters were in the room, except for Sveta Babayeva, the miniature blonde in Putin's press pool, who was, as usual, still in the Kremlin. Suddenly, a glass window shuddered violently. There was a loud explosion outside.

We rushed to the windows in the corridor overlooking Pushkin Square. Gray smoke was rising above the exit from an underground passage connected to a metro station next to the famous monument to Alexander Pushkin, about 300 feet from the *Izvestia* building.

Krutikov looked at us, but we were already running to the elevators. Our previous job had been covering crimes, including terrorist attacks, and we were drawn instinctively to the scene of the incident.

The underground passage had exits on different corners of the square, and two minutes later, when we approached the closest one, men and women were emerging, their clothes bloody, looking shocked and confused. It appeared the explosion had taken place inside the passage.

We talked to witnesses and rescue workers, trying to figure out what had happened. The square, always busy with people, as it was a popular place for Muscovites to meet up, was filling with police officers. Irina's red jacket was the only reason Andrei didn't lose sight of her in the hubbub.

The underground passage was lined with small shops with glass-front showcases. From the look of the wounded, it was clear that all this glass, shattered by the explosion, had added to the devastation. Many people were bleeding. Rescue workers were rushing in and out, trying to locate victims in the smoke as more and more people—men, women, and children—were emerging from the exits, covered in blood and dust. Some were lying on the ground, and it was not clear whether they were alive or dead.

A tall, thin teenager was wandering in the square. There was blood on his face and arms, but he was not injured. He was naked but for his blue underpants, socks, and shoes. The shock wave, enforced by the closed space of the underground passage, had stripped his clothes off. Irina started talking to him. His name was Igor, and he turned out to be a good witness. He remembered the explosion, the panic, and the people around him in vivid detail. As the sun set and it began to get chilly, Irina gave him her red jacket.

Seven people had died on the spot, and six more died later in hospitals. More than a hundred were injured with varying degrees of severity. The masterminds and perpetrators of the attack were never identified.

The day after the attack, President Putin went to Pushkin Square to lay flowers. Dressed all in black, he looked visibly shocked.

Moscow hadn't seen any terrorist attacks for almost a year, and Putin had built his public image on bringing stability and order, at least to the capital. The return of domestic terrorism suddenly reminded carefree Muscovites that the war in Chechnya was still ongoing. It looked as if Putin was doomed to the same fate as his predecessor, Yeltsin, tortured by never-ending instability and all kinds of catastrophes and crises. And the last thing Putin wanted was to become a second Yeltsin.

That day we learned from our colleagues that a young girl who had died at the square worked as a secretary at *Moscow News*, a newspaper with offices across the square from *Izvestia*.

The girl's death forced us to consider that any of us could have been walking along that passage at the time of the explosion. We were talking about her unfortunate fate in Krutikov's office when Sveta Babayeva burst in. She was visibly angry.

"Those fucking policemen!"

"Sveta, calm down," Krutikov said. Babayeva was famously short-tempered.

"They didn't let me drive to the *Izvestia* parking lot from Tverskaya yesterday! I showed them my Kremlin pass, and it had no effect!"

It became clear to us that Babayeva was talking about the immediate aftermath of the terrorist attack, complaining that the police hadn't lifted the cordon for her beloved Suzuki SUV, which she wanted to park near *Izvestia*, 300 feet from the site of an explosion. Babayeva obviously lived in a different world.

Three days later, Putin met in the Kremlin with his security services chiefs. They were discussing the investigation into the attack on Pushkin Square when, roughly 1,300 miles north of Moscow, the nuclear submarine *Kursk*, after an enormous explosion, sank to the bottom of the Barents Sea.

Most of the crew were instantly killed, but twenty-three of them made it to an undamaged compartment of the submarine and locked themselves in. They were now sending up SOS signals, hoping for salvation.

The country learned of the explosion only two days later, on August 14. By that time Putin had already left Moscow, but instead of heading north, where the navy was conducting a rescue operation, he went in the opposite direction—to Sochi, his beloved resort on the Black Sea—on vacation.

It was a planned trip—a holiday combined with meetings with foreign leaders, including the president of Tajikistan. As always, Sveta Babayeva accompanied Putin as part of the president's press pool.

We were not assigned to cover the *Kursk* catastrophe. We just watched helplessly on TV along with millions of other Russians as it unfolded through the agonizing days when it appeared there was still a chance to save the sailors locked in an iron tomb on the bottom of the sea.

In Sochi, Babayeva did her usual job and sent Krutikov her dispatches about Putin's daily routine. "Under the Sochi sun, the president quickly got tanned and even slightly burned," she wrote on August 17. "For two days, Putin actively mastered new sports: water skiing and a jet ski. He starts off at 'third speed,' scaring off the Black Sea fish and forcing the guards to rush after him."

Babayeva did add a few words to her dispatch about the *Kursk* disaster, though: "Every two hours, Putin was briefed about what was happening with the submarine in the Barents Sea. They say that Putin was very worried; he knows (or should we say knew?) the commander of the *Kursk* personally."

To our amazement, *Izvestia* published her report: when the country was talking of nothing but the dying sailors, the newspaper closest to the Kremlin ran a story of what a good time Putin was having in the Black Sea resort.

In the meantime, Russian navy commanders kept reassuring the public that it was still possible to save the survivors. But we at *Izvestia* knew it was over. Admirals were meeting privately with *Izvestia*'s military correspondent, a veteran of the Soviet navy, trying to sell him the conspiracy theory that the *Kursk* had been hit by an American submarine. The rescue operation was still running, but the navy was already trying to divert the blame for their criminal incompetence onto outsiders. On August 21, the chief of staff of the Northern Fleet finally admitted that the entire *Kursk* crew was dead, nine days after the original explosion, which was subsequently traced to a torpedo that prematurely detonated in its firing tube.

The image of a tanned Putin being briefed about the sunken sub between swims and waterskiing haunted us for a long time.

Once Putin's holiday finally ended, and Babayeva returned to Moscow, she dropped by Krutikov's office and casually mentioned that Putin had gone through a hair-transplant procedure in Sochi, and that was why he hadn't been seen in public for some time. Neither she nor Krutikov thought it was worth writing about. Babayeva sounded very protective of the new president, and her bosses at the paper were understanding.

It astonished us. The president of Russia had taken time off for an elective cosmetic surgery during a national emergency, yet our newspaper found nothing exceptional enough about this to share it with the readers. We began to get the feeling that we were not going to last long at *Izvestia*.

At the same time, our own project—the website about Russian security services—was getting ready to launch. The logo for Agentura on the front page would be in black and yellow, with the name followed by images of a few male profiles to symbolize faceless agents and spies. Below these elements would be a slogan—"On behalf of national security"—a phrase that Andrei came up with because he thought it sounded cool.

By September, the website had grown from a skeleton to something that looked like the real thing. The dossiers on Russian security and intelligence services were uploaded, along with bios and photos of known top counterintelligence and intelligence officers. There was a special section devoted to security service failures and scandals. We had a news section that would be updated as often as we needed. Finally, everything looked ready to go.

The launch was scheduled for September 5. That evening, we visited our best friend, Marina Latysheva, whom we'd recruited to work on the popular culture section, which we called, inevitably, Culture007. Latysheva lived with her mother in a leafy neighborhood in southwest Moscow. It was a quiet evening. Dry air from an open balcony cooled Latysheva's room. Andrei pulled out his Sony laptop from his bag, put it on the table, and opened it. Latysheva, a chain smoker, lit a cigarette. Irina did the same.

"So, I do this, right?" Andrei asked.

Latysheva and Irina silently nodded; Andrei pressed the button. Agentura.ru went live.

According to Russian tradition, Andrei had brought a bottle of wine, but Latysheva did not drink at all, and Andrei rarely drank more than a glass, so Irina had no choice but to finish most of the bottle. The celebration was very different from the roaring parties at the Akopovs' apartment. We all felt both nervous and euphoric, and talked all night about the possible future of Agentura.

Three days later, we were back at the apartment of Petya and Marina Akopov on Gogolevsky. The second week of September was still warm in Moscow, so we could have still had our gatherings at the bench outside, but this particular night we met indoors. Putin had gone to the United States for the Millennium Summit in New York, the largest-ever gathering of world leaders. It was his first visit to the

United States as Russian president, and Petya turned on a TV set, waiting to see highlights of Putin's big interview with TV anchor Larry King on CNN.

King was legendary among Russian journalists. CNN was the only American channel available for Russian watchers, and it had attained a special status after it broadcast in real time the shelling of the Russian parliament by Yeltsin's tanks in 1993, footage that was shared by Russian TV channels. Over the years, King became such a familiar face for the Russian audience that the most popular Russian interviewer on TV, Vlad Listyev, religiously copied King's outfit—a shirt combined with suspenders—while on air.

Because of the time difference, the broadcast of the interview was scheduled for almost midnight, and Russian TV immediately aired the most interesting parts of it. Larry King introduced Putin, and there he was on the screen, tanned, dressed in a dark suit and gray tie, and smiling.

King started by asking Putin what had surprised him so far about his job as president. Putin replied that nothing really surprised him because he had been Russian prime minister before being elected. He was well prepared for the interview. His message was that he was sufficiently experienced to run the country.

"Are you enjoying it?" asked King.

"To some extent." Putin kept smiling.

"So, let's get to the part that may not have been very enjoyable." King went on the offensive. "What happened—you tell me. What happened to the submarine?"

Marina was watching King intently.

Putin paused, then grinned. "She sank."

Putin's answer shocked us. Combined with his grin, it felt like the most cynical response that a president, a head of state, could possibly have to that state's failure to save its sailors. We could hardly believe what we'd heard him say.

Then Marina exploded: "How dare this American ask Putin about *Kursk* in such a disrespectful way? Well done for Putin for cutting him off! That's our St. Petersburg way; tell him to go fuck himself!"

It appeared that both Marina and Putin felt the same way: angry at the foreigners who dared to interfere in the country's affairs and try to tell us how to behave, even if it was about saving human lives. Petya, kind and intelligent Petya, seemed to share that feeling.

That night was probably the very first time it dawned on us that we didn't completely understand our friends.

CHAPTER 5

CAST OUT

September treated Moscow well that year, as if summer hadn't yet left town. It was warm and sunny, and we were happy arguing, laughing, and drinking with our colleagues at the office. If we were in the mood, after the daily issue was sent to the printing house, we would walk to Gogolevsky Boulevard to hang out with Petya and his friends. But, most importantly, we were getting our stories published in the pages of a popular and influential national newspaper. *Izvestia* had managed to retain a fair share of the prestigious reputation it had enjoyed during perestroika.

Irina got an assignment from the editor-in-chief to write a long story about Moscow State University—not just a puff piece about the best university in Russia and its great teachers and gifted students, but an investigation into a dark, unknown side of the university. The editor-in-chief did not give Irina any details about what this dark side was, which meant she had complete freedom to go where her reporting led her.

Irina enthusiastically started digging into the university, where 38,000 students studied in forty-three departments. MSU is best known for its iconic main building, one of seven Moscow skyscrapers built on Stalin's orders, topped by a gigantic star. It was the tallest building in Europe until the 1990s and is still the tallest university building in the world, a fact the university is very proud of.

The Soviets built the sand-colored skyscraper, vaguely reminiscent of the Empire State Building, to house a Communist educational paradise intended to amaze the world. Inside the gigantic building was everything one needed for life and for study: not only the university departments, but also student dormitories and professors' flats, a museum, a library, and even a "palace of culture." You could eat, study, and sleep there without going out to the street for weeks. If you broke the law, there was even a police station conveniently located in the same building.

Irina decided to start exploring the hidden side of MSU from its notorious subterranean levels, which had given birth to many different legends, ranging from gigantic rats that wandered beneath Moscow to sinister and clandestine research facilities. It was long rumored that beneath Moscow there was another, secret underground world—bunkers for Politburo members, underground military factories, tank tunnels, and even an underground subway system built for government use only, known informally as Metro-2, separate from the Moscow metro. One of Metro-2's stations was reportedly beneath the MSU building.

A famous explorer and leader of the Moscow community of "diggers," as they called themselves, a guy in his thirties with a pale complexion, agreed to give Irina and her photographer a tour of MSU's underground system of corridors and tunnels. He had been exploring Moscow's subsurface since his Soviet childhood, when his father, a train operator for the metro, would take him into his operator's cabin.

One sunny day, Irina and her photographer, led by the digger, squeezed through a ventilation shaft in a fountain near the main entrance to the university, and they exited a couple of hours later via a sewer well. They hadn't seen either zombie rats or secret nuclear facilities, but the size of the tunnels, some of them more than fifteen feet high and perhaps even wider than they were high, was really impressive. In fact, the multilevel labyrinth beneath the university's buildings had been designed to shelter thousands of teachers and students in the event of a nuclear attack.

Irina's next visit to MSU took her to the university police station, where its chief criminal investigator told her about a gifted chemistry student who had invented a superpowerful drug and organized its production right on the campus.

The third focus of her story was campus violence. As it happened, Irina had a friend, a university student, who had been so violently beaten in his room by another student for making noise at night that he had to have his cheekbone replaced with a metal plate.

Irina finished her long piece, Krutikov enjoyed it, and the text was ready to print.

The next morning, Irina scrolled the pages of *Izvestia* but failed to find her story. She checked again, and finally, there it was, her name on a page above a short piece. Only one part of her long article was there, and, most annoyingly, the text had been cut such that it didn't make much sense.

Irina was furious. Seeking to learn what had happened and who had dismembered her story into meaningless pieces, she grilled Krutikov until he admitted that the decision had come from the editor-in-chief. Which was odd, given that it had been his idea to investigate the dark side of MSU in the first place. It was clear that something had changed, but the editor-in-chief offered no explanation.

Izvestia published the remaining parts of the story later, piece by piece, but they were like well-tailored sleeves worn separately from the dress: there was no way to understand what the dress actually looked like.

Why Krutikov had failed to defend the integrity of the article to the editor-in-chief became clear in mid-September, when Krutikov took Irina to his office and told her with a sad smile that he could not shelter her anymore from a new assignment from the leadership of the newspaper: to write a profile of Putin's representative in Central Russia, a gray-haired man with a massive mustache, another appointee who had come from the KGB.

Irina had a pretty good idea of what kind of profile Putin's official expected of her—a flattering portrait of an honored dignitary—and tried to talk her way out of the assignment. After all, there were many other journalists at *Izvestia* who liked Putin's officials with KGB backgrounds and would be happy to flatter them. Why not give this job to one of them? Krutikov shook his head. It became clear that from now on, *Izvestia*'s leadership wanted every reporter to prove their loyalty to the Kremlin, and the freedom *Izvestia*'s journalists had enjoyed just a few months ago, before the *Kursk* incident, had been curtailed. Irina's reportage about MSU was sufficiently disrespectful to the great institution that she now had to bow her knee to the powers that be. But she said no.

Izvestia was a daily newspaper and needed many stories to fill its pages, but somehow it was getting more and more difficult to get ours published.

Andrei discovered that several French veterans of the Foreign Legion had decided to open an office in Ryazan, a city in Central Russia. One of them had moved to Ryazan some years ago along with his Russian wife. Ryazan was not just any old Russian town. The famous Airborne Command School was located there, and the veterans wanted to set up an office in order to recruit its cadets for the Legion.

Andrei went to Ryazan, spoke with the cadets and the leadership of the school, and found out that the Foreign Legion was very popular among the ranks. At the time of Andrei's trip, the schoolmasters were waging a fierce war with the cadets over the size of their berets: Russian paratroopers wore blue berets, just like the Legionnaires did, but the French version was smaller, and cadets were trying to make theirs look like the French ones.

It was a good story, and Krutikov gave it his approval, but it stalled somewhere on the second floor. Two weeks later, Krutikov announced the reason: the deputy editor-in-chief's country house was next door to the house of the Airborne Forces' commander, and the deputy editor didn't want to risk his personal relationship with the powerful general. Apparently, the access to the country's elite that *Izvestia* enjoyed came with a cost—to be paid by its reporters.

Finally, *Izvestia* did print the story, but by then it was not really news.

This incident typified the intrigues and fierce departmental infighting and showed that the political department was clearly losing favor. But the battles took place mostly on the second floor, and it was Krutikov's job to manage the conflict. However, instead, in his office Krutikov was often lost in a multiplayer *Half Life* shooter game against the ad department (they always won, thanks to their more powerful desktop computers). He was fighting the wrong war and was never going to win either.

On the morning of September 21, news broke of a hostage situation in the Black Sea resort of Sochi. Apparently, a group of militants had stormed a private hotel and taken everyone inside hostage. It was another devastating blow to Russian prestige and a severe embarrassment to a still new president who wanted to pretend that he had the country under control.

Sochi is the closest thing Russia has to the Côte d'Azur—a beautiful coastline indented by bays and peppered not only with hotels, but also with exclusive holiday resorts reserved for government officials and security services personnel, as well as the fancy villas the country's high-level officials had enjoyed on their vacations since Soviet times. Stalin had had his dacha there, and Putin had come to love spending his holidays there too. But Sochi was very close to the North Caucasus, just 300 miles from Chechnya, where the war was still going on. Sochi was also a stone's throw—27 miles—from the border of Abkhazia, a breakout nonrecognized republic that had split from Georgia in the early 1990s after a very bloody and brutal war. Abkhazia was a Russian ally and technically had a government and police, but nobody really controlled the situation there.

Krutikov told Andrei to "get the first flight to Sochi. . . . It's a chance to have an exclusive," so off he went to the airport.

When he got out of a car at the entrance of Domodedovo airport, he was greeted with the words, "Ha, look! *Izvestia* also decided to get an exclusive!" A large group of journalists were standing at the airport entrance, laughing and smoking, mostly familiar faces Andrei knew from the days they had spent together at the scenes of assassinations and explosions on Moscow streets.

Two hours later, the press plane landed in the small airport of Sochi. Several minibuses were hired on the spot, journalists hopped in, and the buses raced off on a serpentine road to the seafront resort village near Sochi where the hotel had been taken by terrorists. It was already dark when the journalists arrived and encountered their first surprise: the place was cordoned off by local police, all dressed in white uniform shirts as if they'd been deployed to protect a festival or sports event.

"Why are you all in white?" someone asked.

"Because of the guests from Moscow!" said a fat police major who looked like he was in charge. "Are you journalists from Moscow?"

Journalists exchanged glances.

"Ha! You are from Moscow!" said the major triumphantly. "Guys, do you need girls for tonight?"

The famous Black Sea resort was living up to its carefree reputation.

The hotel building where the terrorists had barricaded themselves was farther down the road, behind the trees, and after pacing around for several hours the journalists agreed that it was safe to go to sleep. Two photographers stayed behind with the police, just in case.

The hotel next door conveniently had rooms available. The next morning, the biggest news was that breakfast was being served next to the swimming pool; nothing had happened during the night.

But two top generals had taken over control from the locals: a deputy head of the FSB who had brought the elite Alfa special forces group with him, and the deputy interior minister. An hour later it was all finished: the terrorists, who turned out to be three drug addicts, handed over their weapons, released the hostages, and surrendered. All the journalists rushed to report the happy ending to their editors.

Since the sun was still high and the sea warm, the press pack decided to postpone their return to Moscow to the next day and have a night for themselves. As soon as the decision was made to stay, the hotel's manager was told to move a big table closer to the pool for an upcoming feast.

Waiters served the table and brought in bottles of vodka, and the party began. The youngest reporter was one Alexei, barely twenty years old, the son of an FSB press officer, and the oldest was a fifty-five-year-old man named Sergei. Sergei was also the most experienced journalist—he'd covered crimes and terrorist attacks for most of the 1990s, and before that had been a geologist. The latter was a job that, in a time-honored Soviet tradition, was a good one to choose if you wanted to have as little to do with the Soviet rulers as possible.

The first bottle of vodka was half empty and young Alexei was visibly drunk when Sergei addressed him in a loud voice, "Look, kid! I'll give you 500 rubles if you swim naked to the far end of the pool."

He took out the 500 rubles bill and waved it at Alexei.

There was silence at the table. Andrei felt uneasy—it was an insult, and a very rude one, to suggest that a young journalist would do almost anything to make a buck. But Alexei didn't look offended. He stood up, smiled sheepishly, then began to strip. In a second, completely naked, he was swimming to the other end of the pool, where Sergei was waiting for him with the bank note in his hand. Alexei got his 500 and walked back to the table.

Andrei turned to the former geologist. "Why did you do that?" he asked.

"I hate them. The KGB scum," Sergei said through clenched teeth.

The country had voted a former KGB officer into the Kremlin, but that didn't mean everyone had become oblivious to what the KGB—or its successor agency—was.

When two prostitutes showed up, followed by two more, all ordered by another colleague, Andrei and a photographer realized it was time to leave and head for the beach, where they spent the rest of the night.

The next day, Andrei flew back to Moscow and went from the airport directly to *Izvestia*. There he was summoned to see the deputy editor—the same deputy editor who had his country house next to that of the Airborne Forces' commander.

The deputy editor was visibly angry. "On your trip to Sochi, you stole 200 rubles!" he stated, without even greeting Andrei first. Andrei had never been accused of stealing anything before. The accusation was flagrantly insulting. Andrei went berserk and started shouting back.

"Okay, fine, get out of my face," said the deputy editor, and waved him off. Apparently, throwing this kind of accusation around was normal behavior to him; it was the way he talked to his journalists. But the atmosphere on our floor had palpably changed. Every day, Krutikov conveyed a message from the second floor to his journalists on the third floor: the political department was no good; some corrective measures should be taken. Krutikov almost stopped coming to work, and when he did show up, he drank even more Bushmills than usual. All the reporters felt confused and angry: the department had no leadership and was under constant attack.

After three weeks of agony, the axe came down. Krutikov, half-drunk and disheveled, delivered the latest news from the second floor: he'd been ousted, demoted to the position of a columnist, and replaced by Sveta Babayeva as new head of the political department.

The performance of the department had nothing to do with the appointment. The leadership of the newspaper, along with the oligarchs who funded it, understood that the country had a new boss, probably for a very long time, and had reacted accordingly. Those who had access to the president became crucial, and Babayeva, as a member of the Kremlin press pool attached to follow Putin, had it. The editors hoped she could operate as the newspaper's early warning system in these new political circumstances.

A week later, we wrote our letters of resignation. A deputy editor phoned Irina to tell her she was welcome to stay. "We stand with Krutikov," Irina responded. Babayeva also asked Irina to stay and promised she could remain in charge of covering the law enforcement agencies. Irina politely declined. And nobody asked Andrei to stay.

When we came to *Izvestia* for the last time to collect our stuff, we noticed a new face—a nondescript man in his thirties sitting at a desk next to Babayeva's. We were told his name was Andrei Lebedev, and that he was Babayeva's new deputy. He was very timid and seemed hesitant. He was also the only person at the paper to address Sveta Babayeva using her full name with the patronymic—"Svetlana Valeryevna."

To use a patronymic was considered a very Soviet, old-fashioned formal habit. In the new Russia, the first thing newspapers did was to drop the patronymic when writing about Yeltsin—from then on, he was just Boris Yeltsin, in the Western way. Inside the editorial offices, it would be very odd to use a patronymic in addressing other journalists, even in Soviet times.

That was not the only thing foreign to newspaper culture that Lebedev brought with him to *Izvestia*. He also kept his distance from reporters and was very secretive about his past. When we asked about his background, out of curiosity, we were told in a hushed voice that he was in fact an officer of the Russian intelligence agency SVR.

History was coming full circle. After the failed KGB-led putsch in August 1991, the then editor of *Izvestia* had summoned the KGB officers assigned to the paper to his office and told them to resign either from *Izvestia* or from the KGB. He said he was not going to tolerate his people working for two bosses any longer. Ten years later, *Izvestia* seemed to be getting back to old Soviet habits. They had invited the security services back onto the editorial floor.

At the end of October, as an early snow was quickly turning to dirt on the streets of Moscow, we were out on the street ourselves, with no jobs and no idea what to do next, except maintain our own private project, Agentura.

PART II

CHAPTER 6

LANGUISHING IN LIMBO

After almost five years as working reporters, coming every day to the editorial office of a newspaper, first to *Segodnya*, then to *Izvestia*, being journalists had become a big part of our identities. But at once we found ourselves out of a newsroom, and without the sense of mission and the feelings of pride and belonging that we'd found there. We had hoped our names were worth something in the media world of Moscow, but nobody was calling us with job offers.

It was horrible and depressing. Andrei had nightmares that he was back in school, forced to take an exam in math, something he had long forgotten, and failing that exam, night after night. We retreated to a one-room flat with a table, a sagging sofa, and an equally saggy bed on the seventh floor of a Soviet-era high-rise on the northern outskirts of Moscow. There was some irony in the fact that we'd rented our tiny apartment on Ulitsa Svobody, "Freedom Street," one of the longest and ugliest streets in the city. It felt as if we were doomed to that freedom.

We had our website, Agentura, though. The site lived in the computer on the table. We spent hours monitoring the media and talking with other correspondents in Russia's regions, compiling more dossiers.

A big angry woman from the sixth floor often interrupted our working routine—she had the misfortune of sharing a paired phone number with our apartment. In Moscow at that time, the only way to get connected online was dial-up via a landline phone. Because of us, her phone line was constantly busy, for hours, and that not unreasonably drove her crazy. We tried to suggest that she develop some schedule—that she could make calls by day and then not occupy the line after 6:00 p.m. for several hours—but that was not what she wanted. She wanted to have an option to call her elderly parents whenever she wanted and to take a call from them at any time. It was a fair request, and we sympathized, but we needed to work. The only alternative was to have our landlord disengage our lines, but she was not ready to pay for that. We were stuck in an unyielding domestic squabble for months.

The fall nights grew longer and darker in our apartment on Freedom Street as we waited impatiently for something, anything, to happen.

A pleasant break from that routine came with a call from the *New York Times*. A young reporter wanted to come to Moscow to interview Andrei about Agentura. They spoke for a few hours in a lobby of a hotel facing Red Square. It was very flattering, and we waited for the story to come out as if it would change our lives.

In early December, the *Times* article profiling the website finally appeared. "A Web Site That Came in from the Cold to Unveil Russian Secrets," the headline read. It featured a photograph of Andrei with his Sony laptop open in his hands, the FSB Lubyanka headquarters behind him.[1]

We felt excited and proud. Irina immediately sent the article to Evgeny Krutikov at *Izvestia*, who called back and said that he had sent the link to all the editors at the newspaper.

We kept seeing Krutikov during that time. He was always accompanied by his Ossetian friend Alan Kachmazov, at cheap bars or his apartment. Krutikov was drinking more and constantly complaining about the awful atmosphere at *Izvestia*. But while he looked distracted at times, his observations remained smart and thoughtful, and we thought of inviting him to join Agentura.

A friend brought us a printed copy of the *New York Times* from Riga, and Andrei took it to his father. He wanted to prove to him that what we were doing was worth something. But it felt a bit desperate already. We couldn't keep making the rounds in Moscow with a single copy of the *New York Times* article forever.

Nothing changed. We were stuck in the apartment on Freedom Street, with the same sofa and the same bed and the same table, looking out the window at Moscow's dark winter.

If you want to know all there is to know about depression, go to Moscow in midwinter. The sky is hidden by the dark gray smog produced by millions of cars stuck in traffic jams, the streets are covered with a wet layer of mud, and the gloomy faces of Muscovites don't promise anything good. Everyone is condemned to live among dozens of shades of gray.

The Soviet high-rises of Freedom Street looked even more miserable once the trees lost their leaves. The Russian suburbs are called "sleeping districts" for a good reason, and this damned street was way too far from the city center, where things happened; far from the editorial offices, clubs, and bookstores where one had a chance of bumping into an old friend and hearing some news.

Dropping by our friends' apartments was the only way to survive, we came to believe, and Petya Akopov's apartment on Gogolevsky saved us.

No matter what, we could always drive to Gogolevsky—it took forty minutes—and there, on the second floor, were Petya and Marina, usually caught up in some agitated conversation with a friend. Petya fancied himself to be very good at providing relationship advice, and Marina was street-smart—a win-win combination for a good evening. If nobody else was there, we would just sit in their living room, and sometimes in Petya's library, talking and drinking.

Petya also treated us to gossip about *Izvestia*. Sveta Babayeva treated him well and included him in the presidential pool of journalists who accompanied Putin on his trips across the country. Petya acquired good connections at the Administration of the President, he would tell us much later.

Time and again he circled back to a topic he felt very strongly about: he wanted very much to interview one Tikhon Shevkunov, a priest with the Russian Orthodox Church. We'd never heard of Shevkunov, but Petya told us that this young and ambitious priest with a very strong anti-Western stance was something of a confessor to Putin. This priest was well-educated, easygoing, and well-connected in Moscow's bohemian circles—he had actually trained as a screenwriter. We also knew that he served at the Sretensky Monastery, in the Lubyanka district, a stone's throw from FSB headquarters. But he didn't like to give interviews, and Petya had been trying for months to break through. Although he was never a passionate reporter, Petya possessed a great gift: he could identify very early on what kind of people, and ideologies, would be definitive during Putin's rule. Shevkunov, who promoted the spiritual superiority of the Russians over the decaying West—in his view the reason the West was always plotting against Moscow and the Russian Church—became one of them. By 2023 he was named head of the Crimea diocese—a hugely significant and politically charged role.

December came and went.

One late night in January Petya called with an offer. "Guys, there is a new club, called Duma. It's kind of a private club. I've just become a member, so I invite you!"

We met on Tverskaya Street at the front of the massive rectangular Central Telegraph building. Petya told us that the club was somewhere in the alleys, and we would never find it without him.

After a short walk on Nikitsky Lane, we stepped behind a gate into the small, quiet courtyard of the Institute of Europe, an academic center that provided expertise for the State Duma (the Russian parliament), the Administration of the President, and the Foreign Ministry, a ten-minute walk from the Kremlin walls.

The one-story pale yellow building of the institute, a typical Moscow-style mansion, had had two sets of stairs on the left and right merging into a landing at the main entrance, a large black door. But Petya did not lead us up the stairs; instead, he went to the right, where there was a small, unmarked door that clearly led down somewhere. Petya rang a bell, the door opened, and Petya showed a small card to the man inside. After we were waved in, we went down some stairs into the basement, where heavy curtains hid the entry to the club's main room.

Duma certainly did not look like the clubs we usually went to—smoked-filled rooms bursting with loud music and noisy young people. The area where members gathered—a semicircular space with exposed brick walls—was dimly lit, quiet, and very private. It was a place for adults. And judging by the interior, for very serious adults. There was a brown Chesterfield leather sofa and a couple of large armchairs, a low-watt floor lamp, a never-used fireplace, and shelves full of old Soviet-era books lining the walls. On the right, behind a bricked arch, was a long bar counter, and Petya led us to one of the tables to the right of the bar. We ordered wine. We had never been in English clubs before, but Duma struck us as the kind of place we imagined an English club to be. In this club, however, unlike in English clubs, one didn't need to pay for a membership.

The hall was full of people drinking and chatting, but we couldn't hear what they were talking about. There were two editors-in-chief we recognized, though we didn't know them in person, and Olga Kostina, the well-dressed head of the unofficial press center of the FSB, was also there, sitting with some people, who by the look of them were in public relations or government relations business.

Petya lit a cigarette and reminded us of his promise to teach us to play poker. The cards were brought in, and we pretended to get serious about the game as the two of us played for the first time.

"Would you like to have a club card?" Petya asked.

The answer was obvious: we would very much like to join. Petya went off and brought to the table a stylish blonde lady. He said something to her, she smiled back, and that was how we became members of the Duma club there and then. If not for Petya, there was no way two unemployed newspaper reporters would have made it past the gate.

We came to frequent the club almost every other week that winter, and we maintained the habit for years. We felt it was a way for us to stay relevant as political journalists: a keyhole through which to see people who had access to the Kremlin, just ten minutes' walk away. The owner of the Duma club was a businessman and musician who owned several clubs in Moscow, and he was very proud of the fact that in the 1990s Vladimir Putin used to drop by his first club whenever he came to Moscow from St. Petersburg.

The Duma became a place where prominent political journalists met PR men and women who worked for oligarchs and Kremlin dignitaries. They all came to talk about sensitive issues and to try to address problems in a relaxed, private atmosphere while drinking wine and playing pool.

We knew we did not belong in such a place. But we kept coming, partly because that winter we had barely anywhere else to go.

CHAPTER 7

PLAYING WITH THE SPIES

At the very end of January 2001, the popular Russian tabloid *Komsomolskaya Pravda* and *Izvestia* both came out with front-page stories about a Russian soldier-turned-jihadist named Vasily Kalinkin.

Kalinkin's story sounds like a spinoff of the TV series *Homeland*, though *Homeland* wouldn't be made until ten years later. In the early 1990s, Kalinkin served as a warrant officer in the Russian army communications battalion in Nizhny Tagil, an industrial town in the Urals mostly known for its monstrous tank factory. He spent most of his time in the military facility getting bored—his unit was a pointless fragment of a large and mostly dysfunctional Soviet army. He was also very poorly paid, as the army was underfunded for years, and officers of the Kalinkin caliber usually made ends meet selling army communications hardware on the side. But in a highly polluted town like Nizhny Tagil, where good jobs aside from the tank factory were always scarce, he had at least secured a job in a relatively clean office, which would provide him with a very modest income for decades without demanding that he ever become involved in any actual fighting. According to the papers, though, he suddenly deserted the

Russian army and moved to Chechnya, where he joined the rebels and converted to Islam. Why he did so, exchanging his quiet life for the war, was never explained. His Chechen commanders, according to the story, then sent him to Afghanistan. In Afghanistan he went through a rigorous training supervised by an instructor and handler—a mysterious American named "Bill." As part of the training, "Bill" directed the new Russian recruit to kill sixteen helpless prisoners.

If that hint that the ominous CIA was involved was not enough, the newspapers claimed that Kalinkin had signed a document of cooperation with US intelligence. Kalinkin told the reporters that this fantastic document had the Statue of Liberty in the left corner and in the right, the title "Osama bin Laden Sabotage School."[1]

After that, the articles ludicrously asserted that Kalinkin was sent back to Russia as an undercover agent. He reportedly waited six years before he was given an order: to organize the destruction of the Volga Hydroelectric Station—the largest dam in Europe.

But Kalinkin chose not to follow the order and instead gave himself up to the FSB, which leaked the story to the papers. The FSB wanted to use Kalinkin as proof that it was the duplicitous Americans who were behind terrorism in Russia and trying to subvert the Russian state.

It did not surprise us that *Komsomolskaya Pravda* published such a clearly made-up story. The tabloid had cooperated closely with Russian intelligence since Soviet times, and some of the paper's correspondents in the United States were KGB spies under journalistic cover. This tradition had continued uninterrupted into the 1990s, and the foreign intelligence service SVR, the successor of the KGB's foreign branch, kept using the tabloid to provide journalistic cover to its operatives in the United States.

But we wondered why *Izvestia* agreed to run a story about Kalinkin. Even more surprising was that the story was not written by Babayeva's deputy Lebedev, an officer of the SVR. It had a byline of Evgeny Krutikov. Apparently, the paper had succumbed to the idea of assigning a journalist to the pool of reporters briefed by the FSB, and Krutikov had been given the task.

That came as a shock to us. Our friend, or at least ally when sober, Krutikov was much more experienced as a reporter than we were. He had covered wars, and he had no illusions about the intelligence services, because he knew them from the inside and had seen them in action. He was not narrow-minded, either. Extensively well-read in books about intelligence history, he had also read—in English—every novel John le Carré had written. That he was reduced to reporting whatever nonsense the FSB was peddling was difficult to digest.

Krutikov was no fool. He knew that Kalinkin's story was implausible. Years later, Andrei asked Krutikov about the Kalinkin story, and Krutikov, visibly tired and depressed, and much thinner by then, shrugged. "You think it was an active measure of the FSB. Well, maybe it was," he said. Did he try to verify Kalinkin's story, or speak to his lawyer? Andrei asked. "Of course not," Krutikov replied.

So why had he done it? Why had he decided to take part in the FSB disinformation operation?

We remembered from our days in *Izvestia* that while Krutikov had no photographs of his wife and son on his desk, he did have, in a simple frame, a black-and-white photograph of a man in a suit—his father, Felix. When Krutikov was in a sour mood, which happened a lot in the autumn and winter of 2000, the subject of his father's tragic fate often came up. Soon, we knew the story by heart.

Krutikov was very proud of the fact that his grandfather, Alexei Krutikov, had been a longtime deputy to Stalin's powerful minister and political survivalist Anastas Mikoyan. Krutikov's father, Felix, son of Alexei, had finished naval school in 1945, when the war was already over, and had immediately been recruited into Soviet intelligence, thanks to his gift for languages. Felix's first assignment was to be a diplomatic courier—a dream job for any young man in the Soviet Union under Stalin when 99 percent of Soviet citizens were not allowed to travel abroad.

Mikoyan was Alexei Krutikov's main political patron, but Krutikov was wise enough to realize he also needed good, close, and preferably personal connections with the mandarins of Stalin's security services. For many years he had been cultivating personal ties with Ivan Serov, the fearful general of Stalin's secret police. Serov supervised the purges and mass deportations across the Soviet-occupied Baltics, Western Ukraine, and Poland, and he became Stalin's chief of security in occupied Germany after the war. Alexei Krutikov and Serov had grown up in neighboring villages in the Vologda region. They developed a close relationship and often spent weekends together.

Being a courier was a good start for Felix, but his father, whom Stalin had just made deputy prime minister, wanted his son to develop his career close to Mikoyan, at that time minister of foreign trade. So Felix went to the Institute of Foreign Trade in Moscow.

After Felix graduated in 1951, his father got him the much-cherished position of assistant to Mikoyan—and just in time. Stalin, prone to erratically moving his bureaucrats around, suddenly downgraded Krutikov's dad from being deputy prime minister and made him, again, deputy to Mikoyan, at which point father and son were working together under Mikoyan.

As a young intelligence officer, Felix was installed in Mikoyan's large reception room, a good place to establish connections with the high-placed bureaucrats who came to seek favors from the influential minister. But Felix wanted to serve abroad, in France, and soon he was sent to Paris as an officer of the KGB station in Paris, now under the disguise of being an employee of the Soviet trade mission. Apparently, he did well, and in February 1954 Felix was named on the Soviet foreign trade personnel list in France as a bureaucrat with the right to sign trade contracts—a very sensitive and important privilege in the Soviet diplomatic world.

Once he settled in Paris, his future looked bright, but in snowy Moscow, after Stalin's death the previous spring, fierce infighting began to rage among the elites. That infighting included the security services: the once all-powerful chief of Stalin's security police, Lavrenty Beria, had been arrested and shot just a few months before Felix's promotion.

In April 1954 Felix got orders to go to Geneva to pick up some top-secret documents, which he was told were waiting for him in the plane of a top Soviet official, who had flown in for some diplomatic talks.

Felix went by train to Switzerland, and from the train station headed to the airport. When he climbed the steps into the Soviet airplane, security men handcuffed him and threw him inside. The plane took Felix to Moscow, straight to the Lubyanka prison. There, he was thrown into a cell. What followed was a series of exhausting interrogations, accompanied by torture. Sometimes he was tortured in the presence of Ivan Serov, his father's old friend.

Just a month before Felix's arrest, Stalin's secret services had been reorganized into the Committee of State Security, or the KGB (Komitet Gosudarstvennoy Bezopasnosti), and Serov became the KGB's first chairman. The new name did not change much. Krutikov's family legend had it that Serov was beating Felix in Lubyanka's cell to get him to talk about Mikoyan, adding, sometimes, "You'll piss blood if you don't say what the investigation needs!" That Serov had been close friends with the young intelligence officer's father Alexei and had known Felix since his childhood apparently didn't count for much.

Felix was sentenced to twenty-five years in the Gulag on treason charges. The attack didn't spare his father, either, who was stripped of his Communist Party membership. It was a sudden and dramatic fall for both son and father—so dramatic that it was even reported by the *New York Times*: "A former Deputy Premier of the Soviet Union has been expelled from the Communist party in the most serious punishment of a Soviet official since the execution of Lavrenti P. Beria last December. The expelled man is Alexei D. Krutikov, a veteran associate of Deputy Premier Anastas I. Mikoyan," reported Moscow correspondent Harry Schwartz.[2]

But why had Serov attacked the Krutikovs, the crème de la crème of the Soviet elite? Sudden downfalls of high-level officials and their relatives had been very common under Stalin, who was famous for having a straightforward and brutal approach to keeping his people under control—by regularly shooting them. But Stalin was dead.

When Krutikov told us his father's story in Moscow fifty years later, he always insisted that his family had fallen victim to an attack directed at Mikoyan. He believed that the attack had been orchestrated by KGB chairman Ivan Serov and Nikita Khrushchev, first secretary of the Communist Party of the Soviet Union. The CIA appeared to agree: "The expulsion from the Communist Party of A. D. Krutikov, deputy minister of trade, appears to reflect upon Minister of Trade A. I. Mikoyan, one of the six leading figures in the Soviet Union today," claimed the CIA *Central Intelligence Bulletin* in September 1954.[3]

Felix spent six years in the Gulag in Siberia. It was a camp in Vorkuta, beyond the Arctic Circle, and conditions were harsh. Most of the inmates were from Western Ukraine and the Baltics and had been sent to the Gulag because they had fought the advancing Red Army. A disgraced KGB officer was unlikely to become popular among them, so Felix made up a legend, telling his cellmates that he had killed his superior officer in Paris.[4] It helped.

Felix was released and rehabilitated by a special court ruling in 1960 at the personal petition of Anastas Mikoyan, who was at that time the chairman of the Supreme Soviet of the Soviet Union—the Soviet quasi-parliament. Thus, it looked like Mikoyan knew about the attack on him, appreciated the Krutikovs' loyalty—and got Felix released when the opportunity presented itself.

But was this the whole story?

The year 1954 was a very special one in the political history of the Soviet Union. Stalin was out of the picture, but the ensuing infighting in the Kremlin was fierce, and Beria, the chief of Stalin's secret police, was not the only victim of it.

After the war, Stalin had made Andrei Vyshinsky Soviet foreign minister. Vyshinsky was the infamous prosecutor who, in the 1930s, had orchestrated Stalin's show trials and sent many people to their deaths. When Stalin died, Vyshinsky lost his position and was sent to the United States as the Soviet representative to the United Nations. He died in mysterious circumstances in November 1954, at breakfast in the Soviet residence on 680 Park Avenue in New York. According to the official version, the cause of death was heart failure; another version claimed that he had committed suicide; and some historians believe he was poisoned. Police officers were not allowed to enter the building, and the next day the body was extracted by special flight to Moscow.

Many suspected that he died right on time to prevent him from defecting to the Americans. Some KGB officers had already succeeded in defecting: after Stalin's death, five Soviet operatives fled to the West from their postings in Soviet missions in Austria, West Germany, Japan, and even Australia.

The KGB had accused Felix Krutikov of entering into secret talks with the French and British, possibly to negotiate a defection.[5] Some British historians claim that the talks with Felix Krutikov, and his apparent recruitment, were handled not by the British Secret Intelligence Service (SIS) station in Paris but under the direction of the legendary SIS commander Kenneth Cohen.[6]

Cohen, the first Jew to receive a commission in the Royal Navy, spent World War II recruiting French sources from within the unoccupied zone of France, and after D-Day oversaw parachuting dozens of Allied intelligence teams behind enemy lines.[7] After the war he was made the SIS's chief controller in charge of British intelligence operations in Europe.[8] He'd retired the previous year, but apparently was called out of retirement to help recruit Krutikov. One could only guess whose defection—which top-ranking Soviet official—young intelligence officer Felix Krutikov was negotiating about with Cohen. But because of these secret talks, Felix had his promising career ruined by the Soviet secret police, alongside his father's.

So why in early 2001 had his son Evgeny, a leading columnist at *Izvestia*, accepted a part in the operation run by the FSB, a direct and proud successor to the KGB? Hadn't his family suffered enough at the hands of Stalin's secret police?

When Andrei spoke with Evgeny in 2023, he asked this very question. Krutikov countered, "Nobody in my family suffered from Stalin's repression."

Technically, he was correct: his father had gone to jail only after Stalin's death, so he cannot be seen as a victim of Stalin's mass purges. Moreover, his family had only grown more and more important in social standing under Stalin, reaching, at the highest point, the position of deputy prime minister. Evgeny Krutikov believed that his father fell victim to Kremlin infighting only after Stalin's death. To the Krutikovs, Stalin did only good.

But what about the KGB, which had held his father in the Gulag in Siberia for six long years on treason charges? Evgeny Krutikov always denied those charges: when a KGB veteran published an article in a history journal praising the successful KGB operation that prevented Felix from defecting, Evgeny made it a point to find the veteran and force him to print a retraction.

As for the KGB, his father Felix didn't hold them in high regard. He kept his distance from the foreign intelligence service and didn't demand compensation or a special pension. But he wanted a clear record of his past, and he had the KGB put in his personal file, "Until 1960, he was on a long-term business trip abroad." He was able to accomplish this because he found a way to maintain and even develop his high-level connections with Soviet elites after his release from the camps, though in the 1970s and 1980s he was mostly busy writing and translating academic articles about economics. Those connections were supporting the family right until the end of the Soviet Union.

Since his childhood, Evgeny Krutikov had worshiped his father—a revered, rather enigmatic figure, forty-one years old when Evgeny was born, whose best days, coupled with high tragedy, were already well behind him. Evgeny saw his father as a brilliant member of the Stalinist elite and a gifted intelligence officer whose ascent to the top was tragically interrupted by intrigues. He shared his father's sense of belonging to the Soviet elite as well as his disdain for the KGB. Evgeny told us time and again that the KGB of the 1980s was full of mediocrities and had it coming when the Soviet Union collapsed and brought about its dissolution.

In the late 1980s, when Evgeny was at university, his father got him a job working on the journal of the Central Committee of the Communist Party—a very good start for an ambitious man who wanted to climb up in the Soviet hierarchy. In 1990, he took accelerated retraining courses at the Military Diplomatic Academy of the General Staff (military intelligence)—he had a gift for languages, just as his father had—with the prospect of being deployed as a military attaché's officer to the Soviet embassy in Albania. When Evgeny was in his early twenties, the military intelligence service gave him a country house and a good salary.

In a way, Evgeny was clearly following in Felix's footsteps. He became a young intelligence officer with good connections in Soviet high circles, destined for a bright future.

But then the Soviet Union collapsed. Evgeny Krutikov didn't go to Albania. He abruptly left military intelligence and reinvented himself as a journalist. He did fine as a reporter in the 1990s, but not nearly as well as he likely imagined doing as an intelligence mandarin or diplomat had the Soviet Union not collapsed. His chances to make up where his father had failed, and to reach the level of his ambitious grandfather, were ruined by the disintegration of the Soviet empire.

By the fall of 2000, his career in political journalism had reached its peak. He was the head of the political department at the newspaper with the best access to the Kremlin, on his way, he hoped, to becoming the editor-in-chief. And then he lost it—as he firmly believed, because of the intrigues of his competitor, Sveta Babayeva. He was downgraded, almost disgraced. He took it as a sign that his second attempt at building a career was a humiliating failure. He told us that he was thinking of abandoning journalism for something else, and hinted he wanted to do something in diplomacy, to get back where he had been in 1991. He was just waiting for a good offer.

And then, while waiting for this offer, he was offered a part in an FSB-orchestrated disinformation campaign. Did he take it as an invitation to get into the game with the big boys? Under Putin, the FSB was becoming more and more important politically—he saw that clearly.

Apparently, Krutikov never regretted doing the Kalinkin story. After all, he had already lost respect for the profession that had failed him.

The secret police are always good at exploiting people's weaknesses, approaching and seducing them at their darkest hour.

As for former warrant officer Vasily Kalinkin, the official version of the story was that the FSB didn't charge him because he had been so cooperative. He then changed his name and appearance, for his own protection, and even his photographs from the 2001 press conference were quietly taken off the internet.

Kalinkin, if such a person ever existed, simply disappeared into thin air.

CHAPTER 8

WHEN THE COLD WAR WAS OVER

We spent the spring of 2001 building a community of participants and contributors around Agentura. Andrei secured a monthly honoraria budget from his father—a few hundred dollars to pay the authors we would commission to write for the website—and we went on to allocate it to the regional journalists who began sending us stories about their local FSB departments.

We also wanted to recruit Sergei Kozlov, a stocky, energetic, vigorously mustached veteran of Russia's *spetsnaz*, or special forces. Kozlov was well known from his stint in Afghanistan during the Russian invasion of the 1980s, when he had conducted several daring operations against the mujahideen. His rebelliousness and initiative hardly ingratiated him with his commanding officers—if he was given a stupid order, he would say so to a general's face—but did secure him legendary status among his comrades-in-arms. After Afghanistan he was assigned to a brigade in Crimea. The Cold War was not completely over, at least not for spetsnaz: military plans called for Kozlov's brigade to be trained to launch a raid on Incirlik, a Turkish air base also used by the US Air Force, in case of a real war.

When the Soviet Union collapsed in December 1991, Kozlov's brigade fell under the control of a newly independent Ukraine, which demanded that he swear allegiance to Kyiv. Kozlov, ever sharp and short-fused, resigned instead and moved to Moscow. Still in his early thirties, he had no idea what to do with his life.

He had his reputation, though, so some former comrades-in-arms offered him a chance to join a criminal gang—and be paid an astonishing amount of hard currency. He knew what was expected of him and declined. Next came an offer from the Russian security service. Yeltsin intended to bring rebellious Chechnya to heel, and the plan was to invade the Chechen capital of Grozny with unmarked tanks, provided by Moscow and packed with mercenaries. Security service officers proposed that Kozlov lead a group of forty military veterans to carry out a diversionary attack on the presidential palace in Grozny in the early hours of the invasion. He was promised $1,000. Ever a professional, he laid out for his recruiters the close-to-zero chances that the proposed group, doing the job on completely unknown terrain with no local support and no reconnaissance, would survive. To him, the amount they'd offered would be just enough to pay for his funeral. He declined.

Kozlov was wasting his life working in a currency exchange office of a Moscow bank when, during his night shift, he came across a Russian-language edition of *Soldier of Fortune*, an American magazine popular among the US military and special forces. The magazine had acquired a cult status in the Soviet Union since the late 1970s, when copies were smuggled into military academies, including Kozlov's, so current and future officers could read the stories it contained about special operations, written by those who conducted them. Very soon the Russian-language edition of *Soldier of Fortune* became the forum for discussing Russian special forces operations, even though just a few years back the American magazine had covered favorably operations against Russian troops in Afghanistan. Kozlov sent a couple of his articles about spetsnaz operations in Afghanistan to the editor, and the magazine published them. Kozlov made a point of talking to a commander of every spetsnaz group involved in an operation he wrote about. He soon emerged as the most trusted voice in the Russian spetsnaz community.

He also made some money, and when he took his wife to Turkey on vacation, he very quickly left her at the beach and made his way to Incirlik Air Base, where he told the US Marines at the gate, in his hesitant English, "Hi, I'm a Soviet spetsnaz commander, and I was trained to raid your base in case of the big war." Some US Marines took him out drinking, and they spent the night talking about how accurate the Russian military planning of the raid had been. He was convinced he had a much better time with the US Marines than his wife had on the beach.

We invited him to write for Agentura—to run the section of the website devoted to special operations. In his brusque military manner, he asked about the payment, and that was that. He agreed to come on board.

Soon a walk-in asked to join us: Alexander Mikhailov, a bald and mustached retired FSB general. A former head of the FSB press office, he had overseen the Kremlin propaganda effort over the Chechen war just a year before. It had been a nasty campaign—a combination of disinformation and blatant attacks on independent journalists accused of being on the payroll of Western masters or Chechen warlords. But now Mikhailov was kicking his heels as a head of security in a small hotel. We assumed his former bosses had asked him to approach us to keep tabs on Agentura. Instead, the general asked for a monthly stipend of $300 in return for his "advice." We had no intention of augmenting the general's FSB pension, and politely declined his offer.

Next came a foreign intelligence officer, a tall, pleasant man in his early fifties, with a quiet voice, who introduced himself as Vladimir

Alekseenko, lieutenant colonel, retired. He had served in foreign intelligence as a technical expert. During a deployment in the United States, to a Russian consulate in San Francisco, his job had been to protect it from American electronic surveillance. In the 1970s he'd invented revolutionary eavesdropping equipment that could detect listening devices even if they were switched off. Now he worked security at some big corporation, but it was a part-time job. With his keen interest in listening devices and spy cameras, he had become close to Keith Melton, an American millionaire and collector of spy tech who founded the International Spy Museum in Washington. The two of them were now hunting for Cold War spy artifacts for Melton's collection.

Thanks to his connections, Alekseenko had gotten access to museums in prisons, in secret research facilities, and on military bases usually open only to servicemen. We thought he took an interest in us because he believed it might be helpful to have us around, as journalistic cover, while asking questions about spy tech. The pretext of helping curious journalists would explain his interest in something that fell into the gray area between the classified and nonclassified worlds. Alekseenko firmly believed that spy tech couldn't be secret, only the place and time of its deployment—he repeated this formula to us time and again—but paranoid counterintelligence FSB officers could have had a very different opinion.

Alekseenko secured a private tour for us of the FSB museum. It was hardly a real museum—just four rooms in the massive rectangular Soviet structure behind the main building of the FSB on Lubyanka. The rooms were filled with memorabilia from the civil war, the Great Patriotic War (World War II), and the early Cold War period. One hall was devoted to Stalin's purges of his secret services. One could easily get the impression that Stalin's secret services were the primary victims of his dictatorship.

There was also a separate exhibition of trophies—Western weapons and radio sets taken from the resistance groups that had fought

Soviet occupation of the Baltics and Ukraine—to demonstrate that the Western spy agencies always plotted against Russia.

To the FSB, the main enemy was always the same: the West. The FSB, it was clear, considered itself a proud successor to Bolshevik secret police and all its brutal iterations throughout the twentieth century, as protectors of the political regime in Moscow against that archenemy. That enemy was formidable and powerful: the officers on Lubyanka saw the dissolution of the Soviet Union as a huge tragedy, one that was orchestrated by the West—the geopolitical catastrophe that Putin described.

That geopolitical catastrophe, among other things, had led to a shrinking of the country's influence on other continents. That was something many Russian elites felt very nostalgic about.

Petya Akopov loved to tell us a story of his parents' lives in Mogadishu, Somalia's capital. He had been a toddler then and hardly remembered anything, but he talked with deep admiration and excitement about the beauty of the African countryside, as if the memories were his own. He looked at Somalia through the rose-colored glasses of his parents, who had been happy to leave cold and gloomy Moscow in the late 1960s for the sunny city on the coast of the Indian Ocean.

The Soviet Union was an isolated country, and not many citizens ever traveled abroad. Those who were allowed to travel usually went to socialist-bloc countries such as East Germany or Bulgaria. Western Europe and the United States were options mainly for diplomats, spies, and top-level apparatchiks. If someone had been lucky enough to go abroad, even for a short trip, their memories of their journey to the Big World had been carefully kept by several generations of their family along with material keepsakes like fine German porcelain or Barbie dolls.

Africa stood apart. In the 1960s, many African countries broke free of Western colonialism and became destinations for long-term assignments for Soviet experts sent to aid the newly independent nations. Moscow established diplomatic relations with Somalia in 1960, promising military and financial support in exchange for a naval base. Along with money, aircraft, and tanks, the Soviets sent engineers, doctors, and teachers. One of them was Petya's dad, who had seized the opportunity to go off to this exotic country with his young wife. Several years in Mogadishu became the happiest period of their life. They came to love the blue skies and colorful Italianate mansions and villas of the coastal city.

It sounded to us like a bitter fairy tale from another time and space. As we drank wine with Petya on the boulevard, Somalia was notorious for a devastating civil war and a terrible famine. Petya insisted that all of that happened only because the Soviets had been forced out of Somalia after a faulty decision by Somalia's leadership.

We along with other friends made a lot of fun of Petya's African obsession, but he paid us no mind. He was not susceptible to anyone else's opinion. He talked for months about his desire to go visit Somalia, and in the summer of 2001, he took action.

His planned journey seemed slightly insane. After all, *Izvestia* was not CNN or the BBC, and international reporting was not its strong suit—not to mention how expensive the trip to what was a very dangerous part of Africa would be. Mogadishu was at the time divided into pieces ruled by various warlords, and only one part was under the government's control. But Petya was never a guy who could be stopped from following his dream.

It remained a mystery how he got the leadership of *Izvestia* to send him, but in June Petya landed on a sand runway at the aerodrome thirty-five miles from Mogadishu that then served as an airport. He was not alone—his wife, Marina, along with his friend Zhenya Baranov and Baranov's TV crew, arrived with him.

Glamorous Marina, who appreciated comfort over all other things, did not exactly fit in, but she wanted to see the country she had heard so much about. A government minister had been sent to the aerodrome to meet the first Russian journalists to visit in ten years, and the Somali authorities had arranged a military parade to impress their guests.

The country lay in ruins. Once beautiful buildings were in decay, assault rifles were being sold at the city market, and a rotten smell pervaded the city. Next to the hotel was a refugee camp. *Izvestia* published Petya's sharp and well-written reports, but the opening of his first story was rather puzzling.

It was a quiz for readers. It started with a question: What country whose name starts with S (an obvious hint to the Soviet Union) collapsed in 1991? Then he provided a few hints—that the country's capital started with M-O, that it had experienced the October Revolution, that its flag had once featured a five-pointed star, and that the previous year this country got a new president and expected him to restore order. Petya's twist was that it was Somalia, not Russia. Of course, it was very much Petya's version of Somalia—he listed only the facts from Somalia's history that fitted his narrative to make the faraway African country resonate with the Russian audience. Petya's point was that a historical mistake would be corrected if Somalia sought support from Putin's Russia, since there were so many similarities between the two countries.

Few people other than Petya would have ever compared the two. Baranov, for one, didn't share Petya's fascination with the place. When, after his return to Moscow, Petya treated us to stories about Mogadishu, Baranov merely smiled.

On summer weekends we would pick up Petya and Marina in our old gray Mitsubishi Pajero SUV and drive to some nice place in the Moscow suburbs, where Baranov and some of his friends would join us. A certain pattern established itself: we usually started from the Akopovs' apartment, then drove north and northwest, exploring the triangle between Zvenigorod, a small, neat town known for its monastery on a picturesque hill over Moskva River, and the famous Rublyovka Road.

The country's elite—old Soviet apparatchiks, famous artists and producers, KGB generals and oligarchs—had loved Rublyovka since the 1920s. It was a well-maintained area where a collection of luxury villages had emerged, protected from the road by the woods and checkpoints manned by private security, and sometimes the FSB, if the owner had good connections in the Kremlin. Baranov knew how to get beyond the checkpoints to good restaurants with terraces overlooking the river. He sometimes brought his seventeen-year-old girlfriend with him, which embarrassed Irina; she felt uncomfortable having drinks with a teenager.

Andrei didn't drink at all, which the company found very convenient; he became the "designated driver," always there to bring the Akopovs back to Moscow in our car.

It was mostly Baranov who insisted on ending up on Rublyovka Road. The desire to be close to the most powerful and wealthy is a temptation shared by many journalists—one day you might interview an oligarch, and the next you could be invited to fly to his factory in Siberia on his private jet, and on the way, you might get privy to the gossip about the Kremlin and other oligarchs. It's heady stuff.

But Baranov, it appeared, more than anyone among our friends, wanted to find a way into the Russian elite. For that, Rublyovka was the place, and we played along with his obsession all summer.

The second week of September we flew to a small resort town on the Mediterranean coast of Turkey to get some sun and to swim in the warm sea before the first hints of winter. We enjoyed ourselves, day after day, until the evening of September 11.

That night we spent in a lobby, along with all the other hotel guests, watching CNN, which was playing nonstop footage of two planes hitting the World Trade Center. Our fellow Russian tourists were clearly devastated. It felt like the world order had collapsed, and people talked about the prospects of a new world war, this time between civilizations. It was clear that the Russians around us thought of themselves as being in the same civilization as the Americans.

In Moscow, Krutikov was watching CNN's footage in his new *Izvestia* office on the second floor. He had recently been awarded a larger room, next to the bosses. He was assigned to write a story about the attacks. In it, he added a comment by the head of the FSB press office. "This is a clear act of terrorism," the FSB press director said. "I offer my condolences to all the relatives of the victims. I would like to emphasize that in the fight against international terrorism we need to join forces and not apply double standards.... These events will push us to work more closely with the Americans."

This was the same FSB general who had orchestrated the Kalinkin disinformation operation just nine months before, the aim of which was to depict bin Laden in bed with the CIA plotting terrorist attacks on Russian soil. But on September 11, he sounded very different. The FSB had adjusted its position, following Putin's lead.

Baranov was in the Kremlin with the Russian president on September 11. That morning, Putin had been handing out awards to a group of journalists, and Baranov was one of four awarded the Order of Courage for covering the war in Chechnya. Three hours later, Putin made a phone call to George W. Bush, becoming the first foreign leader to express his condolences to the American president.

The following month, *Izvestia* sent Krutikov to northern Afghanistan, to the US-controlled military base, to write about the offensive by the Northern Alliance, the key American ally against the Taliban. For almost two weeks he sent dispatches to Moscow. Their tone was cautious but optimistic. When he returned to Moscow, he maintained the government line: al-Qaeda was a threat not only to the United States and the West, but to the entire world, including Russia, thus there was a need for cooperation.

In November, the American blockbuster movie *Spy Game* opened on screens worldwide, including in Moscow. The spectacular film directed by Tony Scott tells the story of two CIA operatives, played by Robert Redford and Brad Pitt, and takes place in legendary Cold War–era locations—Vietnam, East Berlin, Lebanon, China, and, of course, Langley, Virginia—when the Berlin Wall fell.

Vladimir Alekseenko, the foreign intelligence veteran and technical expert who'd arranged our tour of the FSB museum, invited us to watch it together. He chose a recently renovated theater on Novy Arbat featuring fancy Dolby Surround equipment to make the most of it. We loved the movie, but Alekseenko was ecstatic. "Look, it's authentic! It's just squeezed into one day, but the spy tradecraft they show—it's all solid!" he exclaimed, visibly impressed.

The film had the nostalgic feel of a great epoch, now gone. Alekseenko had been part of it, and though he was on the other side, he shared this feeling of nostalgia—a sign, to us, that the Cold War was truly gone, for good.

In January 2002, another American blockbuster, this one made by Ridley Scott, hit the cinemas—*Black Hawk Down*. We knew the movie was based on real events—the American military operation in Somalia in October 1993 that turned into a bloody disaster.

The civil war and horrible famine in Somalia in the 1990s were not well-known events in Russia, and very few had heard of the UN peacekeeping mission in Mogadishu. We knew close to nothing about the American attempt to take down warlord Mohamed Aidid, a graduate of the Soviet tank school.

We read that *Black Hawk Down* endeavored to portray the US raid in the most accurate way possible, and so we decided to take our spetsnaz veteran, Kozlov, to the cinema. Kozlov immediately agreed—he wanted to watch the movie as much as we did. We watched with bated breath how the mission by US Army Delta Force operators and Rangers to the center of Mogadishu to capture Aidid's lieutenants quickly developed into chaotic and bloody city fighting when insurgents took down two Black Hawk helicopters, one by one.

The visual and audio effects were astonishing even though the film was dubbed in Russian. We noticed that the Russian translators had called the adversary in the movie—the Somalia militia—*dukhi*, which is what Soviet soldiers had called Afghan mujahideen in the 1980s. When we emerged from the cinema, we asked Kozlov whether he'd noticed that as well. He said he did, but apparently he had no problem with it. To him, mujahideen and militants of Mogadishu were on one side—the side of the enemy. He was talking about the American raid and the Battle of Mogadishu as if he were on the side of the American forces. A professional soldier, he immediately associated himself with the US Army forces.

At that moment, Petya Akopov's obsession with the Soviet legacy in Africa felt old-fashioned and marginal, a remnant of a long-forgotten and irrelevant battle of the long-past Cold War. After all, it was the twenty-first century, and a big new war against global terror had just begun. We also thought that Petya was always a bit of a maverick, with his love for countries like North Korea and Somalia, someone always drawn to promoting the most helpless causes. But he was a very shrewd observer when it came to internal politics, of what Petya called the "Chekist management" of the country introduced by Putin (the Cheka was the first Bolshevik secret police), and we invited him to join Agentura.

Krutikov was already listed as a participant. We wanted the network of Agentura to grow, and we began to republish Krutikov's articles—with his permission.

At that time, we strongly believed, despite our exodus from *Izvestia*, that there might still be ways that we could keep our friends all working together.

CHAPTER 9

NEW BEGINNINGS

When we finally found new jobs, we moved to a new rented apartment in the center of Moscow.

Just a few stops away by metro from our flat was Stary Arbat, a picturesque pedestrian-only street in the heart of Moscow's historical center. From there it was a ten-minute walk along nice old streets to the six-story yellow building next to the Spaso House—the grand residence of American ambassadors since the mid-1930s—which hosted the newspaper *Versia*, a weekly tabloid featuring an unorthodox mix of political stories, investigative pieces, and gossip. We'd gotten there thanks to our old friend Marina Latysheva, in whose apartment we had launched Agentura two years before. She'd worked at *Versia* as a reporter for several months, and when she learned that the editor-in-chief was looking for investigative journalists, she put us in touch with him.

The editor, Rustam Arifdjanov, a gray-haired man with an easy laugh, knew who we were, and after a short professional conversation he invited us to set up a department for our Agentura team. Rustam was well-known for his unique journalistic approach—a combination of vivid literary style and shrewd observations spun from apparently mundane details. Unless he was forced to do so, he never wasted his time. We called our department "Of National Security," because we intended to focus on covering terrorism issues and security service activities.

The chance to join *Versia* as staff writers made us happy. We'd spent a year working only for Agentura and missed dearly the intensity of a reporter's life. But we knew it was a risky move. Among Moscow's journalists, *Versia* enjoyed the dubious reputation of being rather indiscriminate—insightful and revelatory investigations appeared alongside the trashy articles obviously planted by competitors of whoever was being smeared. *Versia* owed that reputation to its origins, a reflection of the way the strain of Soviet journalism that had directly served the interests of the KGB had mutated in the wild capitalist media world of the 1990s.

Versia was the latest addition to the media holding company called Sovershenno Sekretno (Top Secret) founded by two men. One was the famous Soviet writer Yulian Semyonov, who wrote very popular spy thrillers—many of them made into even more popular Soviet movies, including the number-one hit *Seventeen Moments of Spring*, Putin's favorite TV spy series—by closely cooperating with the KGB. The second was the reporter Artyom Borovik, the son of a veteran Soviet foreign correspondent.

The Boroviks were a peculiar family of gifted propagandists who were also closely connected with the KGB. Artyom's father, Genrikh Borovik, had covered war zones around the globe, including in Vietnam in the 1960s, attacking American imperialism. Between his assignments he had authored plays about Western militarism, staged in Moscow theaters, and participated in the Kremlin's public campaign against Alexander Solzhenitsyn.

The standing of the family was further strengthened by dynastic marriages—Borovik Sr. had his daughter married to the son of a KGB general, the head of the "American department" of the foreign intelligence branch of the Soviet secret police. His son, Artyom, had married the daughter of a prominent Soviet diplomat who had served in Geneva and New York, and who had ended up leading the Soviet mission at UNESCO in Paris. When Artyom decided to follow his father's path in journalism, in the same media outlet, Ogonyok, he was sent to Afghanistan to cover the Soviet invasion.

But the ascent of Mikhail Gorbachev changed the political climate. Gorbachev wanted to pull Soviet troops out of Afghanistan, and he needed public support. Artyom sensed the change in the Kremlin and turned to writing the "uncensored truth" of the last years of the Soviet invasion of Afghanistan, which brought him international acclaim. In 1988, even the *New York Times* praised Borovik's "gripping accounts" of "war-weary soldiers playing Rod Stewart tapes as they prepare for battle in a strange land."[1]

In the late 1980s, Semyonov had launched *Sovershenno Sekretno* as a monthly tabloid, and Borovik soon joined him with his father's blessing. The tabloid became wildly popular because it published investigations and untold stories about secret Soviet history at a time when nobody in the Soviet Union knew what a real journalistic investigation looked like. It also made very good money, and after the collapse of the Soviet Union the media company successfully started a TV program, a magazine, and the weekly newspaper *Versia*.

By the early 2000s, both founders of the media company were dead. Semyonov died of a stroke, and Borovik was killed in a plane crash under mysterious circumstances two years before we joined *Versia*. The private jet had been chartered by a Chechen oil oligarch, and the plane with the oligarch, Borovik, crew members, and a couple of others aboard crashed immediately after takeoff. Two years afterward, the newspaper was still conducting its investigation, suspecting an assassination plot—against either the oligarch or Borovik. Borovik's young widow, Veronika, then in her mid-thirties and the mother of three sons, took over the small media empire.

We first saw Veronika Borovik-Khilchevskaya as she emerged from a gigantic black Land Cruiser in front of the office. Her chauffeur opened the door, and an attractive brunette wearing a mink coat walked into the building. Her style was very unusual for a top media manager in the twenty-first century, and it was a mismatch for a daughter of a seasoned diplomat—she had spent several years in Paris because of her father's position with UNESCO.

On her desk in her spacious office Veronika kept a photograph of FSB chief General Nikolai Patrushev standing next to a large globe. Her late husband gazed upon the general from a black-framed photograph on the wall. It was not a big secret that Veronika maintained pretty close relationships with the generals of the FSB, inherited from her husband's father, who had written many stories on behalf of the KGB. There were also rumors about too-close connections with some prominent Russian mafiosi.

As we learned all this, our enthusiasm for our new workplace faded a bit, but it was the only offer we had. Besides, because we were allowed to form our own department, we believed we could maintain some independence, as long as we delivered the requested number of stories on a weekly basis. That was the promise our editor, Rustam, had made to us.

Besides, we had company: Evgeny Krutikov had secured a job at *Versia* a couple of months before us, bringing along with him two of his friends from *Izvestia*.

In the spring of 2002 we decided to test *Versia*'s limits. Our department prepared a big investigation of the way the real estate business negotiated with the security services over plots of land in Moscow. In Soviet times, the security services had enjoyed elite status among Soviet organizations and was able to seize any piece of land in Moscow they wanted for their "special objects"—headquarters of different departments, research centers, prisons, listening posts, factories of spy equipment, all top secret, of course. They also extensively built special objects beneath Moscow—bunkers, metro lines for the exclusive use of Kremlin bosses, and tunnels for tanks. Since the regime lasted for seven decades, the KGB ended up with a property portfolio that would have made a feudal lord blush, including mansions, palaces, and huge fenced areas of Moscow, some in the very center of the city around the Lubyanka headquarters.

In the early 2000s, a real estate boom was transforming Moscow. The successors to the KGB had kept their property, and soon the generals realized they were sitting on a gold mine. There were a lot of lucrative opportunities for the greedy generals, especially when it became clear that the approval of the security services was required before anything could be built on the site of what had been a special object, and that building anything over a special object was banned, even if that object lay far below the ground.

Our editor didn't have any objections to the investigation, so we printed the story, illustrating it with a map of FSB property across Moscow that we compiled based on open-source information.[2] We heard nothing from the executive floor after publication. Apparently, Veronika didn't care much, or she didn't notice the story. The FSB did notice, though we learned of that only much later.

On a sunny Saturday in August, we stopped by the Duma club, where we saw Zhenya Baranov with a short, stocky young blonde woman we'd never met before. Baranov introduced her as his colleague from a TV channel, but the way they talked to each other made it clear they were not just colleagues. Petya Akopov told us later that the blonde was Baranov's new girlfriend, Olga Lyubimova. She was ten years younger than he, and their relationship seemed to be serious.

It turned out Lyubimova came from a renowned theatrical Moscow family. Her great-grandfather was the legendary actor Vasily Kachalov, who at the beginning of the twentieth century had worked with the world-famous director Konstantin Stanislavski. A street in the center of Moscow was named for him. Lyubimova's mother was also an actress, and her father worked as a literature director at various theaters.

Lyubimova did not go down that path. Instead, she chose to study journalism and ended up working at a small TV channel, where she had met Baranov and fallen in love with him.

Petya told us that Lyubimova had introduced Baranov to her family, and that he had already become a frequent guest at their dacha in the upscale district of Rublyovka. The family was very proud of their old dacha. They had inherited it from their distinguished ancestor, who had moved there in the mid-1930s. It was a country house surrounded by pine forest in the village of Nikolina Gora, fifteen miles west of Moscow. For almost a century, since the Soviet elite had chosen this place for their dachas, it had been the most sought-after piece of land in the country, Russia's Golden Mile.

Next to Lyubimova's dacha lived the Mikhalkov clan, a remarkable and controversial family of minor Russian aristocracy that had come to prominence under Stalin but found a way to stay important in the new Russia. The family had first been propelled to the highest echelons of the Soviet elite by the poet Sergey Mikhalkov, who was wise enough to write a poem in the 1930s that many believed was a paean to Stalin's daughter. During the Great Patriotic War, Stalin had chosen him to write the lyrics to the new Soviet national anthem. The text praised Stalin as a father of the nation, and the Soviet dictator rewarded him. As part of their elevated status, the Mikhalkovs moved to the dacha in Nikolina Gora. After Stalin's death, when an anti-Stalin campaign took place in the country, the poet was told to change the lyrics of the anthem, which he did, removing Stalin and replacing him with Lenin. In 2000, when Putin came to power, the new president decided to reinstate the old Soviet anthem and asked Mikhalkov, by then in his late eighties, to write yet another set of words. The old man complied and dutifully rewrote the lyrics a third time. Rather than mentioning Lenin, Stalin, or Putin, however, it now just praised Great Russia.

Sergey's son Nikita Mikhalkov, a talented filmmaker and actor—all Russians knew his trademark walrus mustache, a key part of his dashing masculinity, carefully tended—had inherited his father's acute political instincts. In the 1990s he made a thrilling anti-Stalinist movie, *Burnt by the Sun*, which won an Oscar, and he supported Boris Yeltsin in the 1996 presidential election. When Putin came to power, Nikita rushed to the new president, eager to offer public support for his militarism and for his nostalgia for the great Soviet Union.

Seven years older than Putin, Nikita Mikhalkov aspired to become Putin's spiritual mentor. Putin, in return, granted Mikhalkov unprecedented access. Putin didn't hesitate to show his support publicly by coming to the Moscow Film Festival, which Nikita Mikhalkov ran.[3] The star of the Mikhalkov family was, once again, on the rise.

In the best and worst traditions of the Russian aristocracy—which Nikita Mikhalkov never failed to mention that his family belonged to—the Mikhalkovs were at the center of a circle of several families of Moscow's intelligentsia they cared about and promoted. Olga Lyubimova's family was a prominent part of the circle, so close to the protector that their dachas' allotments were not even separated by a fence.

As Baranov visited Rublyovka increasingly often, we joked that, while he seemed to be charmed by the girl, what he really loved was Rublyovka's elite. Soon enough, Baranov and Lyubimova got married.

At work, we encountered a different version of the elite. The editorial office occupied the sixth, top floor of the building, and one summer day on the stairs to the office we came across a corpulent man who was leading a tiger cub on a leash. At least he said it was a cub; it seemed full of adolescent menace.

"What's going on?" we asked when we finally reached our floor. A photographer waved nonchalantly, saying, "It's Taiwanchik. Apparently, he is a pal of Veronika's, so we are doing a photo session with him and a tiger." Taiwanchik, a.k.a. "Little Taiwanese," whose real name was Alimzhan Tokhtakhunov, was allegedly one of the most notorious organized crime bosses in Russia.

Born in Soviet Central Asia, he was involved in illegal gambling and spent some years in Soviet jail before he moved out—first to Germany, later France, and then to Italy. He had just returned to Moscow after being detained for several months in Italy at the request of the United States on conspiracy charges. He was suspected of trying to bribe skating officials to fix the pairs skating competitions at the Winter Olympics in Salt Lake City, where the Russian couple had defeated the Canadians.[4] The Italian authorities ultimately refused the extradition request and released Taiwanchik, but made clear he was not welcome anymore. So he returned to Russia.

Pair skating is one of the most beloved sports in Russia, and it didn't surprise us that Taiwanchik was given safe haven in Russia. But to discover him with a tiger in the editorial office was a bit weird.

It was not the only strange activity at *Versia*. More and more paid articles were appearing in the paper, sometimes literally next to our stories. But nobody interfered with our work, and the editor took it well when we refused to accept the "bonuses" paid in cash that were distributed among journalists every month by Rustam's deputy at the far end on the sixth floor. We knew that accepting those bonuses would mean we would be writing articles at the request of the advertising department, which we had no intention of doing.

So after a lot of soul searching, we decided to remain at *Versia*. There were not so many places in the Moscow media world where we could enjoy equivalent freedom, though the price was high, and sometimes we thought it was too high. We knew full well that the corrupt paper retained us only because our stories helped it sustain the pretense of being a genuine investigative media outlet.

CHAPTER 10

COMRADES IN ARMS

The night of Wednesday, October 23, 2002, we were sitting and chatting in the only room of a tiny apartment that Marina Latysheva had rented on the street next to *Versia*'s editorial offices. We dropped by her place several days a week after work—it was so convenient. It was around 9:00 in the evening, and the TV set was on, when we heard a breaking news alert: a group of terrorists had taken hostages at the Dubrovka Theater, where the musical *Nord-Ost* was being performed.

The initial information was that armed men had come into the hall and opened fire in the air. The audience was not allowed to leave the hall, but people were given an opportunity to make calls to friends and relatives. The entire audience was taken hostage along with theater personnel, at least 1,000 people altogether. Traffic around the theater was blocked, and special forces were deployed to the area.

We left Marina, jumped in our Opel, and quickly headed off to the unfolding disaster.

The theater was not in the center of Moscow; it was in one of the cultural centers built in the city's suburbs in the 1970s, at a former Moscow ball bearing factory in the city's eastern portion. Housed in a massive, squat, brutalist-looking three-story rectangle with a large glass-and-concrete entrance, it was surrounded by Stalin-era apartment buildings. Because the factory's workers and their families were supposed to spend all their free time there, the main concert hall had a capacity to host more than 1,000 people. The large auditorium was the reason why *Nord-Ost*'s ambitious producers had chosen it for their play. They wanted to make the first Russian Broadway-style musical really big, a Russian rival to *Les Misérables* and *Phantom of the Opera*. They had adapted a very popular Soviet book praising the heroism of Soviet pilots—a politically safe and patriotic topic. All of Moscow was plastered with *Nord-Ost* placards, and a high point of the show was a bomber plane landing right on the huge stage.

We drove east down dark Moscow streets toward one of the ugliest parts of the city, built up with Soviet-era high-rises. Unsurprisingly, Dubrovka Street was blocked by police, so we abandoned the car and set out on foot, trying to get closer to the theater to find out what was going on inside. The view was blocked by an apartment building, and the police were busy setting up a perimeter, pushing people out. Young soldiers stood next to armored vehicles, alongside police officers and some journalists. A large crowd of bystanders had gathered in the street.

We immediately bumped into several friends. One of them was Zhenya Baranov, with his TV crew. Rain turned to snow—that wet and heavy Moscow snow that immediately turns to dirt, making everything feel much colder—as we awaited developments. Many journalists were shivering from the cold, but Baranov was conspicuously calm, dressed from head to toe in strange gray-green overalls. "You see?" he exclaimed. "It is an Israeli Air Force pilot outfit I got as a gift—and I'm not cold!" Certainly, he looked much more comfortable than our friend Olga, a TV presenter, who, sent straight from the studio to cover the crisis, was wearing a light jacket and high heels.

With every passing minute it became clearer that the crisis would last a long time, so we set out to find a place to stay warm, and, ideally, close to the theater. We circled around until Andrei remembered that he had an ID from some association of friends of the antidrug department of the Moscow police; the association had given its members badges with numbers on them that looked just like real police badges. We approached the soldiers guarding the perimeter, choosing a place with no officers, and Andrei produced the badge. A soldier got suspicious. "Antidrug police? Why?" he asked. "Don't you see? It's huge; every department gets involved!" Andrei answered as confidently as he could, and we were allowed to pass through.

We knew we couldn't wander among the police for long, so we slipped into the entrance of the nearest apartment building with windows facing the theater. On the third floor, a woman in her forties opened the door: "Journalists? Come on in. Your colleagues are already inside." And indeed, in the biggest room, with windows looking at the entrance of the theater, were two reporters. We knew one of them—Mark Franchetti from London's *Sunday Times*. Our brave hostess, an imposing, intelligent woman who we later learned had participated in the democratic movement in the early 1990s, was willing to accommodate more journalists in her apartment, so when a friend of ours, Nick Paton Walsh, a correspondent from the *Guardian*, called, she agreed to walk him in through the security perimeter. She got back in half an hour, by herself, still giggling. "I told the policemen I needed to fetch my lover—I was ready to compromise myself," she said. "But then I saw your friend. He is a very handsome guy, so it might have worked, but he had brought a TV crew team with him, with cameras!"

We spent three nights in that apartment, making short trips home to change clothes and get some sleep. The hostage tragedy unfolded in full public view: the terrorists gave interviews to Russian media, sometimes calling radio stations directly on air, and let a hostage walk out and read their demands to the authorities in front of TV cameras. They also demanded that relatives of the hostages stage an antiwar protest on Red Square. The terrorists let several opposition politicians, along with a doctor, a famous singer, and some journalists, into the theater. The journalists included Franchetti. Another one was Anna Politkovskaya, a famous Russian reporter trusted in the North Caucasus, who was allowed to bring water to the hostages.

The Kremlin went berserk, lambasting the media. The media ministry issued a warning to the most popular Moscow radio station, Ekho Moskvy, threatening to shut it down for giving a platform to the terrorists, because Ekho's hosts had interviewed one of the terrorists on air. The ministry also temporarily halted broadcasting by the TV channel Moskovia, the one Baranov worked for, because it had aired an Al Jazeera story in which the terrorists' demands were voiced. On the second day of the crisis, the ministry issued a call to journalists to limit their coverage.

We hunkered down in the apartment. In the early hours of Saturday, October 26, our hostess woke us up—the lights illuminating the theater's entrance had turned off. We knew that was a bad sign. The previous day, the terrorists had warned that if the lights were killed by the authorities, they would assume an assault was underway.

We heard a grenade explosion, then the sound of shattering glass. Bursts of gunfire came from the building opposite the side entrances of the theater, followed by machine-gun fire.

From all directions, special forces rushed to the entrance of the theater. At that moment, the radio, always turned on in the apartment, broadcast the hostage-release operation HQ's statement that the storming by special forces had been triggered by the knowledge that the terrorists were preparing to execute the hostages, and that the terrorists had fired the first shots. Journalists in the room looked at each other in horror and disgust. Who, then, had turned the lights off? We all understood that the special operation had started with a big lie and that the FSB was preparing a cover-up if things got ugly.

Two hours later, soldiers started dragging the unconscious bodies of hostages out of the main entrance, laying them out in a line in front of the theater.

The number increased rapidly, and from the way they were unceremoniously laid at the entrance, we realized that many of them were dead. Soon, the bodies occupied the entire area between the steps and the entrance, the line of them extending some 150 feet. Still there wasn't enough room, and the rescuers resorted to stacking corpses on top of one another. The TV was still on in the apartment, and a member of the special forces staff came on air to announce the end of the operation: the hostages were free, he said, and the terrorists had been killed.

Not a single mention was made of any casualties.

Of more than 1,000 hostages, the authorities later admitted that 130 people had died. The terrorists themselves had killed 5 people. The rest were poisoned by a gas that the special forces had pumped into the theater to sedate the terrorists. Something had gone very wrong.

Nevertheless, the operation was declared to be a victory. The interests of the Kremlin and the security services coincided: Putin wanted to be seen as different from his predecessor, Boris Yeltsin, and that meant being tough and decisive in dealing with terrorists. The FSB, desperate for revenge after the humiliations of the mid-1990s, wanted to be seen as victorious.

Just seven years before, in June 1995, Chechen militants led by warlord Shamil Basayev had taken an entire hospital hostage in the southern Russian town of Budennovsk. It was a maternity hospital, and for several agonizing days Chechens held hostage over 1,800 pregnant women, new mothers, and doctors and other medical personnel.[1] Basayev's fighters put women in the window frames as human shields to prevent a special operation and demanded talks with the Russian authorities to end the war in Chechnya. The Russian prime minister, Viktor Chernomyrdin, took it on himself to make an embarrassing and humiliating phone call to Basayev in front of journalists' cameras. As a result, the hostages were released, the terrorists were let go, and, after further talks, the First Chechen War came to an end. Ever since, the security services and the military had held a grudge about the fact that Chernomyrdin and Yeltsin had "let them win," and had shown weakness in front of the Chechens. This weakness, they believed, had provoked Basayev to attack the Russian region of Dagestan several years later, starting the Second Chechen War.

Putin didn't want to look weak, even if it meant sacrificing the hostages, and the security services fully supported him. The last thing he and his generals wanted was to talk about the casualties or why people died. Only much later did we learn from participants in the operation that the FSB had been aware of numerous explosive devices in the theater and had expected the terrorists to blow up the entire building. They had sent special forces soldiers to what they assumed was an almost certain death. They had expected fewer than 10 percent of the hostages to survive. For that reason, no temporary hospital had been set up, not enough oxygen was on hand, and no antidote to the poison gas was at the ready.

We got back to our apartment completely exhausted. Andrei wanted to take a nap but Irina insisted on sitting down to write the story based on what we had witnessed firsthand.

But it would be ten days before we could get our reportage in print in *Versia*, because it was a weekly. The issue was sent to the printer only on Fridays. That seemed like too long to wait for such a story, so we decided to publish it on Agentura. It was up on the website on Sunday and immediately got picked up by a major Italian publication, *La Stampa*.[2]

At our *Versia* editorial meeting on Monday, we discussed what the paper planned to do about the coverage of the tragedy for the next issue. We shared our reportage with colleagues, and our editor, Rustam, immediately decided to print it. Evgeny Krutikov was just as appalled as we were by the government response to the crisis—he wrote his own piece about the lack of coordination and planning and the confusion among the security services during the first two days.[3] A journalist with close ties to political PR people suggested that we also write an op-ed praising the FSB special forces, but we all rejected that idea. Veronika, the head of the media holding company, didn't get involved at all.

Baranov had spent three days on Dubrovka, and he was angry. He'd watched buses filled with dead bodies leaving the theater the morning after the special operation. He read our story and came over to us with his TV crew to film what we had to say. His channel was back on air, and Baranov wanted to get our testimony on the record. He aired it at once.

We kept working feverishly on the story, enlisting all the human sources Agentura could access. We talked to our contacts in hospitals, in the FSB, and at the morgues where the bodies of killed terrorists were stashed. Agentura's spetsnaz veteran Sergei Kozlov came to our apartment to watch footage of the storming of the theater that our colleagues had shared with us, and he helped us analyze the special forces' tactics.

On Friday afternoon, November 1, when the issue was ready to be sent to the printing house, we left the *Versia* office. Our story was on the front page under a big, bold headline: "Not True."

We were halfway home when Andrei got a call from Rustam: the FSB was in the editorial office. The editor was laconic, but we understood that the FSB had come to raid the place. Still, Rustam sounded surprisingly upbeat. Eight FSB operatives had missed their chance to sabotage the issue: the pages had already been sent off. But they were searching the office, and the editor told us not to come back. We headed there anyway and established ourselves in a tiny café on Stary Arbat near the office to wait for news.

Krutikov was still in the office, along with his reporters. The FSB operatives asked them to help identify Andrei's computer: they had a warrant to seize it. Krutikov brilliantly improvised, directing the FSB to a computer used by a reporter with a well-known interest in online porn. The computer was graciously offered to the operatives, and they happily picked it up and went off with it. But before leaving they left a sheet of paper with the FSB's emblem—a summons for Andrei to come to interrogation.

By then every journalist in Moscow had learned of the search. Our friends stormed into our tiny café, which was turned into a semiofficial press office of Agentura, while Rustam was busy giving comments to major TV channels. "I am certain," he said, "that this visit was connected with the intention of finding out what information the editorial office had about the hostage taking and the rescue operation."

In the following days and weeks, the FSB subjected the *Versia* staff to an exhausting series of interrogations. Operatives questioned reporters, the editor, us of course, even the technical staff.

Then the operatives visited the editorial office again, and this time they took personnel files of journalists from two departments—ours and Krutikov's—from HR. Apparently, his computer-full-of-porn prank hadn't gone over well with the investigators.

The FSB clearly wanted to paralyze our work and harass our sources. The paper fought back: a week after the raid, it published a list of twenty-five questions to the government investigation into the Nord-Ost tragedy, demanding to know why the rescue operation had led to the deaths of so many innocent victims.

We never got any answers, and neither did the opposition members of the Russian parliament; when they tried to launch a parliamentary investigation, it was blocked by pro-Putin factions.

In the meantime, the FSB kept summoning us for more questioning. Initially, the interrogations took place in the pleasant old mansion in the city center on Ostozhenka—the headquarters of the military intelligence department—but soon the FSB ordered us to come to the infamous Lefortovo prison, where the investigative department of the FSB—the main body of the agency that conducts investigations—was headquartered.

Lefortovo, the old Russian prison continuously in operation since the late nineteenth century, has a horrible reputation. Under Stalin, it was in the Lefortovo basement where the victims of mass purges were routinely shot. In the 1970s and 1980s, the KGB held political dissidents and those accused of high treason there, and in the first post-Soviet decade the Russian security services had continued the tradition of imprisoning those charged with treason in Lefortovo. Under Putin, Lefortovo was still hosting political prisoners: by the time we got our summons to the interrogation in Lefortovo, Eduard Limonov, the radical and nationalist writer beloved by Petya Akopov, had already been languishing there for more than a year on charges of illegal possession of weapons.

It was very useful for the FSB to conduct interrogations inside Lefortovo when dealing with those who were not yet arrested, like us. People invited for questioning never knew whether they would be freed or just moved to another part of the same building—to the prison. They were more likely to be afraid, which was how the FSB wanted them.

The first interrogation in Lefortovo was daunting. The reputation of the prison filled us with foreboding. And besides, it's quite difficult to find. The squat prison building, in the form of the letter K, is hidden behind an eight-story Soviet-era apartment building on Energeticheskaya Street, east of the center of Moscow, behind a large city park.

There were no guards at the entrance, and visitors were expected to wait in a hall for their guide. There was no one in the hall, either; all instructions were issued over a loudspeaker. The guide—an officer in his mid-twenties—was waiting behind a heavy door to accompany us down a pale blue and beige corridor and up to the second floor.

Along the corridor, the doors to the offices of investigators were marked only with numbers, and at the end of the corridor a heavy metal door led to the part of the building housing the prison. We had to sit for hours answering endless questions in a small room—just a table, three chairs, and a huge metal safe, with white paper veils covering the office windows. The only distraction was an FSB calendar on the wall featuring photos of special forces operators posing with their guns. Soon this became part of our weekly routine.

If the FSB thought this tactic would intimidate us, they miscalculated. The official reason for the FSB investigation against us was that we had supposedly disclosed some state secrets. The FSB remembered our investigation about the security services' "special objects" and the lucrative generals' real estate business in Moscow that we had published in the spring. Now, all of a sudden, in the eyes of the investigators, the information about those "special objects" had become classified.

But in 2002 it was legally impossible to accuse someone of disclosing state secrets if that person didn't have security clearance. We clearly had no such clearances. The FSB tried to put pressure on us to make us reveal our inside sources. That was the very last thing we wanted to share with the FSB, and so the investigation hit a dead end.

But the FSB kept trying, summoning us in turns. One December morning, it was Irina's turn. When she arrived at Lefortovo around 8:00 a.m., a sleepy woman behind the glass took a look at the summons and pointed out to Irina that her interrogation was actually arranged for the next day. Irina realized she had gotten the day of the interrogation confused. She asked the woman to call the FSB investigator and ask if he was ready to talk to her, so she wouldn't have to come to Lefortovo two days in a row.

In a few minutes a young man in a gray jacket showed up. "Hi, you are welcome! Did you recall something?" He looked agitated and friendly, but his excitement was premature. During the interrogations, Irina used the tactics that she, Andrei, and a lawyer friend had come up with beforehand. For every question she gave the same answer: "I don't remember because it was a long time ago."

The investigator soon got angry and asked another question: "What's your relationship with your superior, Andrei Soldatov?"

That came out of the blue. Irina's partnership with Andrei was not a secret, but Irina did not want to discuss it with the FSB, because it had nothing to do with the FSB. She got confused, then angry. So, she asked the officer back, "What sorts of relationships, in your opinion, exist, in general?"

"Friendly, normal, hostile...," the interrogator listed.

"Well, in this case, please write, 'My relationship with Andrei Soldatov is friendly and is not hostile.'"

After that, the conversation ended. It was the last time Irina was interrogated.

A month later, Andrei got a call from a major in the Moscow department of the FSB who worked in the counterterrorism section. He was around our age, intelligent, and easygoing. He'd graduated not from the Academy of the FSB but from the prestigious Moscow Engineering Physics Institute, and he had gone to work for the FSB a few years before to fight a very real terrorist threat. Sometimes he provided good information, including during the Nord-Ost crisis, and Andrei believed they'd struck up a good working relationship.

This time he sounded very serious and requested an urgent meeting, on a street near the entrance of the Moscow Zoo. When they met, Andrei offered to get into our Opel—it was freezing cold outside. But the major flatly refused. "I was told to tell you they are ready to close your criminal investigation, but we have to make a deal. Forget about Nord-Ost."

It came as a bit of a shock that the FSB major had been reporting our conversations to his bosses, apparently for several years. Now he had a message from them to us.

The major told Andrei that the number of Nord-Ost victims was purposely understated, and the operation portrayed as a victory, to discourage terrorists from attempting similar attacks in the future. "Andrei, you know, according to the suicide bombers' rules, if each jihadist kills six people, they win. We cannot let that happen."

It was a loopy justification, and Andrei was skeptical about the jihadist mathematics.

The FSB major warned that if we didn't stop, the FSB would keep summoning *Versia*'s journalists for interrogation. Finally, Andrei got angry and responded that in this case, every interrogation would be reported by our journalist friends—and that would put pressure on the FSB.

A few months later, the FSB quietly killed the investigation. *Versia* got its computers back, including the one full of porn.

By that time, very few people wanted to remember what had happened at the Dubrovka Theater in October 2002. Only the relatives of the victims kept up the doomed fight for truth, and they were more and more isolated. Even in the offices of *Versia*, some people became annoyed by our persistence. "Stop it, we want to trust our security services!" the paper's layout designer, a woman in her early thirties, exclaimed in frustration.

The country moved on, convincing itself that it had left the horrors of the hostage tragedy behind it, and that the security services would do everything in their power to prevent such a thing from ever happening again.

CHAPTER 11

BESLAN

The FSB attack on us didn't much affect our positions at *Versia*. Rustam, our editor, had our backs, and we were not made privy to what was said between him and Veronika, the head of Sovershenno Sekretno.

On the eve of the New Year, heading into 2003, a corporate party was held at the giant nightclub Metelitsa on Novy Arbat—a neon-lighted place with a warning sign at the entrance urging visitors to give up their firearms. Several burly men guarded the stairs leading up to the dance floor, and there was a casino on the ground floor.

Upstairs, Veronika, in an elegant dress, stood on stage with a mic, while reporters, editors, and photographers sat at the tables around the room. She was presenting awards to the journalists of her media outlets. At one point, Veronika called Andrei up and handed him a big mock cardboard credit card for, she said, the costliest story of the year. Her joke sounded a bit sour to us. *Versia* hadn't even provided us with a lawyer, and we'd had to ask our friend to accompany us to Lefortovo. But others laughed at her joke, apart from some colleagues who came to believe that the mock card would be followed by a cash bonus. It took some skills to convince them that was not the case.

Then, in the summer of 2003, Veronika suddenly forced Rustam out, without much explanation, and replaced him with a twenty-four-year-old woman who had almost no journalistic experience. It was not very difficult for us to gain the new editor's trust, but we all felt we needed a much more experienced person in that role, as the political atmosphere in the country had begun to change.

In April, Sergei Yushenkov, an opposition member of the Russian parliament who had been investigating the role of the FSB in the terrorist attacks in Moscow, was shot dead walking to his apartment building. In July, the prominent investigative journalist Yuri Shchekochikhin, also a member of the parliament, was poisoned. In two weeks, the healthy fifty-three-year-old reporter turned into a very old man. He almost completely lost his hair, his skin began to peel, his internal organs failed one by one, and then he died. He'd been in the middle of a huge investigation into FSB corruption. All Moscow knew him—he'd been a legendary journalist since the 1980s and commanded universal respect. Rustam went to the funeral. He was usually cheerful and optimistic—even the FSB interrogations couldn't really disturb him—but after seeing Shchekochikhin's shriveled body in the casket he was deeply shocked.

In the fall, the Kremlin and the FSB came after the most powerful Russian oligarch—Mikhail Khodorkovsky. Khodorkovsky had challenged Putin in public and didn't show a lot of respect either, as most other oligarchs did.

First, his oil corporation came under an all-out attack—every law enforcement agency in the country seemed to need to ask questions about its operations—and in late October Khodorkovsky himself was arrested by FSB special forces and thrown in jail. The security services began preparing a big show trial of Khodorkovsky and his top managers. The charges thrown at them ranged from tax evasion to embezzlement to assassination.

Olga Kostina, once the brain behind the unofficial press center of the FSB and a regular at the Duma club, stepped up as a witness against Khodorkovsky's top managers, claiming that Khodorkovsky's deputy had ordered the head of Khodorkovsky's security to assassinate her five years before for personal reasons.[1] The head of security was sentenced to twenty years in jail; Khodorkovsky's deputy fled the country and received a life sentence in absentia.[2] Khodorkovsky would spend the next ten years in a labor camp near the Chinese border.

There were some good moments that year though. In early June, Petya Akopov called. "Guys, Baranov had a son! Let's go celebrate!" We drove to Povarskaya street, where Zhenya Baranov was already celebrating in a Georgian restaurant.

At Baranov's table there were members of his TV crew, Petya, and his father-in-law—Olga Lyubimova's father. Baranov was excited. We all toasted his newborn son, Nikita, who, just by pure accident, had been given the same name as Nikita Mikhalkov, the main patron of Lyubimova's and Baranov's careers.

The celebration progressed, and at some point late in the night Baranov stood up suddenly, and in his deep voice announced, "I'm very happy that I have friends who are drinking today for my son and me in Moscow, friends who are drinking for me in Tel Aviv, friends who are drinking for me in Paris, and in Belgrade!"

It was very clear that Baranov found it important to be part of a global culture at one of the most exciting moments of his life. But the friends he was speaking about were either former Soviet citizens—in Paris and Tel Aviv—or Russian-speaking Serbs. Baranov didn't speak any foreign languages. Sometimes we wondered what kind of global world he was truly a part of.

Meanwhile, at *Versia*, we kept figuring out ways to work with the new leadership and began to feel that we could keep going with the new editor. The only problem was that she was so unsure of herself and of her own opinion that she agreed with whoever happened to be the last person to come to her office.

It made for a hectic atmosphere, but things were tolerable for many months. That remained so until the early spring of 2004, when Andrei crossed a line by writing a long piece about conspiracy theories popular in the Russian security services. We'd long wondered what people in the agencies had come to believe after Communist ideology was disposed of in the early 1990s. As we found out, the ideology was mostly replaced with conspiracy theories, all of them fiercely hostile to foreigners.

One such theory, very popular among the army ranks, claimed that "Judeo-Christian civilization" posed a threat to Russians, because these forces wanted to turn us into slaves and place the country under the control of the "global satanic predictor"—some sort of secret center in the West. So Russians, this theory went, needed to get back to paganism. Another theory, equally popular among the FSB rank and file, was that Russia had always been under attack from the West because there were hidden treasures of the long-lost Hyperborean civilization—secret knowledge—under the Ural Mountains, which the West was after. A Russian writer, Sergey Alekseev, had written books about the hidden treasures of the Hyperboreans—and they were very popular. Andrei discovered fans of the theories in many places, from the Russian parliament to the FSB to the Russian cabinet offices. This was both scary and entertaining—and a good story.

The article was about to be sent to print when Andrei received an urgent summons to Veronika's office. She never showed any interest in what we did, and Andrei, intrigued, rushed to comply. Veronika was sitting at her desk with a layout of the article in her hands. She was visibly angry. She attacked the caustic tone of the article and its criticism of the theories. She sounded sincere and emotional, and Andrei began to realize that Veronika had known about the theories and partly believed them. She also turned out to be a big fan of Sergey Alekseev and felt deeply offended. After a long, angry exchange, she told Andrei that the article was to be killed.

Clearly, it was time to go.

Thankfully, an old friend from our days at *Izvestia* came to our aid and got the story published in *Moscow News*, a weekly publication with a long liberal tradition.[3] Soon *Moscow News* invited us on board.

In the summer of 2004, we felt happy. *Moscow News* kept publishing our investigations. It was a good newspaper, one that had attained legendary status in the years of Gorbachev's perestroika. Though it had lost its popularity and some of its touch in the 1990s, it was still capable of decent reporting. It had been funded by Khodorkovsky, the oligarch who was now in jail. That didn't make it a particularly stable publication, but in the early years of Vladimir Putin's reign we'd already learned not to make any long-term plans. After all, we had had four different employers in four years.

The constant movement of journalists affected our friends as well. Petya had left *Izvestia* and moved to a new political magazine. The magazine, funded by a nationalistic oligarch with a soft spot for the Soviet empire, was small, but its editor gave Petya very much a free hand in what to write about.

Evgeny Krutikov, meanwhile, disappeared from Moscow. Some rumors had it that he'd gone to his beloved South Ossetia. We had lost touch with him after *Versia*.

September 1 puts many Russians into a nostalgic mood. It is the day when children go back to school after three months of summer holiday. Whether you liked school or hated it, you never forget the feeling of melting happiness and light melancholy associated with this day.

But September 1, 2004, put all of Russia in a state of horror. A school in Beslan, a small town in the North Caucasus, was taken hostage by terrorists. A group of armed men captured more than 1,000 people on the day of a festive ceremony, including children, parents, and teachers.

As soon as we heard of this, we rushed to the office of *Moscow News*. We wanted to be granted funds for a trip to Beslan.

It was no easy task, as there were other journalists who could get there ahead of us. In the office, Andrei went to Misha, the deputy editor and a very experienced war correspondent, who had covered several conflicts in the Caucasus himself. He promptly arranged travel expenses for us.

On our way to the airport, we learned that hostages had been herded into the school's gymnasium. Their mobile phones had been taken away, and several explosive devices had been hung up on the basketball hoops. It was reported that among the terrorists were several female suicide bombers wearing explosive belts on their waists—an ominous echo of the Nord-Ost tragedy.

There was not much information about the terrorists, other than that they appeared to have gotten to Beslan on several trucks from the neighboring republic of Ingushetia. It was clear that they were behaving more aggressively than the Chechens who had taken the theater in Moscow hostage two years before. In Beslan, terrorists had immediately shot dozens of captured men and thrown their bodies out of a school window.

In Moscow's Vnukovo airport, where flights to the North Caucasus departed, we saw a crowd of journalists. Baranov, wearing only a light cotton shirt, was near the information desk talking on his mobile phone. He looked confused. His cameraman explained to us that Baranov had been in his office when he had heard the news and had had no time to get home to change clothes. He had left his passport at home and was trying to find a way to fly from Moscow without his documents.

We never learned how he managed to do it, but in less than an hour, all the journalists, including Baranov, boarded a plane bound to the Mineralnye Vody, or Min Vody, airport, the one nearest to Beslan. Baranov's passport remained at his apartment.

It was already dark when we landed. Baranov suggested we take a car together, and off we drove to Beslan, a journey of approximately 120 miles. We expected plenty of checkpoints on the road, and we were trying to come up with a plausible explanation for why Baranov had no identification. But we encountered just one, and nobody asked for any documents. In three hours, we arrived in Beslan. On a dark street just 300 or so feet from the school, a young soldier blocked our way. We turned around and went looking for somewhere to spend the night in the neighboring town of Vladikavkaz.

Early the next morning, we returned. Beslan was a small town, and it seemed that every person we met had a relative or a friend inside the captured school. Two local men in plain clothes, armed with Kalashnikovs, approached us. They realized we were journalists and offered to get us closer to the school building.

They led us into a shed in front of the school. Through a big gap in the wooden planks, we saw the bodies of several men, killed by terrorists the day before, still lying under the school windows. A dark figure appeared in the school window and stayed there, looking out. "Don't move, he could see us," one of our guides warned us.

The local militiaman spoke again after the figure moved away. "We don't want our children to get killed like what happened in Nord-Ost," he said. "We want negotiations and release of hostages at any price. Let the world see what is going on here." His eyes were red from fatigue and fury. At the beginning of the Beslan crisis, the Kremlin had instructed state media, including TV channels, to lie about the number of hostages and say there were only 300 of them, while in reality there were more than 1,000. The militiaman feared that the Kremlin, to avoid talking to terrorists, was trying to prepare the public for another "special operation."

He was correct—the Kremlin did not want any negotiation. We knew that Putin had sent the FSB director and the interior minister to Beslan on the first day of the crisis, but after they landed, they never went near the school. The generals stayed in the airport, had a brief conference, and caught a return flight to Moscow.

Anna Politkovskaya, a reporter from *Novaya Gazeta* and the most trusted voice in the region, who had brought water to the Nord-Ost hostages two years before, was on her way to Beslan to take part in negotiations, but she was mysteriously poisoned on the plane, hospitalized, and never made it to Beslan.

On Thursday, September 2, the second day of the hostage taking, we were wandering the streets of Beslan when we spotted a familiar stooped figure. It was Krutikov. He was thrilled to see us and told us he had arrived from South Ossetia a day before.

South and North Ossetia are separated by the Caucasus Mountains. North Ossetia is in Russia, while South Ossetia is in Georgia, behind the mountains. Because the Ossetians are mostly adherents of the Orthodox Church, surrounded by the Muslim nations of the North Caucasus, the Russian authorities, from the tsars to Stalin to Yeltsin, had always supported them, relying on them militarily during Russian wars in the Caucasus. When the Soviet Union collapsed, South Ossetia didn't want to stay in Georgia and a short but bloody war erupted. Since 1992, South Ossetia had been a breakaway republic, supported by Russian troops and funded by Russia. The two Ossetias are connected only by the 2.5-mile-long Roki Tunnel. But they are one people, and Ossetians from both sides of the mountains had always fought for each other. Each Ossetia had in fact had its own war in the early 1990s—while the Southern Ossetians had fought the Georgians, in another bloody conflict in the region the Northern Ossetians had fought the neighboring, predominantly Muslim Ingushetia.

"We came in two cars, all the personnel of our state security service!" Krutikov added proudly. That puzzled us. What security service? And what sort of security service could fit in just two cars?

He didn't tell us then, but when we were in London Andrei later asked him about the episode. "I was an adviser to the director of the newly formed foreign intelligence agency of South Ossetia back then," he admitted. The agency had been set up by the government of the breakaway republic a year before the Beslan crisis. Krutikov had finally made it to the other side: he'd moved from journalism to the spy world and secured a place in an intelligence agency. It was a tiny agency in a small, separatist republic, but, from day one, the intelligence agency of South Ossetia was under Russia's control.

Krutikov was in a sober, gloomy mood that September day in Beslan. "It is also very bad on the other side of the mountains," he said. "We had a horrible week back there, under heavy Georgian howitzer fire." It sounded like the war between Georgia and the separatist republic had never really ended.

He said they'd come to Beslan as a group of South Ossetians, led by their president, to help, but it was evident from the way Krutikov looked that he was not entirely sure how they could be of any help.

It was still summer in Beslan—hot and sunny. The streets of the town were full of soldiers and local militiamen. By the second day of the crisis, it had already become clear that both sides—the terrorists and the Russian security services—had learned some lessons from Nord-Ost. Terrorists had broken all the windows in the school so the gas couldn't be used; the authorities had evacuated residents from all the houses and apartments adjacent to the school to keep out any journalists who might find a viewing spot in direct line of sight of the school. The locals left, but with one caveat: one man from each of the resident families remained in almost all the apartments. Many local police officers lived there, and now they stood guard outside with machine guns.

The soldiers were not happy to have the locals around carrying guns, but it couldn't be helped—it was their kids inside the school, after all, and many local families had kept weapons hidden in their yards since the war with Ingushetia in the early 1990s. The Russian authorities had never made a serious attempt to confiscate those weapons.

In the afternoon, the authorities announced good news: the terrorists had agreed to release twenty-six hostages. But when the hostages were let out, they told journalists that their captors had stopped giving water to the hostages.

The night was uneventful, and on the morning of the third day, Friday, the information was leaked that the terrorists were ready to let medics remove the bodies of the dead hostages that had lain on the grass near the school for two days. Soldiers around the school looked a bit more relaxed. Arab journalists told us that the terrorists would definitely release more hostages that day because it was Friday, a holy day for Muslims. A local doctor—a highly respected profession in the North Caucasus—took us through security to the operations staff, and at the entrance we bumped into an FSB general, a friend of Krutikov's. He was now deputy head of Russian state television, but for years he had overseen "active measures," or, simply put, disinformation operations, like the Kalinkin story, on behalf of the FSB. His presence indicated that the FSB was making a special effort to control coverage of the crisis.

At 1:05 p.m., we heard two explosions go off inside the school. What followed was a chaotic, messy nightmare, which quickly turned into an urban battle.

While the soldiers froze, waiting for orders, rescuers, special forces operatives, and local militiamen rushed into the school. They reemerged with children in their arms—in bloody scraps of clothing. Men kept running to the school, firing in all directions. "Look, the school is burning!" we heard someone say. Thick smoke rose above the building.

The chaotic shooting rapidly expanded to the nearby streets, park, and railway tracks, where a tank was positioned. The tank suddenly rolled into a firing position and opened fire at the school. For several hours, we moved from place to place around the area, from the park to the small square in front of the school, trying to track what was going on without getting killed.

Even toward the end of the day the shooting was not over, despite the assurances of the pro-Kremlin media. At 6:00 p.m. Andrei was called on the phone by current news radio station Ekho Moskvy, asking for an update—the station didn't have a reporter in Beslan, and Andrei helped with coverage of the crisis. At this very moment there was another explosion: "What's going on?" the news anchor asked. Andrei said it was a tank shot. "But we were told the operation was long over!" the anchor exclaimed, annoyed.

The tank didn't fire its last shell at the school until 11:15 p.m.

By then we knew that there would be dozens of burned bodies inside the gymnasium. It was much, much, worse than Nord-Ost. In total, 334 hostages were killed, including 186 children.

It was such a terrible scene that many of our colleagues simply didn't know how to react. They were experienced reporters who had gone through the two Chechen wars, but this was different.

The next day, when we met Baranov with his cameraman on a street, he looked shaken. His eyes were inflamed, and his voice trembled. "Did you listen to Putin's address to the nation?" he asked us incredulously.

Putin had not made any public statements during the three days of the crisis. Finally, the day after 186 children died, he made a trip to Beslan and found the courage to talk to a nation in shock. He spoke about the "direct intervention of international terror against Russia." But he also spoke of the collapse of the Soviet Union, which, he said, had made the country unready for the challenges: "Our country, with what was once the most powerful system for protecting its external borders, suddenly found itself unprotected from either the West or the East."[4] We felt confused and angry. Why had he tried to blame the terrorist attack on some external enemy, when everyone could see that his security services had failed to protect people, and that his generals had done nothing to save the hostages' lives?

But Baranov did not feel the way we did. "I think it was like Stalin's 'Brothers and Sisters'!" he exclaimed with admiration, comparing

Putin's speech to Stalin's address to the nation when Nazi Germany had invaded the Soviet Union.

We were astonished. There was only one possible similarity between those two events, as we saw it. In June 1941, Stalin had disappeared for several days while the Germans were destroying the Soviet army and advancing deep into the country—not exactly anyone's idea of leadership in a crisis. Didn't Baranov see through Putin's hypocrisy? Wasn't he angry at Putin's cowardice? And when did Stalin, who had killed millions, suddenly become a good guy?

But we said nothing. It was not a moment to debate national history. Besides, we thought, maybe Baranov's response was just an aftereffect of the profound trauma we'd all just witnessed.

Three weeks after Beslan, the national television channel NTV aired a long documentary called *Misha* about the president of Georgia, Mikheil Saakashvili.

That it took a very hostile stance against Saakashvili was clear from the title—"Misha" in Russian is a diminutive form of Mikheil and was meant to be an insult, implying that the president of Georgia was some naughty boy who didn't deserve any respect, not the leader of another country.

But the documentary went much further. Saakashvili was accused of receiving funding from the Hungarian American financier and philanthropist George Soros, of providing support to Chechen militants, and of having "mental problems."[5] The undisguised aggressiveness of the documentary made it a huge scandal. All journalistic Moscow talked about the film. It was one of the first of its kind to be aired on Russian television, though many more were to follow. It contained wild accusations against Russian opposition and human rights activists. But in 2004 the Russian public was not yet accustomed to encountering that scale of open hostility toward a neighboring country's leader. In fact, the backlash was so intense that the

NTV producer was forced to go public and admit that the film was "an extremely bad job," that the kind of journalism it reflected was unacceptable, and that "the way it was done was propaganda of the worst Soviet kind."[6]

The production company that had made the documentary was Sovershenno Sekretno—the same corporation that included *Versia*. We learned from our sources that the thesis for the documentary had been provided by the SVR—Russia's foreign intelligence agency. We also learned that the contract for the documentary had been arranged through Olga Kostina—the woman in a business suit who had overseen the establishment of the unofficial FSB press office four years before. That didn't surprise us at all. But it looked as if in just a few months, Sovershenno Sekretno had become much closer to the security services than it had been when we were there.

It came as a complete shock to us that one of the two authors of the *Misha* documentary was Baranov. Baranov was paid for this job, but had he really done it for the money? Or was it a reflection of some sort of professional crisis he was having? It was not an aftereffect of Beslan, that we knew for sure—Baranov had told us on the way to Beslan that he was working on a film about Saakashvili. We knew he was very critical of Saakashvili. But it is one thing is to be critical, and quite another to conflate actual journalism with the notes given to you by an intelligence service.

That year, two of our friends, Krutikov and Baranov, had moved to the other side. Krutikov began to work for the intelligence service as a fully paid employee, and Baranov, while remaining officially a journalist, joined the ranks of Kremlin propagandists, working under the guidance of the security agencies.

CHAPTER 12

OLD FLAME

Despite the best efforts of the tsars and Communist rulers, Moscow is still a city of concentric rings, radiating from the center, reflecting the way the city grew. The leafy Boulevard Ring, closest to the Kremlin, is surely the prettiest of them, but here and there, the rulers cut highways through it radiating from the Kremlin to the outskirts. Novy Arbat is one of them, a highway built for party bosses' limousines to speed from the Kremlin to their Rublyovka dachas. Novy Arbat separates Gogolevsky Boulevard, where the Akopovs lived, from Nikitsky Boulevard. Unlike Gogolevsky, Nikitsky Boulevard is built up mostly with imperial classic buildings—with porticoes and rusticated windows—which in the early 2000s housed museums, restaurants, and theaters.

Late on a December night in 2004, on the top floor of the three-story mansion at the very beginning of Nikitsky, two dozen people gathered in a spacious room around a large table laden with vodka bottles and plastic cups to celebrate the imminent new year. The room was the editorial office of a new online media project—Ej.ru, short for *Yezhednevny Journal*, "Daily Journal" in Russian, as it was supposed to be updated on a daily basis—that had been launched just a month before. There was a good deal of laughter and many jokes, but no speeches about grand hopes or great expectations for winning a national audience, because we had none. The goal of the project was to give a public platform to those who disagreed with Putin—journalists as well as politicians, experts, and commentators. Until recently, many of these people had been frequent guests on major Russian television channels. They were household names in Russian liberal circles, some since the perestroika years of the late 1980s. But in Putin's world, they had become a nuisance. After the tragedy in Beslan, Putin completed his marginalization of the liberal opposition. TV channels ceased inviting the liberal politicians, experts, and commentators to their shows; major newspapers stopped publishing their columns. The parliament was cleansed too: a year before, liberal parties had lost their seats at the Duma in the Kremlin's tightly controlled parliamentary elections. The Kremlin wanted to make Russian liberals completely irrelevant. Putin and his people were to be the only voices representing the nation; the outcast opposition, in his version, represented nobody.

Vladimir Gusinsky, the once powerful media mogul, had been forced out of Russia by Putin long before, but he still had money, and some financial assets in the country. He was also very angry, so he provided the funding of Ej.ru as a platform for anti-Putin liberals.

In the room were several liberal historians; a poet, one of the founders of Russian conceptualism; a comedian, who had been expelled from Russian television because his show had angered Putin; and the head of the country's largest human rights group, who'd spent years investigating Russian war crimes in Chechnya. And there was also a bespectacled, taciturn man with a fierce look—a former member of parliament, but, most importantly, still a big shot in the Russian Union of Journalists. That was crucial, as it was the Union of Journalists that owned the mansion where Ej.ru had just set up shop.

The people in the room made no secret of their opposition to Putin. Many of them were members of the Committee 2008 initiative, the aim of which was to help get rid of Putin at the next election.

A month before, in a building next door to Ej.ru's office on Nikitsky Boulevard, the very same people had been among a crowd celebrating the launch of another project: a restaurant named "Jean-Jacques." It was a classic Parisian brasserie, with huge mirrors on the walls, which were painted red; tables covered with paper; and glasses on the tables filled with the inevitable pencils. Jean-Jacques had been designed by Muriel Rousseau, a French artist with a Russian husband and the proud descendant of the French liberal philosopher, hence the restaurant's name. But the brains behind the project were two Muscovites and close friends—a successful lawyer and a restaurateur. It was not their first project.

In Cold War Moscow, with the KGB closely watching Soviet intelligentsia, there were only two sorts of places where one could have a decent drink: the restaurants at the government-sanctioned clubs, like the Union of Writers, where access was granted only to those who proved their loyalty to the regime; and the apartment kitchens of Moscow's liberal-minded intelligentsia, where people gathered for conversation.

When the Communist regime finally collapsed, several prominent Moscow intelligentsia families—the Borisovs and Papernys first among them—came up with the idea of opening places to drink, eat, and talk. Not private clubs like Duma—they were as sick and tired of party membership–only places as they were of the stuffy kitchens of Soviet times. They wanted to open the kinds of places that bring a normal city to life: clubs, pubs, and accessible restaurants.

Despite doubts about the business skills of Russia's intelligentsia, those families became successful entrepreneurs, running a dozen places in Moscow. Jean-Jacques was yet another Borisov-owned place.

The families also wanted the new places to feel European, because they believed that would make the city more civilized. The first thing the owners of Jean-Jacques did after the launch was to bring a

Beaujolais Nouveau festival to snowy, cold winter Moscow. We went to the event, though we had no idea what Beaujolais was or why Beaujolais Nouveau was so special.

Being European was not only a cultural choice but also a political one. In late Soviet times, the prominent families of the liberal intelligentsia were on the wrong side of the regime. The restaurateur, Borisov's father, had been a prominent historian who had published an open letter in support of Solzhenitsyn in 1974 (the year the writer was expelled from the Soviet Union), became his literary agent in the late 1980s, and, as deputy editor of *Novy Mir*, secured the first publication of *The Gulag Archipelago* in the Soviet Union in 1989.

Overnight, Jean-Jacques on Nikitsky Boulevard became the place that hosted liberal Moscow intelligentsia, not only the authors of Ej.ru but also actors, writers, and artists, every other night.

By the spring of 2005, we were once again without jobs. Our time with *Moscow News* proved to be short—with Mikhail Khodorkovsky, the financial backer, in jail, the weekly was struggling, and at some point, the *Moscow News* managers decided to fire half the editorial office. Misha, the deputy editor who had sent us to Beslan, was among those fired, and we decided to quit in protest.

Once again, we began looking for places to publish our stories. So as not to waste time, we decided to write a long report about the mistakes the FSB had made in Beslan, as well as the national counterterrorism system the Russian security services built in the aftermath of Beslan. Nobody asked us to do that, but we felt it was important to try to identify what had gone wrong with the FSB's response to terrorist attacks, several times in a row, since Nord-Ost. At that time, we still hoped that the Russian security agencies had the potential to be reformed to become something reminiscent of a normal, functional security service.

But the country wanted to forget about the horrors of Beslan and move on, again. For almost a year, Andrei had maintained a weekly presence on the radio station Ekho Moskvy, writing a current events column and reading it on air every Sunday. After Beslan, that program was canceled. Andrei, eager to remain, approached the legendary Ekho's editor, Alexey Venediktov, whose lion's mane was known to all Muscovites—Venediktov had been respected by Russians with democratic views since August 1991, when Ekho bravely challenged KGB-led putschists, supporting Yeltsin. Venediktov tried to keep his radio station, the most popular in Moscow, critical of Putin in the early 2000s, but it came with a cost. Andrei offered to do a radio program about terrorism. "Look, we don't have a special program about ballet, why should we have a special one about terrorism?" was Venediktov's response.

We had no other place to publish the report but on our website. But then Petya Akopov came to our aid. He somehow got the editor of *Political Journal*, where he worked, to agree to publish the report—in full.

Unfortunately, it was only a one-off. The other more permanent option was Gusinky's Ej.ru, so we started writing for them, initially just short pieces.

In December, a prominent Russian political journalist, Evgenia Albats, who was on the board of Ej.ru, suggested we write a series of reports about the dramatic expansion of the security services. She came up with a title for the series: "Back to the KGB." In the early 1990s, Albats had authored the book *KGB: State Within a State*—the first book about the KGB written by a Russian journalist. A fierce and larger-than-life personality, she called the editor of Ej.ru and convinced him to accept the idea of the series.

We loved the idea. On the surface, it sounded a bit sensational, but in 2005 Moscow, it sure felt accurate. Putin kept reinforcing the FSB, the direct successor to the KGB, and expanding its powers.

When he'd merged it with two other agencies two years before, he'd made it the largest and most powerful security agency in the country. The officers of the FSB felt more confident every day. Now they were to be found everywhere, from ministries to banks to universities to cultural venues. We learned that the FSB major who had passed us an offer from his superiors to stop investigating Nord-Ost, in return for closing the criminal case, had been assigned to supervise the Moscow acting school. Once he had wanted to fearlessly fight terrorists, and we assumed he was a decent officer, the kind every country needs. Now he apparently had no reservations about spying on theater students.

The FSB launched a systematic effort to rewrite its own history, including the history of political prosecution conducted by the KGB and its predecessors under Stalin, and restricted access to the archives that had been opened to the public under Boris Yeltsin. A friend of Irina's tried to obtain records of the criminal case against her grandfather, who had been shot as an enemy of the people in 1937, and the FSB refused. The FSB's justification was that because the participants in those events might still be alive, information about them could not be disclosed. The seventy-five-year period restricting access to documents revealing "compromising information about the victims [and] third parties," and that "jeopardize[d] their privacy," had not yet expired. But to date, those records have never been released.

As part of this effort, the FSB also arranged a reputational renaissance for Yuri Andropov. Before his brief tenure as Soviet leader in the early 1980s, Andropov had been a major KGB hero, the agency's longest-serving and much-feared chairman who had a key role in sending Russian troops to Czechoslovakia in 1968 and Afghanistan in 1979. Inside the country, it was Andropov who'd come up with the idea of imprisoning dissidents in psychiatric clinics. Now, under Putin, a school was named after him, a ten-foot-tall statue was erected in a town where he had worked, and a scholarship for intelligence recruits was established in his name.

Against that background, Ej.ru started publishing our "Back to the KGB" articles. Ej.ru united a diverse group of people of different generations and backgrounds, but they all had something in common: they did not like the KGB.

The editor-in-chief of Ej.ru, a former reporter turned political activist, was always busy with opposition party activity and was thus often absent from the Ej.ru office. The real heart and soul of that place was Anna Pavlova, a bright, flamboyant editor in her mid-thirties. We knew Anna from when we'd worked together at *Segodnya* in the late 1990s, where she had overseen fact-checking. She was old friends with Petya Akopov; they had gone to university together, along with Zhenya Baranov and Evgeny Krutikov.

We were really happy to see her at Ej.ru, because it meant that things would get done, and quickly. While Anna was on duty, running between the desks in the spacious room on the top floor of the mansion on Nikitsky, telling a layout designer what photo to use for a story or urging an editor to hurry up, no one else needed to worry about the deadline for updating the website—she would make sure it was met. As a child Anna had performed Russian folk dances, and it looked as if she'd never stopped spinning around, with her hair flying in all directions. She'd grown up in Moscow, the child of regular Soviet parents, but her father was of Roma origin, a fact she was very proud of. We often joked that whoever dared to disobey Anna would be cursed.

Anna had always felt very strongly about politics and had become an activist as early as the late 1980s. While studying history at university, she—along with Krutikov, Petya Akopov, and Baranov—had joined a civil initiative involved in collecting Soviet dissident movement documents. And she had been the woman whom Baranov had loved since they were at university together.

Every time we dropped by Ej.ru, we would take her to Jean-Jacques afterward—unless she was already there, since that was where she had her meetings with authors and friends, which were usually one and the same. Jean-Jacques became a favorite spot for a very liberal crowd—independent journalists and other writers, artists, producers, and others. Baranov also became a regular at Jean-Jacques, though he never mixed with the Ej.ru writers. By now Baranov and Olga Lyubimova were raising their son. The boy was not Baranov's first child—he had a teenage daughter from an earlier marriage.

Anna Pavlova had just divorced her husband, a reporter at a national TV channel who was assigned to head a bureau in the Middle East. She had stayed in Moscow. Every day she drove from a northwestern suburb of the city, where she lived with her young son, to the office on Nikitsky, often ending her day at Jean-Jacques. Some nights the conversations at Jean-Jacques were not enough, and she went with her friends off to clubs where she could indulge her passion for dancing. Her career was on the rise, and she felt she was in the right place at the right moment.

We hadn't seen much of Baranov since Beslan. When we finally saw him one day on Gogolevsky Boulevard, he looked the same and was as friendly and talkative as he had always been, but something about him had changed. Usually calm and levelheaded, he seemed nervous, even anxious. We knew Beslan had affected him deeply, but something else seemed to be going on.

Later, at the Akopovs' apartment, Marina told us that Anna Pavlova had come to one of their parties and that Baranov had been there, alone, without his wife. Marina didn't like that he'd been there without his wife, but Irina told her not to exaggerate the power of what had just been a teenage crush.

But Baranov was definitely going through something.

Another day, Irina bumped into him at Jean-Jacques. He was with Anna. The conversation somehow veered to the topic of the Russian Orthodox Church, and Baranov became agitated. He started talking about his mother—something he'd never done before. He told Irina that in the days of the Soviet Union, his mother had cooperated as an editor with Politizdat, supervising the publication of "scientific atheism" literature. "Scientific atheism" was aggressive anti-religious propaganda. It had nothing to do with academic research: Politizdat was a Soviet publishing monster directly subordinated to the Central Committee of the Communist Party, and it had a monopoly on publishing party propaganda. Baranov now accused his mother of hypocrisy. He told Irina that his mother had entertained priests at their apartment while writing her atheism articles. Irina wasn't sure what was making Baranov so agitated—couldn't someone who was friendly with priests still be a genuine atheist? But Baranov was adamant.

We had always known that Baranov was an ardent Orthodox believer, but he seemed to be getting even more passionate.

CHAPTER 13

BARANOV ON THE EDGE

We didn't see Zhenya Baranov much over the next two years, but when we did, religion came up often. He talked a lot about Russian monasteries and priests. It felt a bit odd to us.

We had both grown up in secular families, like most Soviet kids in the 1980s. None of our parents had gone to church during the Soviet era, and after the Soviet Union fell, only Irina's mother began attending regularly, because she had come from an Old Believer family. The Old Believers had split from the Russian Orthodox Church in the seventeenth century because they did not accept the Church reforms of the period. They were fiercely persecuted by many of the tsars, but those who survived the torture and executions retained their beliefs. Some of them burned themselves alive rather than give up their faith; others ran to Lithuania, the Volga region, or Siberia to stay loyal to their traditions.

Irina's grandparents kept the family's ancient icon at home in Syzran, a town on the Volga River—the small house they had built after wandering for decades, after they were expelled from their house by Communists and thrown out onto the street in the 1930s. As a child, Irina had visited her grandmother every summer at her house with a cherry garden on the river, and she would see her grandmother praying in front of the icon. Her grandmother prayed in an old Slavonic language, so Irina couldn't comprehend all the words, but she loved how the prayers sounded. Though her grandma was a strict believer, her children, Irina's parents, had not followed her path. Irina's mother became an exemplary Soviet engineer.

Officially, the state and the church have been separated since the days of the revolution of 1917, and Russia is a multifaith country, with regions as big as Tatarstan and Bashkiria, not to mention the North Caucasus, that are predominantly Muslim. But over 70 percent of Russians consider themselves Orthodox, and the Kremlin has treated the Russian Orthodox Church as the national church.[1]

The Orthodox Church is led by the Patriarch of Moscow, who has always been a recognizable figure, a presence on Russian television, and directly connected to the Kremlin. Russians got used to seeing the televised ceremony in the main Russian cathedral Christ the Savior in Moscow, conducted by the patriarch, attended by the president, every Easter. The Church's cooperation with the state is a question that tortured the Russian intelligentsia for decades, because the relationship between priests and the authorities was never black and white.

Stalin eased up on the repression of the Church that had been initiated by Bolsheviks when he found out, at great cost to the country, that when Hitler had launched the brutal Nazi invasion, Russian soldiers were not that ready to die in a war that Communist slogans framed as "the universal battle against imperialists." Stalin's propaganda began preaching nationalism instead of communism, coupled with the concept of total war—the annihilation of Germans whether or not they were Nazi officials or military combatants. He dubbed his war the Great Patriotic War in an homage to the Patriotic War that Russians had waged against Napoleon's invasion years before Karl Marx was born. In 1942, Stalin's poet Konstantin Simonov published a poem titled "Kill Him" in *Krasnaya Zvezda* (Red Star), the main newspaper of the Red Army. The poem was essentially a call to kill any German, the more the better:

> *If your brother killed a German,*
> *If your neighbor killed one too.*
> *It's your brother's and neighbor's vengeance,*
> *And it's no revenge for you.*
> *You can't sit behind another*
> *Letting him fire your shot.*
> *If your brother kills a German,*
> *He's a soldier; you are not.*[2]

Stalin remembered that when Napoleon had invaded Russia in 1812, the Russian Orthodox Church had helped the state by preaching total war against the French army—and hadn't hesitated to declare Napoleon the Antichrist.

In his war, Stalin wanted something similar. The Church supported the war, preaching resistance against the "pagan swastika" and hosting fundraising drives for the Red Army.[3] But this was not a simple sellout on the Church's part. Many inside the Church felt they had to support what they rightly saw as Russia's existential fight against Germany. The Church took it as its duty to help resist the enemy, a tradition dating back to the revered Russian saint Sergey of Radonezh, who in the late fourteenth century had given the monks his blessing to take up arms and fight the Mongol invasion alongside Russian soldiers. It didn't much matter to the Church what the political regime was in the country, as long as it was deemed "patriotic."

Long after the end of the Great Patriotic War, Church hierarchs continued to use patriotism as an excuse to justify their cooperation with Communists. Yet the state remained anti-religious until the end of the Cold War. When Andrei's mother baptized him in the early 1980s, in a church in the center of Moscow, it was done in secret, with a passerby serving as a godmother, because baptism was strongly discouraged.

Once Communist ideology was visibly dying, during the perestroika years, liberal, well-educated priests began to emerge in Moscow. They became an important center of gravity for an intelligentsia tired of the empty words and meaningless slogans still used by the political regime.

When the Soviet Union disintegrated, the Church suddenly received a boost when Boris Yeltsin, the first president of a new Russia, decided to promote it as a spiritual alternative to the godless Communist regime of the past, thinking it would help build a new democratic Russia.

But would the Church actually provide that alternative? Within the circles of the intelligentsia, many people discussed this question. All the high officials in the Church, the patriarch included, had started their careers under the Communists. Many had cooperated with the KGB. And whenever dissident voices in the Church raised the issue of its cooperation, the Church quietly silenced the conversations.

In the 1990s, the Russian Orthodox Church became one of the very few institutions granted a national license to import tobacco and alcohol, tax free, to Russia, courtesy of Yeltsin's government. This certainly didn't do much to improve the reputation of the Church hierarchs as uncorrupted spiritual guides to the Russian people. Many became disgusted by the sight of priests driving around in luxury Mercedes and wearing expensive watches.

Zhenya Baranov and Petya Akopov didn't have any illusions about the Church hierarchs' shady business dealings. In the mid-1990s the two of them had worked for several years for a businessman who had made a fortune selling cigarettes on the Church's license.

Nevertheless, they both believed that the Church had a special role to play in Russia's destiny. Petya maintained his interest in the Church as a political organization, which is what had led him to Tikhon Shevkunov—the young priest with the very strong anti-Western stance who was something of a confessor to Putin. Petya was also charmed by the monastic traditions and philosophical thought of Russian Orthodoxy—an alternative to Western philosophers. Those monastic traditions became a frequently discussed topic in his apartment on Gogolevsky when we gathered there.

While Petya spoke of the Church, Baranov spoke of the faith.

Baranov loved talking about how inspired he was by his latest visit to yet another Orthodox monastery, often in Russia, but, as he began making more frequent visits to the Balkans and Israel, in Serbia or the Holy Land. He had just made a breakthrough in his career: he had gotten a job with Channel One, the main Russian national television channel, as a reporter for its flagship show—the Sunday evening newscast *Voskresnoye Vremya* (Times on Sunday), hosted by Petr Tolstoy, a great-great-grandson to Leo Tolstoy. Baranov's stories, such as a report from Jerusalem on the celebration of Orthodox Easter, or one on how the hand of John the Baptist and other relics from Montenegro, a small Orthodox country in the Balkans, had traveled across Russia, were commissioned by Tolstoy. The hand of John the Baptist had been kept in Constantinople until the fall of the city in 1453, when it was taken by the Knights Hospitaller Order to Rhodes and later to Malta. In 1799, the Hospitallers gave it for safekeeping to the Russian emperor Paul, and it remained in Russia until the civil war, when the defeated Whites brought it with them to Europe. It ended up in Yugoslavia, where it was rediscovered in a monastery in Montenegro in the early 1990s.

Baranov also became easily offended. Once, he greatly embarrassed his friends at Jean-Jacques when he overheard a conversation at the next table among a group of Russian emigrants to Israel who were visiting Moscow. He thought the tone of the conversation was offensive toward Russia, approached the table, and suggested, in a raised voice, that they go outside to discuss what they didn't like about the country they had left. On another occasion, at the Akopovs' apartment on Gogolevsky, he accused Andrei of insulting the Russian people. Irina managed to calm him down by reminding him that Andrei was the only Russian at the table, given her own part-Gagauzian heritage, Petya's Armenian Italian background, and Baranov's Jewish origins.

Still, we didn't take Baranov's new obsession with Orthodoxy and Russian nationalism entirely seriously. We assumed all the conversations about the unique spirituality of Russian Orthodoxy were no more than table talk.

Baranov's wife, Olga Lyubimova, certainly did not seem churchy, especially when she was downing drinks and uttering gleeful profanities. One winter evening on Gogolevsky, Irina was having a smoke with Lyubimova in the Akopovs' kitchen. Lyubimova was sitting in a chair, crossing her legs in a way that made it impossible to miss her striking-looking shoes. They looked like a moose's hooves. "What is this? Are these hooves?" Irina asked. "Where did you get them? I've never seen such shoes before!"

"Yes! These are my favorite vintage shoes. Do you like them?" Lyubimova smiled and exhaled a puff of smoke.

She definitely wanted to look bohemian, in her green blouse and the hoof shoes with a cigarette dangling from her hand.

Irina decided to ask Lyubimova about her great-grandfather, the legendary actor Vasily Kachalov. The question was not about the actor himself, but about his dog. The famous Russian poet Sergei Yesenin had written a poem titled "To Kachalov's Dog" in 1925, and it was familiar to all Russians—the poem was included in every school's curriculum. So Irina asked the inevitable question: "What breed was Jim, your great-grandfather's famous dog?"

"He was a Doberman!" Lyubimova replied, delighted that Irina had given her an excuse to emphasize that she was Kachalov's direct descendant, and with that, Irina won Lyubimova's trust, at least to some extent.

Lyubimova didn't come often to the apartment on Gogolevsky. But when we did see her, it sometimes seemed that she was getting quite possessive about her husband. One evening, when we bumped into Baranov and Lyubimova on the street next to Nikitsky Boulevard, we hardly had time to say hello before Lyubimova told Baranov in a very firm voice that they needed to go. She literally dragged him away. It sounded and looked a bit rude, since we hadn't been talking for more than a minute. We wondered why a young, attractive woman from such a prominent family, and with a very promising career on television, apparently felt so vulnerable.

However, Lyubimova had had a very complicated childhood. Her parents had sent her to an Orthodox school, or "gymnasium." She had spent only three years there, but they were formative years for her. It was not easy for a teenager to attend that kind of school in 1990s Moscow.

"By the 7th grade, the Orthodox Gymnasium became an Al-Qaeda camp for me," she confessed in an interview years later.[4]

The rules were extremely strict at the school. One boy was expelled for eating a cheese sandwich during Lent. Students were told that it was a sin to have a refrigerator at home because it meant you cared about tomorrow, and that a TV set was a devil with horns. Lyubimova came to hate long skirts, because she was forced to wear them in school. It was so traumatic that at one point she decided that she would not "stay in the fold of the Russian Orthodox Church."[5]

She decided to become a journalist and enrolled in the journalism program at Moscow State University. When the time came to decide what area to focus on as a journalist, she realized that the Church was something she knew a lot about. Her first job as a journalist was with the wire agency of the Russian Orthodox Church, which produced a TV show called *Orthodox*. It probably helped that the filmmaker Nikita Mikhalkov, the powerful backer of Lyubimova's family, had a personal connection to the patriarch. The year Lyubimova landed her first job on TV, the patriarch attended the grand reception of the Russian fund of culture, headed by Mikhalkov, in person.[6]

The Orthodox news agency was based in Ostankino, a concrete, rectangular building in northeast Moscow that had served as headquarters for major Russian TV channels since Soviet times. There, Lyubimova, then twenty years old, met a group of men who were at the time top managers of the TV channel Moskovia, and who were also close to the Russian patriarch.

They were a new generation, all young people who had begun to rise in their careers when Putin decided to make Russian Orthodoxy a national ideology. This was where Lyubimova had first met Baranov.

Lyubimova's connections with Orthodox media managers helped launch her career. In a few years, she became editor-in-chief of a TV show called *The Russian View*, a strange mix of stories about monasteries and church-service broadcasts coupled with a nationalistic message.

That only helped her career. By 2006 she was hosting her own TV show, called *A City Girl*, and had become recognizable in the households of Moscow.

But she never cut off her ties with the Orthodox media and continued to do projects for them on the side.

In 2006 we were working for *Novaya Gazeta*, a newspaper with a reputation for fearlessness: several of its journalists had been killed, including Yuri Shchekochikhin, the investigative reporter who had been poisoned three years earlier.

We joined Shchekochikhin's former department. The paper always suffered funding shortages, but that summer the mood was uncharacteristically cheerful: it had just secured the backing of Alexander Lebedev, a curious character in Moscow's banking world. A former spy—he had served in the Soviet embassy in London with the economic intelligence section at the KGB station—he had made money in the early 1990s by founding a bank that handled Russia's debts. He had also nurtured political ambitions—he ran for mayor of Moscow, unsuccessfully, and got himself elected to the Russian parliament. And he had struck a very close relationship with Mikhail Gorbachev.

Lebedev had been helping the paper for several years. That summer he became the owner of 49 percent of it, alongside Mikhail Gorbachev, who was still active in politics, though without the international prominence he'd held previously. Gorbachev had been added to guarantee the paper's integrity. Of course, many journalists had their misgivings about Lebedev, but, true to his word, he didn't interfere in our work, at least as far as we could detect. He brought money to the paper, including funds for foreign trips.

Hezbollah was fighting with Israel that summer, and thanks to the improved financial situation, the paper was able to send us both to Lebanon to cover the war. That didn't happen without our efforts to force their hand: when the clock was ticking, and the deputy editor was dragging his feet, we told him we would call Lebedev's brother, whom we knew, because a friend of the Akopovs regularly brought him to the apartment on Gogolevsky Boulevard to drink. After that, we were given first-class tickets on the Aeroflot flight to Damascus (Lebedev owned a significant stake in Aeroflot), as it was already impossible to fly directly to Beirut—the airport had been bombed heavily by the Israeli Air Force.

When we returned to Moscow, the editor told us to go to Israel to get the second part of the story. We had no contacts in Israel apart from some personal friends, so we called Baranov, asking for his advice. We hadn't seen him for a while but thought he would share a few tips about the country with fellow journalists.

In a café next door to the television center in Ostankino, Baranov briefed us about what he knew of Israel. "I know everyone in the country!" he proudly said. "I can get you access to any monastery in the Holy Land—I know all the abbots!"

We were taken slightly aback. We needed contacts in the military and in the security services, we needed contacts with the Palestinians, we needed a way to get into constantly blocked Gaza, and the very last thing we were interested in was news from the Orthodox monasteries.

Baranov seemed agitated and restless, as if he couldn't sit still. We were wondering why, but his wife probably had a clue. For several years, Lyubimova had kept a very candid online blog on LiveJournal, a social networking site. A year before, she had written on LiveJournal about the condition her husband had arrived in from Israel. She described what a pitiful sight he was in the morning. She cited his weakness and withdrawal, his shaking hands and complete reluctance to live, his depression, irritability, and tearfulness.

She wrote that she decided to use it as a cautionary tale for their son. "Look, Nikita, how it got your dad," she told him.

She then warned him against using: "Are you going to use drugs, Nikitochka?"

"Nope," Baranov Junior responded sluggishly.

She also thought it was a good moment to warn their son against drinking. "Will you be an alcoholic?" But their son was not very enthusiastic. "'Nope,' our son replied even more noncommittally," she wrote.

Then she turned to the subject of smoking—as she put it, by "hammering pedagogical nails." But Nikita was equally noncommittal. "The answer was the same," Lyubimova admitted. "And when you grow up, you will become a military man...," she told her son.

"Yeah," the son agreed happily.

"'Fuuuuuuuuuuuuuuuck' came from under the blanket. The hangover was not easy on my husband," she concluded.

It looked as if Baranov was having some sort of crisis, and the hangover his wife described was just an attempt to block it out. It was surely taking a toll on him. What on earth was this obsession of his with the monks? We thought that the Church had become a career vehicle for his wife, pure and simple, but for Baranov it was probably more complicated.

Baranov's role with the Russian TV channel he worked for had moved him quite far away from reporting. It looked as if he was more focused on taking part in the propaganda activities of intelligence agencies, where the Church also had its role.

Two months before Baranov boasted to us about his contacts in monasteries in Israel in the Ostankino café, he had done a big story from Montenegro for Tolstoy's newscast. By 2006, the union of Serbia and Montenegro was all that was left of Yugoslavia after the horrible Balkan wars in the 1990s, and now Montenegro was holding a referendum on becoming an independent country. Belgrade was not happy to lose Montenegro, nor was Moscow.

Baranov's reportage aired the day of the referendum and had everything that makes a good conspiracy theory: an exposé of an attempt to bribe Montenegran peasants by sinister strangers to make them vote for independence; a pro-independence priest who mobilized his flock under the American flag; an ominous warning, from a fisherman, that the referendum could turn ugly; a hint at the prospect of a new civil war. And there was a pro-Serbian priest from the Montenegran town of Kotor who bluntly said, "This city is a Serbian city and Montenegro is a Serbian land, just as Ukraine is a Russian land."[7] It sounded more like an attempt to influence the outcome of the vote than a piece of journalism.

In the café in Ostankino, Baranov told us he was going to Israel at the same time we were going. We made a plan to meet up there. But when we got to Tel Aviv, Baranov proved to be hard to find, even though we were staying at the same hotel. When we caught up with him, his local fixer, a tall, handsome journalist named Mika, complained that he had gotten tired of accompanying Baranov to Orthodox monasteries. But Baranov didn't want to go anywhere else. When we told him of our plans to go to the West Bank and Gaza, Baranov scoffed. "I'm not very interested in the Indians," he said, dismissing the Palestinians as the Indians of James Fenimore Cooper's novels.

The war with Hezbollah was over, and there was not much to do in Israel, so we went off to the West Bank and Gaza to do our stories. Before that, we had a nice dinner with Baranov and Mika in a restaurant overlooking the ancient walls of Jerusalem, and that was that. It would be the very last time we would find ourselves on a reporting trip alongside Zhenya Baranov.

CHAPTER 14

THE ARRANGEMENT

As the first decade of the new millennium progressed, Andrei felt increasingly uneasy—he feared he was betraying his father's expectations. Andrei's father had had our backs when we'd gotten into trouble with the FSB, and his company was still supporting Agentura, but he'd told us that he saw his role as providing the initial funding to get the website off the ground. He didn't want to support it indefinitely. Andrei felt more and more as if he were some overindulged son of a rich father who bought him expensive toys, so we tried desperately to find a new investor for the website. We had already spent years seeking access to different people and organizations with a view to gaining their support, but so far we had come up short.

Besides, in the six years since we'd started Agentura in 2000, our idea of what the site could be and what Andrei's father thought it should be had diverged. Andrei's father believed it would become a sort of elite private club for serious, respected people to talk about national security. Instead, we had published more and more stories about the FSB's nationwide hunt for spies (mostly imaginary) and the security services' horrible handling of terrorist attacks. Andrei's father always insisted that the success of the website depended on open-source research and our cooperation with the media. But while in 2000 our media partner had been the mainstream *Izvestia*, now it was the openly anti-Kremlin *Novaya Gazeta*. Andrei's father didn't openly protest, but he was not happy—that we could clearly see.

In the spring of 2006, he summoned us to his office in the north of Moscow, in an apartment building in the vicinity of the Kurchatov nuclear research institute where his internet company rented two floors. Andrei's father had worked at the Kurchatov Institute for more than thirty years; it was where he had started the very first internet provider in the Soviet Union in 1990.

When we went to his office, he looked somber. Without much polite chitchat, he told us he didn't see any future for Agentura. He believed there was no choice but to shut the website down.

We'd expected some trouble, but not this definitive cease-and-desist pronouncement. Eventually, we talked him out of the closure, and he agreed instead to let us move the website out. Andrei reregistered the domain name under his own name, and we moved the server to a hosting company independent from Andrei's father. From then on, we supported the website on our own as a volunteer project.

We didn't completely lose hope that we'd find an investor, though. In Moscow in 2006, there were still people with money investing in media independent of the Kremlin. The projects were now all online—it was much cheaper and politically safer than launching a newspaper or magazine. Some friends of ours, for example, former colleagues at *Moscow News*, had just secured funding for an online daily news and opinion website from a wealthy businessman who made his money making pipes for energy companies.

Nobody expected these new projects to win huge national audiences; the number of visitors for each website never exceeded 50,000 people. Liberal-minded intelligentsia accepted that Putin was the most popular politician in the country. But they gave journalists places to publish, and they provided salaries and offices in good locations. Our former *Moscow News* colleagues who ran a website had gotten an office in a basement next door to the Duma club on Mokhovaya Street; an editor of an online journal with a very anti-Kremlin agenda had an office just a five-minute walk from Jean-Jacques on Nikitsky, and rented an apartment for himself above the restaurant. He soon became a fixture at Jean-Jacques, entertaining his guests at the table in the left corner that was reserved for him every night.

Because we no longer had an office for Agentura, we developed a routine of wandering around. When in Moscow, we moved constantly between the *Novaya Gazeta* office on Potapovsky Lane and Ej.ru on Nikitsky Boulevard, bumping into friends and colleagues. We abandoned going to the Duma club completely when we discovered it had become a favorite watering hole for the police from the Interior Ministry building farther down the street. The club's owners gave up the idea of restricted access and opened the doors to everyone. The last thing we wanted was to spend time among drunken law enforcement officers celebrating promotions.

Reporters frequently gathered at Bulingua, an arts club with an independent bookshop located across the street from *Novaya Gazeta*. Those who didn't find a table in Bulingua could walk a few hundred feet down the street to join friends in the OGI club, which occupied a roomy basement in a yellow mansion. There, they could have some drinks and pick up a book, as OGI also had a small but decent bookstore. It was mostly pleasant to wander. We just needed to map our everyday journey between the various places in Moscow where we felt welcome and could be among people who were on the same page, socially and politically, and we learned to do that pretty well.

It felt as if we and our friends had discovered some sort of arrangement where we could coexist with the country's political regime. As we understood it, the arrangement was that Putin called the shots, while liberal journalists, blacklisted by mainstream media, found a place in the corner, which they turned into a comfortable reservation.

They could express their opinions freely online and gather to talk in comfortable offline spots in liberal cafés and clubs and editorial offices. Many believed that this coexistence could last for years and that one day Putin would just be gone. And when that happened, liberal-minded people would reemerge, and things would get back to "normal"—whatever that meant.

But not everyone was sipping coffee in the corner and waiting for a return to cozy liberalism. Petya Akopov's *Political Journal*, the rather obscure magazine funded by a nationalist banker, where he worked, suddenly became much talked about in the corridors of the Russian parliament when Petya published a long article discussing the prospects for the restoration of monarchy. It was a project, he believed, that could be launched after the next presidential election with the full support of Putin.

Petya apparently envisaged a scheme reminiscent of that in Spain in the late years of Francisco Franco's dictatorship, when an all-powerful caudillo had chosen and groomed Juan Carlos as the future king to secure his legacy. Petya wasn't wistfully dreaming of the day that Putin and his legacy would be gone. He wanted Putin's turn to authoritarianism to become permanent.

That year, 2006, *Novaya Gazeta* sent us to investigate how Russia's security services responded to terrorism in the most troublesome region in the country—the North Caucasus. Several months before, Nalchik, a sleepy capital of the small republic of Kabardino-Balkaria, had been turned into a battlefield between the police, supported by troops, and jihadist militants who attacked the town. The Russian troops eventually suppressed the invasion of the militants in a traditionally bloody and messy way.

It was a predictably difficult assignment. People were angered by our questions, and the level of interference was a clear a message to us, two journalists from Moscow, to get back to where we had come from as soon as possible.

But people did talk to us, and they were willing to talk on the record. Local activists and nationalists, police officers, and even relatives of terrorists all spoke with us, though for one reason only: because we were from *Novaya Gazeta*.

It was a fantastic feeling to be working for a newspaper that everybody in the region knew and read. *Novaya Gazeta* was not popular among our friends in Moscow; lawyers, IT engineers, financiers, and the like found it too depressing. But it was clearly the most influential news outlet in the North Caucasus, and that was because of its star reporter—Anna Politkovskaya.

Politkovskaya fearlessly covered the war in Chechnya and became deeply involved in the region. She wrote about things people were afraid to talk about—rapes, abductions, and killings by Russian military—war crimes, in short. She kept writing her stories even when the public didn't want to read them. Everybody remembered that she had been poisoned on her way to Beslan, but she kept returning to the region and publishing front-page investigations.

She did this increasingly dangerous work for years, and it earned her an unparalleled network of contacts. We experienced the effect ourselves: people we had come to interview would give us stacks of documents, saying, "Please, take this to Politkovskaya."

The first thing we would do when we got back to Moscow was to head to the early Soviet-era printing building where *Novaya Gazeta* had its office, walk over to Politkovskaya's office, and quietly put the documents on her desk. A graceful woman with gray hair, wire-rimmed glasses, and the determined look of a strict teacher, she was usually on the phone taking notes.

It was great fun working for *Novaya Gazeta*. Our stories were widely read. We knew that for sure when we were summoned to an interrogation at the Moscow prosecutor's office after we published our investigation on the Nalchik attack.

THE ARRANGEMENT

We worked really hard, partly to help us recover from the blow of losing the funding for Agentura.

On October 7, 2006, a Saturday, Irina's parents hosted a dinner in their cozy apartment in a small town twenty miles east of Moscow. They were entertaining an aunt who had come from Siberia, and we had been invited.

Shortly after 6:00 p.m., Andrei took a call from a reporter we had worked with back in *Segodnya*'s crime bureau in the 1990s. He had remained a good friend, and the last time we'd seen him was in Beirut, two months before.

"Andrei, it's me. Politkovskaya has just been shot. At the entrance of her apartment. She is dead."

We hurriedly said our farewells to Irina's shocked parents and jumped into our Opel. The east of Moscow was not the most prestigious of Moscow's suburbs, to put it mildly, and the roads leading to Moscow from there were always jammed. It took us two hours to get to the office on Potapovsky Lane.

The editorial office was filled with people. They kept coming—not only reporters, but also friends of *Novaya*. People talked in hushed voices. Everyone was in shock.

We didn't know what to do or how to react, so we simply walked into the office of the deputy editor who oversaw the investigative department and asked how we could help. We instinctively tried to treat the assassination as a crisis that needed to be approached professionally. The deputy editor, Politkovskaya's friend for many years, had a deliberately calm expression on his face. He tried to act as if it were nothing more than a usual assignment, but he gave us some names to run by our sources, and we hurried to the exit.

There, in the corridor, we saw a bald, muscular man—a journalist we knew from our days as crime reporters. Five or six years before, we had trampled the snow for hours together at murder scenes. Now he worked for the government TV news channel, and we struggled to think of him as our colleague anymore. He rushed to Andrei and hugged him; he was visibly shocked. "Who the fuck did that?" he exclaimed. He then said something about the need for solidarity. "She was one of us!"

He obviously hadn't gotten any instructions from his bosses yet. They were no doubt waiting for Putin's reaction. But October 7 was also Vladimir Putin's birthday, and the Russian president apparently had better things to do than to react to the assassination of a famous journalist in the center of Moscow. It wasn't until the third day after Politkovskaya's murder that Putin commented on it.

He said that the murder had caused "much more damage" than her publications critical of the authorities.[1] He added, "I think that journalists should know, and experts perfectly understand, that her capacity to influence political life in Russia was extremely insignificant."[2] Essentially, he denied the relevance of her life and work by saying she had become important only because she had gotten killed.

For any liberal journalist who had thought there was any possibility for any kind of coexistence with Putin, the illusions they had harbored disappeared after Anna Politkovskaya's death. Politkovskaya had many powerful enemies, including the president of Chechnya, Ramzan Kadyrov, who had been personally chosen and groomed by Putin. Kadyrov introduced a brutal and totalitarian regime in Chechnya by harassing the population with his death squads. He first used them in his region but was also sending them out to mainland Russia and abroad to kill his opponents.

Putin's comments made it clear that the authorities would never conduct a proper investigation into who was behind Politkovskaya's assassination.

Soon those illusions were gone for everyone else, too. Less than a month after Politkovskaya's murder, the former FSB officer Alexander Litvinenko was poisoned in London. Litvinenko was a whistleblower who had defected to Britain; his revelatory book about

Putin's security services had been very popular in Russia, even if it was officially banned. An online copy was available. When we'd interviewed him in London three years before, he'd looked energetic and optimistic. Now he was dying in a London hospital.

His poisoning caused a scandal between Russia and Britain. The British identified the assassins and demanded their extradition, and when Moscow refused, London expelled four Russian diplomats.

The Kremlin and the FSB vehemently denied their involvement, but it dawned even on those who wanted to trust in Putin's benevolence that the people sent to London to kill Litvinenko had acted on Moscow's orders. Litvinenko had died from radioactive poisoning, and it was inconceivable that the assassins could have procured the polonium that killed him without the approval of the Russian state. Soon afterward, the principal assassin identified by the British was given a seat in the Russian parliament, where he became a member of the security committee—essentially taking the place once held by the fearless investigative journalist Yuri Shchekochikhin, from *Novaya Gazeta*, who had been poisoned in 2003.

It became increasingly clear that the political regime was set on a murderous course. The liberal intelligentsia didn't want to accept that change silently. But what was to be done? The street seemed to be an obvious option, perhaps the only place left.

CHAPTER 15

TO THE STREETS

Russia experienced several revolutions in the twentieth century, but by 2006, this tradition of street-level protests and social actions was long gone.

In the Soviet Union, the demonstrations allowed had been those in support of the Communist Party. Carefully choreographed columns of Soviet citizens, armed with portraits of Soviet leaders, marched on Red Square and the main streets of Soviet cities on designated Soviet holidays.

The only mass protest rally in the post-Stalin era of the Soviet Union was the one that had taken place in 1962 in the southern town of Novocherkassk, when workers had gone to the streets to protest a sharp increase in food prices. It was brutally suppressed with live ammunition, people were killed, and it was completely forbidden even to mention this event. Other street protests were held by tiny groups of dissidents and were completely ignored by the general population.

In the late 1980s, when Mikhail Gorbachev's perestroika policies loosened the regime's grasp over society, Soviet citizens amassed in big numbers in the streets of Moscow and St. Petersburg—then still Leningrad—enthusiastically embracing a right to protest they had been deprived of for decades. Every month the numbers of protesters grew until, in February 1990, 300,000 had gathered on Manezhnaya Square in Moscow to demand the cancellation of Article 6 of the Soviet Constitution—the article that awarded the Communist Party a key role in Soviet society. A year later, almost half a million people protested the decision to send Soviet troops to Lithuania to suppress the Lithuanian independence movement.[1]

Half a million people had also gathered on Manezhnaya Square in March 1991 on the eve of the referendum on the future of the Soviet Union—Gorbachev's desperate attempt to save it—to protest keeping the Soviet Union and to support the popular democratic leader Boris Yeltsin as president of Russia.[2]

A demonstration of that size was never to be seen again: once Yeltsin established himself in the Kremlin, his administration began to manifest open disgust toward the mass rallies that had helped him get there.

(There were mass protests in Moscow in 1993, which ended up with the shelling of the Russian parliament in October by the tanks, but they were never as numerous as those in 1991.)

Liberals in Yeltsin's government did not try to prevent people from gathering on the streets, but they made a conscious effort to make street protests seem old-fashioned, outdated, and even reactionary. Communism had been defeated and there was a new country with a new liberal economy. Everyone was free to make money. Why protest? Protest rallies were for losers—like communists and those nostalgic for the Soviet empire.

Liberal-minded journalists soon coined a term—"red-browns"—to describe the opposition to Yeltsin as a mix of communists and fascists, alluding to their nationalistic revanchism. The media, including the newspaper we worked for at the time, *Segodnya*, mocked all forms of protest activity as a pastime for old losers who had failed to find a place in the new Russian reality.

The mass gatherings were still permitted, although the places where they were to occur needed to be agreed upon with the local authorities; they just went out of fashion among those who went to work for banks and commercial companies and others who gained access to the perks of the new capitalist economy. Manezhnaya Square, once the place of the biggest popular protest rallies, was rebuilt as a giant shopping mall.

When Yeltsin decided to send troops to Chechnya in December 1994, and Yegor Gaidar, a liberal icon—Yeltsin's former prime minister and the architect of the Russian shock therapy economic program—realized he couldn't persuade Yeltsin to change his decision, he called on like-minded Muscovites to come to Pushkin Square to protest the war. Very few responded.[3]

Ever since, democratic protests had been attended by a few thousand people at most. By the mid-2000s, the people who'd thought of themselves as beneficiaries of the liberal reforms of the 1990s realized they'd surrendered their country to Putin and the FSB, and that they'd completely forgotten how to protest.

When Anna Politkovskaya was killed, more people took to the streets in Paris than they did in Moscow.

In the spring of 2007, the coalition of diverse opposition parties and movements that called itself "the other Russia" announced an anti-Kremlin protest rally to be held in Moscow on Saturday, April 14. The coalition named the rally the March of Dissenters. This time, liberals—artists, writers, even journalists, who never went to protests—decided to join.

The authorities responded by banning the march and launching a massive smear campaign in pro-Kremlin media. An article titled "Real Treason," published on the pro-Kremlin website Vzglyad (View) three days before the march, put it this way: "Why do they need this? Why do serious people put on clown clothes and go to the circus? Apparently, they have some kind of super-goal, for the sake of which they are ready to endure humiliation in the media and contempt from friends. As it turns out, there is such a goal. And it lies in their total corruption, as well as in what exactly they are selling. The leaders of the 'Other Russia' are selling our Motherland, Wholesale and Retail."[4]

That same day, the State Duma Speaker, Boris Gryzlov, leader of Putin's United Russia party—warned of the possibility of "provocations" during the March of Dissenters. This was a pretty ominous message: Russians knew well from Soviet times that once the authorities started talking about "provocations," it usually meant they were ready to turn to repression. And if Gryzlov's warning was not enough, the Moscow police department issued a statement that the police were going to "suppress harshly" all attempts to hold unauthorized rallies in Moscow, a phrase that meant the police would be encouraged to be very physical and hand out beatings whenever they pleased.[5]

If you want to gather people for a rally in Moscow, mid-April is the best time to do it. The weather is already warm and dry, and the snow has long since melted, but the time for dacha weekends has not yet arrived. Saturday, April 14, was clear and sunny, and it promised to be a beautiful day.

That morning, when we got off the metro at Pushkin Square, the first thing we saw were hundreds of special forces soldiers in blue camouflage armed with batons and shields. Police buses with barred windows lined Tverskaya Street and an adjacent boulevard, ready for arrested protesters. Not far from the monument to Pushkin, we saw Alexander, a solid man with a mustache, a military observer at Ej.ru and a retired Soviet army colonel.

He had come with his wife, a lady in an elegant coat holding a first aid kit in her hands. "I am a doctor, and I sense my skills might come in handy today," she told us.

We stood surrounded by protesters, many in their twenties and early thirties, too young to have been in the democratic crowd on

Manezhnaya Square in 1991. It was clearly the first time they had overcome their disdain for protests and taken to the streets.

At that moment, the police blocked Tverskaya, Moscow's main street, and began squeezing protesters out of it. At the other end of the square, Mikhail Kasyanov, once Putin's prime minister, now in opposition, emerged, and several soldiers closed in.

Kasyanov, a big man, turned to them and said something in a very angry voice—it was clear he was not afraid of them. Suddenly they stopped, visibly confused: the former prime minister, whom they'd seen for years standing next to Putin on Russian TV, now stood in front of them, yet they had an order to detain him. They retreated; Kasyanov stood his ground.

But the police then turned to other organizers of the march. They swiftly snatched world chess champion Garry Kasparov, and the young political activist Maria Gaidar, a daughter of Yeltsin's prime minister, and threw them into police buses. Maria Gaidar was detained at the same place where her father had spoken at the antiwar rally of liberal-minded Muscovites twelve years before.

We were moving with the crowd along Rozhdestvensky Boulevard when, at a corner, a female figure wearing a bright silver jacket jumped out. It was Anna Pavlova, our friend and editor at Ej.ru. "We need the other Russia!" she chanted loudly, the slogan of the march, her black hair waving in the breeze. Max Blant, an economic observer and another friend, tried to guide her away from the soldiers, but she was unstoppable. Anna climbed up the fence dividing a pedestrian walkway from the road.

Soon after, the special forces column emerged in front of us and blocked both the road and the walkway. They stopped, waiting for the order to charge. The protesters stopped, too, and photographers' cameras were clicking, trying to capture the scene.

In a second, a policeman in full anti-riot gear charged toward a Japanese news photographer, who stood next to us, and hit him in the head with a baton. The journalist collapsed, blood pouring down his face. No one could understand why the policeman had done it: no one had been threatening him, and the Japanese photographer had a brightly colored press card around his neck.[6]

The photographer was not the only victim of police violence that day. Facing the first liberal mass protests of Putin's rule, the Kremlin reacted violently. The anti-riot police beat dozens of people on the streets of Moscow.

We emerged unharmed. On the boulevard, we parted ways—Anna stayed with her friends from Ej.ru and we rushed to the *Novaya* office nearby to write a story about the brutal police methods and the anti-riot gear they had used on Muscovites.

Several days later, we all gathered in our usual place, Jean-Jacques on Nikitsky Boulevard, along with other friends, to talk about the march.

Emotions ran high, predictably, and there was the sense of excitement one feels after being in a crowd pushed and attacked by police. But this excitement could not disguise one fact: at most, the March of Dissenters had amassed 20,000 people. It was probably more than the democratic forces had managed to gather in their protests in the late 1990s and early 2000s, but 20,000 was not a lot of people in a city like Moscow, with a population of 11 million in a country of nearly 143 million citizens.

CHAPTER 16

THE GAME OF SUCCESSION

In May 2008 Vladimir Putin had stepped down as president, barred by the Russian constitution from standing for election for the third time in a row. He had designated as his successor a short, energetic lawyer in his early forties named Dmitry Medvedev. Putin apparently hadn't gone for Petya Akopov's scheme of reintroducing monarchy. Medvedev was a safe option—also from St. Petersburg, just like Putin, and the person who had led Putin's very first presidential election campaign.

Medvedev was sworn in as new president on May 7 after an election that was a formality. He was known to be a keen fan of Apple products and the rock band Deep Purple. Most importantly, he had never served in the KGB, unlike Putin's other appointees. He was expected to deliver a partial liberalization of the stiff and repressive political regime Putin had built. Or so many desperately wanted to believe.

Anna Pavlova's long-standing friend Nikolai Svanidze, a prominent TV journalist, spent much of that spring talking to Medvedev in his mansion on Rublyovka Road, taking notes for a forthcoming book intended to introduce the new president to Russia.

It became a sort of Russian tradition to have such a book written for a new president. While Boris Yeltsin was well known to Russians long before he was elected president, because of his fierce activity as a public politician, it was different for Putin, a bureaucrat who had been picked by Yeltsin from relative obscurity. Putin didn't have a public profile, thus he needed to be introduced to the audience, in the country and abroad, and that had been done through a book written by three Russian journalists who had sat and talked with Putin for several weeks nine years before. Now Putin had picked Medvedev, and it was Medvedev's turn to give the interviews. Svanidze had been chosen as the writer.

A bespectacled, gray-bearded man in his fifties with a sad look and quiet voice, well-suited to his role as a prominent member of the Moscow intelligentsia, Svanidze tried hard to recognize any sign of Medvedev's supposed liberalism.

He noted Medvedev's good manners: the new president himself had accompanied him to the hallway and given him his coat, which "is not common these days." He underscored the point that Medvedev was the first Russian president who had not been the first in his family to go to university. Medvedev was introduced as an admirer of Frank Sinatra and French singer Mylène Farmer, in addition to Deep Purple. The book, due in August, was lyrically titled *Medvedev: Conversations Accompanied by Music*.

We often saw Svanidze at Jean-Jacques, where he regularly came to lunch with Anna. In June, Moscow was bright and warm, and Jean-Jacques placed tables on the boulevard in true Parisian style. The four of us were usually seated at one of them. It seemed like every passerby recognized Svanidze, but he maintained his characteristic withdrawn manner and spoke quietly if anyone approached him.

A historian by training, like Anna, Svanidze worked on television alongside Anna's former husband, who was also a popular TV journalist. The three had been friends for decades. Svanidze was also a shrewd, experienced political operator who for years had held key positions at the All-Russia Broadcasting Company—a state-owned media behemoth with television channels in every Russian region. He enjoyed a reputation as a liberal-minded intellectual from a distinguished Soviet family. His grandfather was a relative of Stalin's first wife, and his father was deputy head of Politizdat, the Soviet publishing monster subordinated to the Central Committee of the Communist Party, where Zhenya Baranov's mother had published her anti-religious books. For several years, Svanidze had run an ambitious project on Russian television with episodes devoted to particular years in twentieth-century Russian history; each show profiled key political, cultural, and historical figures from the year being featured. In a way, he had created a narrative about the most important events and individuals in contemporary Russian history.

It was clear that Svanidze had been hired to sell Medvedev to Russia's intelligentsia as someone very different from Putin. Putin was by then known as a street-smart, KGB-trained strongman fond of Russian "chanson"—a masculine music genre that lionizes jail and the criminal lifestyle. The book was a public relations project, far from real journalism, but Svanidze treated it as something more important. When we spoke with him at Jean-Jacques, he sounded as if he truly believed that Medvedev could be a different kind of president than Putin.

People with more skeptical minds wondered: How big could that difference be? And did it really matter what Medvedev thought? After all, Putin might have left the Kremlin, but he'd hardly given up power. As part of the arrangement between the two, Medvedev appointed Putin prime minister. In late June, Putin was forming his government. It felt a little as though Medvedev was in office but Putin was still in charge.

One evening, after a long day in the editorial office at *Novaya Gazeta*, Andrei was inflating a tire on our old Opel in the parking lot on Potapovsky Lane when he took a call. "Andrei, I'm a correspondent at a news agency. Can you comment on the appointment of your father as deputy minister of communications?"

Andrei went speechless. After his father had cut off his support for Agentura, they'd drifted apart, and they hadn't spoken for many months. Alexey Soldatov certainly hadn't reached out to tell his son about his new position. A colleague who happened to be standing nearby exclaimed, "Leave your old Opel—a black BMW is surely coming your way!" It was a good joke that helped us mask our confusion.

Andrei didn't want to call his father immediately, so we checked what the media had to say about the appointment. The government newspaper's story ran under the headline "Founder of Russian Internet Becomes Deputy Head of the Ministry of Telecom and Mass Communications."[1] According to the ministry's press office, Alexey Soldatov was to oversee the strategic, scientific, and technical development of the IT industry.

That sounded reasonable. Apple fan Medvedev talked incessantly about new technologies, and Alexey Soldatov's expertise and his reputation seemed to make him an appropriate choice.

Andrei was pleased for his father but decided that his promotion was simply a testament to the fact that they were all grown-up people with their own careers. Alexey's new role in the government was amusing and perhaps a little ironic, but no more than that. It seemed that it was perhaps tactful to let him get on with his new job and not make it more complicated for their already strained relationship by reaching out to him.

As prime minister, Putin appointed Sergei Ivanov, a KGB foreign intelligence veteran, as his first deputy in the government. But, unlike for Alexey Soldatov, for whom appointment to the government was an honor, for Ivanov it was a humiliating defeat.

Fifty-four-year-old Sergei Ivanov considered himself to be a close friend to Putin. They had worked in neighboring offices in the late 1970s as young lieutenants in the Leningrad (now St. Petersburg) department of the KGB, and Ivanov was one of the KGB veterans

Putin had brought to power. Most of Putin's appointees from the security services had held a rank equal to or below Putin's, but not Ivanov. With his rodent face, mousy hair separated by a neat parting, and creaky voice, he was never a woman charmer, but he was smart and fitted well in the KGB—Ivanov had made a successful career in foreign intelligence and become a general, a rank Putin himself had never attained. When Putin became president, he made Ivanov his minister of defense, and when the time came to choose Putin's successor, Ivanov was seen by many as the most probable candidate for the top job in the Kremlin.

That was certainly what an energetic tiny blonde, Sveta Babayeva, the head of the political department at *Izvestia* who loved to drive her beloved Suzuki SUV around Moscow, had counted on.

Babayeva met Ivanov in 2000 at Putin's "private," off-the-record briefings for the presidential journalists' pool, when he was Putin's secretary of the Security Council. She was the journalist who landed the first big interview with Ivanov, meant to introduce him to a Russian audience. When *Izvestia* published the interview, Ivanov was ecstatic.

Ivanov kept Sveta Babayeva close when he became minister of defense. She would come by his office, and he would brief her about his vision for military reform, and sometimes share his insights on the Kremlin. Babayeva provided him with her full support. The relationship suited them both: while Ivanov had *Izvestia* on his side, Babayeva secured access to one of the most influential insiders in the Kremlin. She would go to Ivanov to ask for guidance before making her career moves.

Ivanov took Babayeva with him on many of his trips, both across Russia and around the world. He considered himself worldly and sophisticated—he had studied in the United Kingdom in the mid-1970s and served as a spy in Finland and Kenya; he spoke English and Swedish; and he was only too happy to give Sveta advice. Ivanov introduced her to important people—for instance, US

Secretary of Defense Donald Rumsfeld, who came to call her "Sveta the skinny."

At some point Ivanov offered her the position of editor-in-chief of *Red Star*, the main newspaper of the Russian army, but she declined. She wanted to go to London instead, so she secured his support when she became boss of the UK office of the government news agency RIA Novosti in 2004. RIA had fancy digs in a red-brick Victorian townhouse in affluent South Kensington. In those years Moscow went crazy about London, and most of the fancy places in the city respectfully copied British design, down to the sign fonts. Babayeva enjoyed her life in the most cherished city in the world for successful Russians.

After two years in Britain, Babayeva returned to Moscow as Putin's two presidential terms were coming to an end. It appeared as if her powerful patron was destined for the Kremlin.

In mid-2007, Babayeva published a long article about Russian ideology. She started by pointing out that there was a new focus in the Russian narrative—moral values—and noted that Putin had begun using a language of moral values designed to unite all Russians. Babayeva cited her sources, saying that "some in the Kremlin" believed that "the future president, whoever he will be, would have to deal with issues not only to do with oil and gas, but with the moral and ethical standards of society."

Babayeva claimed that there was an ideological vacuum in mid-2000s Russia, and that this was why "glamour" was flourishing in some classes, while unmotivated aggression was omnipresent in others. She acknowledged Putin's focus on traditional values but claimed they were "not enough for an open, global, information society." Moreover, such a traditional focus would slow down the development of society rather than pushing it forward. Her skepticism extended to the role of the Church:

> Now one may notice something else: careful attempts to turn to church experience. But unfortunately, this is an appeal

> not to Christian commandments, but to Church dogmas. By turning to God, we risk encountering the institution whose conservatism, if not to say reactionism, is recognized even by many religious people. But since there is nothing else to turn to—again with the connivance or soft approval of the ruling elites—one can expect a somewhat convulsive turn toward traditionalist values.[2]

She praised many Western values, from respectful driving to the treatment of prisoners of war. Her two years in London had deeply affected her.

The Kremlin foreign policy journal published her article.

Apparently, her criticism was tolerated, if not encouraged. That same summer, Ivanov proclaimed himself an Anglophile and a fan of Western music, just like Medvedev. London's *Times* repeated that Ivanov was a fan of the Beatles, Pink Floyd, and Led Zeppelin, as well as British spy novels. Ivanov was clearly working the Western audience, but many believed he overplayed his hand, taking Putin's approval for granted. He was getting more self-confident, a quality Putin didn't particularly like in his subordinates. The Beatles can't buy you Putin's love, it seemed.

Putin crushed Sergei Ivanov's hopes of becoming Russia's president in December 2007 when the pro-Kremlin party United Russia named Medvedev as the party candidate in the upcoming election. Ivanov endorsed the decision; he had no choice. His discipline and submissiveness were rewarded with the post of a deputy prime minister.

Soon, Sveta Babayeva flew off to the United States. There was no reason for her to remain in Moscow after the election once her main source and patron had been demoted, and she accepted a position as head of the RIA Novosti bureau in Washington, DC, the most prestigious job in the news agency. There she became the hostess of a grand three-story Beaux-Arts building on Eighteenth Street NW in the

Dupont Circle neighborhood, acquired by the Soviet embassy to host its press center in 1957, right in the middle of the Cold War.

Evgeny Krutikov learned that Putin had chosen Medvedev as his successor when he was in Nalchik, the capital of a small republic of the North Caucasus where he worked as a political consultant for a local president.

Krutikov had left his beloved South Ossetia soon after the Beslan tragedy in 2004, when he had a fight with the local elites. He discovered, to his disgust, that people in power in South Ossetia, which he loved and cared so deeply about, had become greedy and corrupt, even if they were brave fighters.

He moved back to Moscow. But he never lost his affection for South Ossetia, a tiny, isolated mountain republic in the North Caucasus of no more than 50,000 people, most of them living in its capital, Tskhinvali. In Moscow, he set on editing a "black book" of the South Ossetian victims of the war with Georgia—one of the bloody conflicts following the collapse of the Soviet Union—modeled on *The Black Book of Soviet Jewry*, compiled by the Soviet writers Ilya Ehrenburg and Vasily Grossman to document the crimes of the Holocaust on Soviet soil. Georgian victims were not listed in the book, which Krutikov finished just before moving to Nalchik. He didn't have any particular interest in Nalchik or that part of the Caucasus, but he was offered a good contract, and he agreed to spend several months there. He had become a kind of consultant for hire.

The news that Putin had chosen Medvedev made Krutikov rather happy. He never believed Medvedev would be a different sort of president than Putin, but he believed Medvedev to be more predictable and reliable than the ambitious Ivanov. He didn't expect any big changes.

Once his PR contract in Nalchik ended in the spring, Krutikov, now back in Moscow, didn't want to return to journalism, so he started writing fiction—spy thrillers, predictably. By then he felt exhausted:

his deteriorating health needed to be attended to, and he decided to remain in his Moscow apartment for a while and focus on his writing.

The plot of his first thriller was built around the assassination of a "famous human rights journalist" who resembled Anna Politkovskaya. The protagonist was a former military intelligence officer and a veteran of local military conflicts, now a private investigator who seemed very much like a spy version of Krutikov himself. British intelligence was playing games with Russian agencies, and the conspiracy his detective would uncover originated in Western Ukraine during Stalin's reign. Krutikov told his readers from the start that he didn't understand why the media would be in opposition to the Kremlin, and he made journalists the most unattractive characters in the book: the assassin was a journalist and former KGB officer. The book ended with Russian military intelligence inviting the protagonist to get back to work for them. On the last page, Krutikov thanked two generals of the FSB.

What was peculiar about the book was that Krutikov published it seven months before Anna Politkovskaya's murder. What kind of conversations about journalists was Krutikov now having with his friends at the FSB and military intelligence? we wondered when we heard about the book.

South Ossetia also remained a huge presence in Krutikov's life: South Ossetians in Moscow were the people he drank with. The most trusted and closest friend among them was Dmitry Medoyev, a balding man with a mustache and chubby cheeks who had accounted for a significant portion of the daily consumption of Bushmills at *Izvestia* and *Versia*. Medoyev rented an apartment in the building next door to Krutikov's. His career, unlike Krutikov's, was on the rise.

In the summer of 2008, Medoyev acted as an unofficial ambassador of South Ossetia to Moscow—unofficial because the tiny republic was not recognized by any country in the world, including Russia. But it was clear that his connections to Russian agencies were extremely close. Six years before, Medoyev had studied at the Russian diplomatic academy, and according to Krutikov, Medoyev had something to do with Russian military intelligence at that time.

That summer, Medoyev's main job was to brief Russian media on the shelling between South Ossetians and Georgians, which became a daily occurrence. He would not tell journalists, though, that Russian special forces were being secretly moved to South Ossetia.

Medoyev and Krutikov believed that something big and bad was coming.

On August 5, Medoyev convened journalists at a press conference in Moscow. He announced that the situation in the area of the Georgian-Ossetian conflict had sharply deteriorated, and that Georgia had moved troops and artillery close to South Ossetia. He also claimed that the Georgian units that were shelling South Ossetian positions had previously participated in the joint Georgian-American exercises, and that Georgian snipers were armed with rifles like those used in North Atlantic Treaty Organization (NATO) countries.[3] It was an obvious attempt to imply that Georgian authorities were acting as puppets of Western powers, the United States first and foremost.

Medoyev promised Georgia a "railroad war" if the crisis reached the stage of a large-scale armed conflict. He was referring to the tactics invented by Lawrence of Arabia, who had used guerrilla warfare against the Ottoman railroads, blowing up the bridges and rails, in World War I—tactics Soviet partisans had used again against the Germans during the Great Patriotic War.

Medoyev also announced a big influx of volunteers—fighters ready to come from Russia to fight for South Ossetia.[4]

He was preparing the public for a major conflict.

PART III

CHAPTER 17

RETURN OF THE EMPIRE

Is that true that Muscovites do not know what to do with all their money?" "Do all Muscovites now live in penthouses?" We were often asked these or similar questions by our contacts and relatives in regions far from Moscow, in tones of admiration and envy.

In the mid-2000s the middle classes in Moscow enjoyed a sharp increase in the quality of life never before experienced in Russian history. Oil prices skyrocketed and so did salaries as Russian and Western companies expanded their presence in Moscow and aggressively recruited local staff. Shopping malls and giant chain stores such as IKEA were mushrooming across the city and its suburbs. Accountants, lawyers, sales managers, and advertisers rushed to buy new cars and get mortgages for their fancy flats in the capital. Brand-new suburban settlements with lines of cottages took the place of old Russian villages in a fifty-mile-wide belt around Moscow.

In 2000 we could have driven from our apartment in a northern suburb to *Izvestia* in twenty-five minutes and parked our car for free on Tverskaya, Moscow's main street; seven years later, the same trip took an hour and a half, and parking in the center of Moscow became impossible. Mercedes of all shapes, Audis (the Russians developed a big thing for luxury German car brands), and Lexuses lined the streets, invading sidewalks if they had to.

Muscovites learned how to make good money, and they wanted to spend it. One New Year's Eve, Irina went to a perfumery and makeup boutique called Île de Beauté near *Novaya Gazeta*'s offices. It was full of excited shoppers pushing shopping carts full of colorful boxes of Chanel, Dior, and Shiseido. Muscovites had swiftly adapted to a lifestyle that was unimaginable to their parents in the Soviet Union.

Moscow, along with several other big Russian cities, became a consumer paradise, and Muscovites were proud of it, but it was not enough. Now they needed something bigger to be proud of—something about the country and its place in the world. Soon the Kremlin duly provided the reasons.

In August 2008 Moscow felt half-empty. Many families were on vacation or spending time at their dachas. Those who remained in the city preferred having cold drinks on the shady terraces of bars—all the outside tables at Jean-Jacques were taken—to following the news, especially if the news concerned a faraway place like South Ossetia or Georgia.

Very few people in Moscow seemed to remember the tragic and bloody history of the early 1990s, when the South Ossetians, backed by Moscow, had split from Georgia, which caused a military conflict. The bloodshed was eventually stopped, and a ceasefire signed, guaranteed by the presence of Russian peacekeepers.

But the Georgians never gave up hope of taking the breakaway region back, and the South Ossetians hated the idea of living with the Georgians. The sporadic and senseless conflict smoldered for years.

At the beginning of August 2008, the shelling between the two sides intensified, but the press conference where Krutikov's friend Medoyev, South Ossetian envoy in Russia, threatened to launch a "railroad war against Georgia" went mostly unnoticed in Moscow.

All that changed in the early hours of August 8, when the Georgian army's Grad multiple rocket launchers set off shelling the South Ossetian capital of Tskhinvali and Georgian tanks rolled into its streets.

What happened next surprised most Russians. President Dmitry Medvedev addressed the nation on Russian television. He accused the Georgians of acts of aggression against Russian peacekeepers and civilians, in that order. He added that most of the casualties in South Ossetia were Russian citizens and promised a swift retaliation. He sounded almost like Vladimir Putin, except without Putin's signature obscenities.

As Medvedev was speaking, the Russian army was moving into South Ossetia through the long and narrow Roki Tunnel. Within a few days, Russian troops pushed the Georgians out of Tskhinvali, but they didn't stop there and swiftly invaded Georgia. Russian tanks occupied the Georgian town of Gori and several villages, stopping just forty-seven miles from the Georgian capital, Tbilisi. A ceasefire agreement was signed.

In Moscow, the victorious five-day war was received with enthusiasm bordering on euphoria. Medoyev and Krutikov were happy because finally Russia had backed with full force the separatist cause they had promoted for years.

But there was also jubilation among Moscow's middle classes. To them, Russia's victory was a sure sign that Russia was back on the global stage. They also understood that for all Medvedev's tough talk, it was Putin who had called the shots. Medvedev as president was commander in chief, but everyone knew that as part of his deal with Medvedev, Putin retained control over the security services and the army.

"It was so cool how we put the Georgians in their place. Finally, we are strong again, and all thanks to Putin!" Kirill, a pink-faced, chubby-cheeked, twenty-something manager of an advertisement agency that Agentura worked with, was in a state of rapture. We were meeting with him on Manezhnaya Square shortly after the ceasefire to talk about our business relationship. Manezhnaya Square was the place where a huge crowd of democratic Muscovites had gathered to support Boris Yeltsin in 1991, which had led to the dissolution of the Soviet Union, a fact Kirill was hardly aware of. Well-educated, mild-mannered, and always optimistic, Kirill was sincerely and visibly excited about the Russian invasion of Georgia, Putin's first external war.

Nine years before, Putin had gotten public support for his war in Chechnya because the Russians feared terrorist attacks, and Putin promised to deal with terrorists, as brutally as possible. This time, he secured wide public support because of wounded pride. Putin's approval rating reached a record high of 88 percent in September, and even Alexei Navalny, who would become Putin's main antagonist, supported the Russian war against Georgia, calling its citizens rodents.[1]

"Before this, no one respected us on the globe. For how long could we tolerate this?" Kirill exclaimed. "Yeltsin destroyed everything in the country, especially the army, and now we've made the world go round, and the Americans respect us."

Kirill was a decent, smart guy, and his shallow nationalism made us sad and angry. The true story of the war was much more complicated than the message promoted by the Kremlin. *Novaya Gazeta* published several investigations outlining how the Russian army had been carefully preparing for war, secretly buffing up its military presence in South Ossetia, well before August 8. But for Kirill, and many like him, that didn't register. What mattered was that Russia had rediscovered its swagger.

A week after the five-day war in Georgia, Nikolai Svanidze's long-awaited book about Medvedev made it to the bookstores. But on the way, it had lost its subtitle, *Conversations Accompanied by Music*.[2] Apparently, in the ramp-up to war, Medvedev had deemed it inappropriate to promote himself as a sensitive and intelligent leader. Instead, the book had no subtitle at all.

On August 26, Medvedev signed two presidential decrees recognizing South Ossetia and Abkhazia, the second breakaway region from Georgia, as two independent states, and establishing diplomatic relations with both.

When they heard the news, Krutikov and Medoyev rushed out of their apartments into the street in Moscow where they both lived. There on the tiny, usually very quiet lane at the back of Moscow's Prospekt Mira highway, the two men danced, hugged, and screamed in jubilation. They'd gotten what they wanted. Medoyev was immediately appointed the first ambassador of South Ossetia to Russia. Krutikov felt that justice was done: South Ossetia had become independent. But he didn't want South Ossetia to be incorporated into Russia.

"Russia can't do that," he would tell us years later. "It would be an annexation, full stop, and we don't want it. Because it would harm Russian interests in other parts of the world. Next time Russia would send soldiers abroad to help other nations, the world would scream 'annexation!'"

Petya Akopov saw it differently. The first issue of the magazine he edited after the war had on its cover a drawing of Medvedev on a Russian tank, a statue of Stalin, and a big, bold headline: "Return of the Empire."

Zhenya Baranov missed the war altogether. His TV channel had sent him to Abkhazia, where the second front against Georgia was expected to open, but that never happened. Baranov wasted his time until he got a broken toe and was evacuated to Russia.

For quite some time, Baranov and Olga Lyubimova had been going through an uneasy period in their relationship. They had two kids, a son, Nikita, and a daughter, Varya. Lyubimova complained on her blog that she'd gained too much weight and was feeling exhausted after a difficult childbirth, while Baranov, not paying a lot of attention to her feelings, brought an Ossetian veteran soldier, a veteran of the Balkan Wars, into their dacha. Lyubimova found herself having to cook for them while looking after the newborn and the toddler at the same time. A few months later she again wrote about "ignorance" and "negligence" on the part of the people closest to her, including her husband.

When the war with Georgia started, she had been in Belgrade on vacation. She kept posting her thoughts on her blog and attacked liberal journalists critical of the Russian invasion: "This is especially wild to read in Belgrade. Here even a child would explain to you what does not fit in the heads of Moscow's exalted journalists." She meant the liberal journalists who were not excited that Russia had dragged itself into a war with Georgia.

To Lyubimova, the war in Georgia, like the wars in the Balkans, was part of one big, never-ending Western attack against Russia and their Slavic brothers, the Orthodox Serbs. Baranov thought the same way—as husband and wife they may have had their problems, but they were on the same page when it came to Serbia being unfairly treated by the West.

A year later, the main Russian TV channel, Channel One, aired a fifty-two-minute documentary titled *08.08.08: The War on Air*, marking the anniversary of the war with Georgia. The film was produced by a company that had previously filmed advertisements for the Kremlin's United Russia party and for Dmitry Medvedev.[3]

The film was narrated by Baranov. It was a full-frontal attack on Western media, accusing them of consciously twisting the truth about the war in Georgia.

Baranov's deep voice told his audience the Kremlin's version of the war. On the screen, women in tears spoke of atrocities committed by Georgian troops; there were destroyed buildings and burned tanks on the streets of the capital of South Ossetia.

Then the focus shifted to a frivolous masseuse, Doctor Dot from Berlin, who claimed she had provided a "biting massage" to President Mikheil Saakashvili of Georgia—she bit a man's back on camera to demonstrate what she meant. It was a weirdly deviant scene, which recalled the film about Saakashvili's supposed madness that Baranov had made five years before. It was intended to hammer home the idea that Saakashvili was peculiar.

Baranov next moved to his primary target—Western media, which, Baranov told his audience, distorted the truth by presenting the Russian troops, the saviors of South Ossetia, as invaders. According to Baranov, it was a familiar Western narrative. Western spin doctors had developed that same narrative against the Serbs during the Yugoslav wars in the early 1990s, using black propaganda methods to present the Serbs as the bad guys in the war and to accuse them of committing war crimes, which Baranov called "a hoax."

A historian by training, Baranov had always been obsessed by the history of what was seen as a glorious Russian-Turkish war of the late nineteenth century, when Russian troops had helped to liberate Bulgaria and Serbia, both predominantly Orthodox and Slav, from Turkey. In Tsarist Russia, the encounter had resulted in increasing fascination with Pan-Slavism, an ideology that sought to unite all the Balkan Slav peoples under the guidance of the biggest Slav and Orthodox country: the Russian empire. Baranov was also fascinated by the heroism of Yugoslav partisans during World War II, which he saw as similar to the Russians' heroic fight against the Nazis.

Baranov had gone to Serbia as a reporter during the NATO bombing in 1999—an operation launched to prevent the Serbs from attacking Kosovo. The experience had a huge impact on him. He understood the NATO operation as a cynical Western attack on the brotherly Slav and Orthodox people. In this, his attitude was shared by many Russians. The NATO bombing operation was condemned by the Kremlin and the Russian public.

In the *08.08.08* documentary, Baranov claimed that the Western spin-doctors were now using the same smear methods to blacken the reputation of South Ossetians and the Russian army. He presented witnesses who refuted charges against the Russian army. The Russian bombing of the Georgian town of Gori had caused a wave of outrage in the West. To deal with these accusations, Baranov called on Mikki, his fixer, whom we had met during our 2006 trip to Israel, and who was introduced in the documentary as an Israeli TV cameraman. Referring to news accounts of Russia targeting civilians, Mikki spoke of Western lies, and when pushed to identify the liars, he declared, "It was CNN!" He said he'd gone to Gori and hadn't seen any destruction. "There was an abandoned market, but not a single body, not a drop of blood," Mikki said. "People just fled. There was broken glass, two damaged apartments. . . . I saw an abandoned town, but completely intact!" Baranov had used his fixer as his witness, which was against all journalistic standards.

In fact, the Russian army had destroyed several apartment buildings in Gori, and there were civilians killed. When Russian cluster bombs hit Gori's main square, a Dutch cameraman was killed and an Israeli journalist seriously wounded, while shrapnel perforated a Reuters armored vehicle.[4]

Baranov's key witness in this trial of Western media coverage was, of course, Putin. In one film clip, a reporter from the *Guardian* asks Putin about the Russian bombing of Gori, and Putin angrily responds, "Your question doesn't surprise me. What surprises me is how powerful the propaganda machine of the so-called West is. It is just amazing. I congratulate you, those who do this. This is great work! But the result is bad, and it will always be like that, because this work is dishonest and immoral. Immoral politics always loses in the long run!" Putin, indeed, as Sveta Babayeva had remarked a year before, came to love invoking morality in his speeches. His instincts didn't betray him: most people in the country shared his feelings of anger toward the West. After the war with Georgia, Putin's approval rating went up to a fabulous 88 percent.[5]

And so, Putin learned that an external war could give him unprecedented popular support inside the country, even if the aggression was condemned by many Western countries. That condemnation left many Russians nursing a grudge—that when the time came to be proud of their army, the entire West had turned against them.

CHAPTER 18

THE URINALS IN OSTANKINO

In September 2008, journalists at *Novaya Gazeta* were gradually losing hope that Anna Politkovskaya's murder would be properly investigated by the authorities. The second anniversary of her assassination was approaching. Several people had been arrested, but law enforcement had failed to find a mastermind, and there was no theory about why she had been killed. The editors and journalists suspected that investigators were not looking very hard and that the process was rigged, partly because the investigators had decided to divide the criminal case into two parts—where people accused of direct involvement in Politkovskaya's murder landed in one case, and suspicions surrounding an FSB officer in another.

Novaya Gazeta had foreseen that events could unfold in this way and had therefore been conducting its own research into the killing from day one. The deputy editor-in-chief tasked Irina and Andrei with uncovering the role of a certain FSB lieutenant colonel in Politkovskaya's assassination. Little was known about this officer, apart from the fact that he had provided Politkovskaya's home address to a person connected to her assassins.

In October, *Novaya Gazeta* published our big profile on the FSB lieutenant colonel. We were proud of what we had found—that the FSB officer's role and position were much more important than had been previously believed.[1] Officially, he was just an operative in a regional unit, but in fact he served in the very secretive and elite FSB foreign intelligence department and was probably involved in supervising financial transactions.[2]

Three weeks later, we went to London on vacation, which promised to be a happy and exciting time in the best city in the world. And for several days it was. Then came the day we were visiting the reconstructed Shakespearean Globe Theater.

We were standing in the stalls, surrounded by other tourists, listening to the guide, when Andrei's phone rang, to our embarrassment. But the number was one of *Novaya Gazeta*'s, so Andrei answered. A very short conversation followed, and Andrei hung up.

"We are fired. *Novaya Gazeta* fired us," Andrei whispered.

We rushed to the exit, and Andrei explained in more detail: "It was *Novaya*'s HR chief. She said that we were fired due to staff reduction. She refused to elaborate." We called the deputy editor, but he refused to talk to us, other than to confirm our firing.

It was a bolt from the blue, and we knew for a fact that *Novaya Gazeta* was the very last media outlet in Russia that would have us on staff. Who else would dare to hire two reporters whose specialty was investigating the Russian security services?

As soon as we returned to Moscow, we went straight to *Novaya Gazeta*'s offices on Potapovsky Lane. But there, the editors flatly refused to talk to us.

Two months later, we learned that the FSB lieutenant colonel involved in Politkovskaya's assassination had been released, and more than that, reinstated in his position.[3]

We thought it was hardly a coincidence. It looked like we had dug deeper in our reporting than we had been expected to do. For the first time, we both began watching our backs.

For months we asked ourselves: Why did *Novaya Gazeta* fire us? Why did the editor refuse to talk to us? What was going on? We felt angry, and stupefied.

In the meantime, Moscow's intelligentsia in general still spoke of Dmitry Medvedev as a hope for democratic change, his direct involvement in the Georgian war explained away by his inexperience in foreign policy and Vladimir Putin's lingering influence.

Around the time the FSB officer was released, *Novaya Gazeta*'s editor interviewed Medvedev. It was the first interview the new Russian president had granted to a Russian newspaper, the Kremlin's press office emphasized. Medvedev was also the first and only Russian president who talked to a newspaper that had been so critical of the Kremlin.

In the interview, Medvedev tried to sound as liberal as humanly possible. He claimed that "democracy was, is, and will be"; hailed civil society; called the internet "the best platform for discussions"; and so on and so forth.[4]

Novaya Gazeta would keep Medvedev's interview on the front page of its website for many months. We thought the reasons were entirely practical: the newspaper wanted to use it as a shield, to create at least an appearance of protection by the Kremlin.

How seriously did the paper take Medvedev's pro-democracy rhetoric? We couldn't tell: *Novaya*'s editors and others on the staff completely ceased communications with us.

We felt increasingly isolated—although Ej.ru still accepted our opinion pieces and we saw Anna Pavlova regularly. She shared the news about our friends' lives.

Our guess that there was no newspaper left in town that would want to employ us proved correct. Having lost not only our jobs but also our salaries, we had no choice but to give up our rented apartment and ask for refuge in Andrei's mom's tiny flat. With every passing day we grew angrier.

Finally, a surprising new turn helped us. Andrei's friend Ilana Ozernoy, an American journalist with Russian origins, suggested that we write a book about Russia's security services. "Ha, in this country? Nobody would dare to publish it!" Andrei said.

"Not in this country—why not try to get an American publisher? I can help with the agent," she replied.

Thanks to journalist friends in London and New York, our proposal for a book about the FSB found its way to a publishing house launched by a former Moscow correspondent for the *Washington Post* during the Cold War. Soon we found ourselves with a contract to write the book. As a result, we spent the next year in a small room in Andrei's mom's apartment working on a book in a foreign language, something we had never done before. The work probably helped to keep us sane.

That autumn, all Moscow, it seemed, was talking about the death of a thirty-seven-year-old tax adviser named Sergei Magnitsky. Magnitsky had died in prison in particularly horrible conditions: he had faced health issues during his year in jail, but the prison's doctors had failed to provide him with medical help. Before that, he had been working for an American investor, Bill Browder. Everyone among our friends believed he had been thrown in jail because of a dispute between Browder and the Kremlin. After eight years of Putin as president, we were used to the assassinations of political opponents of the Kremlin—but this was something different. President Medvedev, as president, had made a promise to protect businessmen. He had clearly failed—and Magnitsky's life was written off as some sort of collateral damage, something that was now completely acceptable.

At some point we decided we needed to give Andrei's dad an advance warning that our forthcoming book would be very critical of the Russian security services and that it would be published in the United States. It could have been very awkward for him, since Alexey Soldatov still held a prominent position in the government. But he took it well, and that helped to repair the relationship between him and Andrei.

All those months, as we worked on the book, the Obama administration was trying to repair its own relationship with the Kremlin in what became known as a "reset" initiative. The Kremlin's top officials were responding in kind. President Barack Obama flew to Moscow to meet Medvedev and Putin, and Medvedev planned a state visit to the United States for June 2010.

A month before Medvedev's visit, Sergei Ivanov—now deputy prime minister, once Medvedev's unfortunate competitor—went to DC. When he spoke to Russian journalists in the Russian embassy, he predicted a blossoming of Russian-American relations.

"New winds have blown in relations between the United States and Russia," he announced grandly. Ivanov, it appeared, believed it would be possible to persuade the Obama administration to give up the Bush administration's plans to deploy a missile defense shield in Europe—something Putin and his people took as a direct American advancement toward Russia's borders, thus a threat—in return for the integration of Russian radar in the European air defense system.[5]

Sveta Babayeva was still based in DC as head of the RIA Novosti bureau, and Ivanov visited her every time he went to Washington. It was probably mutually beneficial—he was updated about the latest gossip in Washington, and she maintained her most important Kremlin connection.

She also developed her own connections with the Americans.

Babayeva had been using back channels to communicate with American officials for several years. She had first started back when she worked in Moscow. As early as 2006, the US embassy had stated in a cable to Washington that Babayeva "has long been a valued Embassy contact who has given us some fascinating insights into the Kremlin's workings."[6] In the years to come, Babayeva kept briefing US diplomats about the Kremlin—of the intrigues and gossip in the inner circle, of upcoming appointments—and her assessments were cabled to Washington.[7]

Why? American diplomats had extensive contacts in Moscow, and there was nothing wrong with Russian journalists, human rights activists, and opposition politicians talking to American and other Western diplomats. We had done it ourselves. But we spoke with foreign diplomats in order to push back on what we saw as an attempt by Western powers to normalize Putin's regime. And we knew and accepted our risks—that Kremlin propaganda would call us Western agents of influence. Why would a pro-Kremlin journalist and insider talk to US diplomats? Babayeva never struck us as an adventurist, eager to take risks and play dangerous political games on her own. It seemed likely that she was channeling views to the United States that Ivanov wanted her to seed without the Americans realizing they came directly from the Kremlin.

During Medvedev's trip to the United States, he happily accepted the role of a diligent boy from a provincial school coming to the big city to ask for access to Western technological innovation. Medvedev traveled first to Silicon Valley. He visited Apple and Twitter, met with top executives from Cisco and Google, and got Google's chief executive, Eric Schmidt, to join the board of the Medvedev-sponsored technological school, Skolkovo.[8] In DC, President Obama welcomed Medvedev, and everyone around was flashing optimistic smiles.

Three days after Medvedev left the United States, the FBI arrested ten Russian illegals, agents of the foreign intelligence agency SVR who had spent years in America living under cover. Eight out of the ten held American, Canadian, and Peruvian passports and used false names; two pretended to be recent Russian emigrants, including a redheaded party girl, Anna Chapman, who had acquired her Western name legally, by marrying a Briton.

The scandal posed a tricky political problem for the Kremlin. Medvedev was hardly affected by it: the arrangement between Medvedev and Putin made Putin responsible for the country's security and intelligence services, not him. Some could even say that Medvedev was Russia's path to a shining future based on international cooperation, while Putin was stuck to his Cold War toolkit of spies. Indeed, a big part of Putin's image, in the country and outside, relied on his background as a proud veteran of the spy department of the KGB—and the SVR was a direct successor to that department.

Media loyal to Putin tried desperately to find a way to present the failure to the Russian audience as something other than an embarrassment for the country's intelligence agencies. It was not easy—the Americans kept providing juicy details about the Russian spies, with Anna Chapman dominating the media coverage.

It turned out that the twenty-eight-year-old socialite Anna had blown her cover in New York when she had called her father in Moscow to share her concerns about meeting with an undercover FBI agent who had posed as a Russian operative.[9] Anna's father was a senior Russian intelligence officer who had formerly served abroad under diplomatic cover. He was the one who had put Anna into the intelligence business to begin with. Anna told her father that she thought she had been identified, and that call was intercepted by the FBI.

We were not very much surprised by all this: spying has been a family business since Stalin's times. But we felt taken aback that a young woman who had married a Brit and moved to New York still returned to old Soviet-era habits at a moment when she was struggling to find a good job in the United States. Anna had been in primary school when the Soviet Union collapsed; she had had plenty of opportunities in the new global world. But she still chose to stay with the family business, Russian intelligence. It was like a mafia family: no one ever really left.

While Chapman was being held in a federal jail in Brooklyn, in Washington, DC, Babayeva, as the head of the local bureau of the Russian government news agency, was fighting the US narrative of the scandal, though, as a journalist, she had never written about spies, and she had no expertise on the matter.

She blustered unconvincingly on NPR's *On Point*: "It seems to be the strangest espionage history. . . . Either Russian intelligence agencies worked so unprofessionally that [they] allowed the enemy to disclose the whole illegal network, or the FBI and other American law enforcement agencies do not reveal the whole story."[10] She ridiculed the details of the scandal as something that "sounded like movies from the sixties." She also tried to downplay the importance of the story for the Russian audience.

It was hardly a surprise that Babayeva stepped into the scandal—after all, not only was the building where she was based owned by the Russian state, so was the news agency she worked for. By the Kremlin's logic, that meant the journalists who worked there were owned by the Russian state as well.

The Kremlin spin doctors found a way to change the narrative two weeks later, when Russia and the United States agreed to a spy swap. As part of the deal, the Americans agreed to trade ten Russian spies for four Russian nationals held in prison for high treason. Three were long-term CIA assets—a colonel in military intelligence, Sergei Skripal; an operative of the SVR, Alexander Zaporozhsky; and a KGB veteran, Gennadiy Vasilenko. The fourth was a scientist, Igor Sutyagin.

The prisoners were swapped in the Vienna airport, and two days later Zhenya Baranov presented a new, updated account of events leading to the swap to the Russian public on the country's most-watched Sunday newscast on Channel One.

Baranov framed his story by recounting the recent mysterious death in the United States of a Russian defector, Sergey Tretyakov, who, Baranov insinuated, could have been a source about the illegal Russian spies—an ominous bit of news that gave viewers the impression that the Russian agencies had already punished the traitor.[11] Tretyakov's widow insisted he died of natural causes.

Baranov then insisted that the spy swap was a victory for the Russian secret services for two reasons. First, the two countries had traded the spies "in a ratio of 10 to 4 in our favor."[12] But, most importantly, it was a victory because, by including them in the swap, the Americans were admitting that all four Russian nationals were their assets, including the scientist Igor Sutyagin. As proof, Baranov quoted then vice president Joe Biden, who said to NBC, "We got back four really good ones."[13]

If Sutyagin was a US agent it would be a huge blow for Russian civil society, because for many years, Russian human rights activists and journalists had been advocating for the government to free Sutyagin, who had been sentenced to fifteen years for espionage. Before his arrest, Sutyagin had provided information to a mysterious London-based consultancy firm, Alternative Futures, which had paid Sutyagin on a regular basis. The FSB determined that Alternative Futures was a front for American military intelligence.

But the FSB had investigated and prosecuted Sutyagin's case in a very odd manner—he was accused of making up military secrets out of open-source material. It was unclear how, if the material was in the public domain, it could be considered secret enough to sustain a conviction. Many doubted Sutyagin was guilty. He was certainly not given a fair trial. We had been following Sutyagin's case for years and had exposed the fact that the FSB had secretly planted an agent of the SVR on his jury to influence the verdict. It emerged later that Alternative Futures was indeed a front for Western intelligence—not, however, for the American agency, but for Britain's MI6.[14] Sutyagin always claimed he didn't realize whom he had worked for.

THE URINALS IN OSTANKINO

Our friend Baranov appeared to have come to the aid of the Russian spy agencies at the very moment when they needed him.

In December 2010, Medvedev was planning to visit Ostankino, where most of Russia's major TV channels were headquartered, to be interviewed on Channel One. It was supposed to be a grand event that would boost his status as a true Russian leader.

On the eve of his visit, Olga Lyubimova blogged about the preparations for his arrival on her LiveJournal page. In a few sentences, which would go viral, she managed to touch on several sensitive issues for the new president: his height—and Medvedev was known to be short even by Putin's standards—his penis, and the atmosphere of sycophancy that surrounded him.

She wrote that Dmitry Medvedev was going to visit Channel One in Ostankino the next week. "I'm not revealing any military secrets here—he will have his interview on Channel One after Putin's interview on the TV channel Russia," Lyubimova explained.

She warned, though, that she was indeed about to reveal "military secrets." Those secrets concerned the cleanup before visits of Putin and Medvedev to Ostankino, which she described as something "like in Alice in Wonderland. . . . They paint roses and cover up all sorts of cracks, Tajiks wash the barriers, [there are] many pointless preparations."

Then she exposed the real secret: "BUT! This time, the fantasies of Ostankino's officials had no boundaries," she wrote. "How can we make it easier for the president, how to touch his wounded heart with sincere concern?" she asked ironically in her post.

"I don't know who came up with the only correct answer to all these rhetorical questions. But he was truly a genius. The men's restroom near the studio, where the interview will be conducted and modern history will be made, has undergone minor cosmetic repairs. The level of the urinals was lowered by 10 cm."[15]

Bloggers and journalists at once picked up Lyubimova's post and had a lot of fun with it. It was talked about in the editorial offices, in the Russian parliament, and in Moscow's cafés and restaurants.

Embarrassed, Lyubimova deleted the post, but to no avail. It was copied hundreds of times and still could be found all over the internet. A few days later, she had to take back her words. She wrote a new post in which she explained that she had succumbed to a hoax; she had asked her male friends to go to the gentlemen's restrooms to check the height of the urinals, and they confirmed that the urinals stayed at the same level.

Why did she write the first post? She was not a rebellious teenager anymore; she was an adult woman and the mother of two kids, and she had consciously and voluntarily agreed to work at a heavily censored Russian television network. What did she want to get out of it? To show that she was an independent-minded person? To draw attention to herself? We believed her motivation was entirely different. We knew very well that she was not a fan of Medvedev, nor was her husband, Baranov. They were Putin's people, along with the Russian Orthodox Church and the Mikhalkov clan.

For any other journalist, such a post about the president would inevitably jeopardize her or his career on Russian television. But in the end, the scandal didn't affect Lyubimova at all. Perhaps her high-placed friends in the Church and in the Kremlin protected her. Or maybe it was because they were also no fans of Dmitry Medvedev. Medvedev, on the other hand, never had the capacity to be as vengeful as Putin.

A few days after the urinals scandal, we stopped by Jean-Jacques and saw that Baranov was there. He was on his own, so we immediately joined him. We were chatting happily until Irina mentioned the scandal and praised Lyubimova for her sense of humor and her daring.

"She was acting irresponsibly. It was very stupid to write such things about the president," Baranov said. He was not defending

Medvedev, but he clearly believed it was reckless in Russian circumstances to attack someone that high in the Kremlin's hierarchy. He was very angry, in a way we had never seen before.

"It was not stupid, Zhenya. It was funny and caustic," Irina defended Olga.

"You just don't understand. It might be funny for you who has nothing to lose, but she has her father, who is a head of Moscow's Higher Theater School and thus a government employee. She could have cost him his job with this post. She has to think about her family!" Baranov was incensed.

Given how emotional he was, it was not entirely clear whether Baranov was actually talking about the risks to Lyubimova's father or about the risks to himself.

Irina looked at him. "Really? You think we don't understand? Maybe I need to point out to you that Andrei's father is a deputy minister of communications, but this fact doesn't prevent us from doing what we do. Or do you think that an acting school is higher than a ministry in the Kremlin hierarchy?"

Baranov said nothing in response, but he got visibly annoyed.

Soon afterward, Andrei's father left Medvedev's government. He did it voluntarily—he didn't want to promote the strange ideas, such as the concept of Russian internet sovereignty or the government-funded development of a national search engine, that were gaining traction in the Kremlin. So he chose to resign and moved to academia, becoming one of the deputies to the head of Moscow State University.

CHAPTER 19

LOSING ONE'S SOUL

One warm summer evening in 2010 our friend Alexey invited us to his mother's dacha. His mom, a good-looking businesswoman in her late fifties, served us supper on the terrace of her house, a pretty two-story cottage bordered by a birch grove. We were enjoying our spaghetti with a bottle of wine, listening to rustling leaves and singing birds. We had known Alexey, a successful lawyer, and his mother for many years, so it felt almost like a family supper. It was not a good moment to discuss politics, but one of us mentioned the recent protests in Moscow, where the police had beaten protesters.

Alexey's mother reacted, visibly irritated. "This thing has nothing to do with normal people. Normal people, they mind their own business and don't have time for that! Only losers go to the protests."

She had a point. We felt like losers, and she was not the only one who told us that. People attacked us all the time when we tried to mention politically sensitive topics in their presence. Muscovites loved their prosperity, believed it would last forever, and didn't want to encourage anyone to rock the boat.

We felt that the divide was becoming insurmountable between us and our peers, who were busy pursuing their successful careers in big corporations as financial managers, lawyers, and PR specialists, and we began avoiding the crowded parties we used to enjoy. We were in our mid-thirties and felt out of step with our own generation.

That suddenly changed in early 2011.

One February night we drove from Moscow toward the Sheremetyevo airport, past the gigantic IKEA, and turned off the packed highway onto a road leading to Eden, one of the brand-new cottage villages that had popped up around Moscow in recent years, where our friend Alexey had his brand-new house.

A security guard in a booth checked his list and lifted a barrier, allowing our old Opel in. The rows of three-story colored townhouses with front lawns looked absolutely identical—so much so that we failed to find Alexey's house on our first attempt.

Eden, five miles northwest of Moscow, was meant to be a paradise for wealthy families eager to imitate the American suburban lifestyle and its combination of security and comfort in a more natural environment than is found in a city setting. Alexey lived there with his wife and son, and most of his neighbors were young professionals with small children. We loved Alexey, but we had often found ourselves lost among his friends. Their conversations usually focused on real estate, cars, or their skiing holidays in the Austrian Alps.

That evening at Alexey's was no different, and we, as usual, withdrew into the background. All of a sudden, a pretty raven-haired woman in her mid-thirties, whom we knew as someone who had never been interested in politics, began talking excitedly about a satirical show on a new TV channel called Dozhd (Rain).

The show, called *Citizen Poet*, was political satire, often mocking corrupt bureaucrats and the Kremlin. Written by a poet, Dmitry Bykov, it would attack Vladimir Putin and his ministers using famous Russian and Soviet classic poems. Bykov would replace rhymes that all Russians knew to make deadly funny parodies, and the star, the actor Mikhail Yefremov, beautifully narrated them in character. One of the shows made fun of the duo of Putin and Dmitry Medvedev, portraying Medvedev as a nominal president who misbehaved, angering Putin. Alexey's guests listened intently, nodding their heads. They had watched the show and apparently loved it.

It was the first time in many years we'd seen "normal," successful folks talking about politics. If Putin had been able to listen in and hear what they were saying about him, he wouldn't have liked it. It was as if fresh air were suddenly blowing into a stuffy, sealed room.

In the spring of 2011, all of a sudden all of Moscow started talking about politics. Conversations about Medvedev, *Citizen Poet*, and the mass protests in the Middle East were heard at Bulingua, at Jean-Jacques, and in a fancy new spacious place called Masterskaya, a club and theater housed on the second floor of the former public baths next door to Lubyanka, the FSB headquarters. Masterskaya was owned by the Papernys, a prominent literary and artistic family of Moscow. Administrative staffers and corporate employees on their lunch breaks were talking about the show or the latest political op-ed even in the coffee shops.

Our book about the FSB, *The New Nobility*, had been published in the United States in September 2010, and, to our surprise, the Russian version of *Forbes*—which was mostly known for publishing the list of wealthiest Russian oligarchs—printed an extract. A publisher specializing in business books acquired a license to publish *The New Nobility* in Russia, and several months later, the Russian translation hit the bookstores. It became an instant bestseller. Even *Afisha* magazine—a Russian version of London's *Time Out*—reviewed the book.

The country was buzzing with anticipation ahead of the 2012 presidential election in Russia. Although first there would be parliamentary elections, the question that obsessed everyone was who would run for president—Medvedev or Putin. Neither of them was eager to say who would run. That raised hopes among the liberal-minded middle classes that Putin would finally agree to step back.

People were tired of Putin everywhere in Moscow. The main reason was that many Muscovites now worked for big corporations that had established very clear rules about how business was to be conducted. They offered their employees spacious offices, good salaries, guaranteed bonuses, and medical insurance. People got used to living by the rules at their workplaces, and they expected the same clear rules to pertain elsewhere. But there were no rules beyond the glass windows of their corporate offices.

You could secure a decent mortgage to buy an apartment in a new building just about to be finished, but the developing company would disappear into thin air. You could drive your fancy car and get hit by another car on the street, and the police would step back because the driver that hit you turned out to be an officer of a security agency. You could plan an expensive tourist trip to Dubai but discover that the tourist company had been shuttered and nobody knew how to get your money back.

The discrepancy between the civilized, predictable rules in the corporate offices and the complete chaos outside was not going away. It inspired the middle classes to make the extraordinary claim that the rules should be extended to apply to the entire country. "The president is just a hired manager, isn't he? We, the citizens, are, so to speak, the board of directors, and he answers to us, as any CEO is answerable to his board!" a hipster in his late twenties, with a fancy beard and big-framed glasses, explained to his friends at the next table in the Masterskaya club. It was clear that Putin, and his KGB friends, wouldn't deliver a society that ran by such rules, but Medvedev constantly and happily talked as if he might.

Young professionals and IT entrepreneurs began frequenting public lectures in theaters and clubs. The performances of *Citizen Poet* in theaters, once the show was adapted for the stage, became increasingly popular. Soon it became clear that people would not be satisfied listening to and talking about politics in places that the liberal-minded intelligentsia opened for them—they wanted to expand the political conversation to the streets of Moscow.

Our friends from our *Izvestia* days didn't like the new mood in Moscow.

Petya Akopov attacked the politically active middle classes on his LiveJournal page. He called them "a driving force" of the upcoming revolution, comparing them with the Soviet intelligentsia of the 1980s who had foolishly supported perestroika. Petya himself had supported Mikhail Gorbachev's reforms in the 1980s as a student, but in the 2000s he came to believe that perestroika was an evil that had destroyed the Soviet Union.

Petya thought the main target of the new revolutionaries was Putin. He identified a young, popular anticorruption blogger, Alexei Navalny, as the leader of these new revolutionaries, and suggested several strategies to counter him. According to Petya, the best strategy for responding to Navalny's criticism of widespread corruption was to clean house of Putin's corrupt elites.[1] As for Navalny himself, Petya suggested expelling him to New York.

Olga Lyubimova felt an urge to respond to this new political awakening as well. On her LiveJournal page she posted what she called the "Lyubimova Manifesto":

> That's what scares me—I can't understand what civil society is. Who are these people? What should civil society look like?
>
> I can feel it in my gut how the situation is heating up before the elections. My friends started going to protest rallies. When I was a child, it was drunkards and slackers who went to rallies; they were given vodka there. Then unhappy, desperate people went to the rallies.

I also had friends. Unhappy and desperate. But they didn't go to rallies, understanding that it was all pointless and they could only freeze their guts.

And now they've started going [to rallies]. And not only the enthusiastic and sensitive fools (and I do have such friends), and not reflective whiners (those who hang out at Jean-Jacques), but thoroughly hardened cynics....

So, I wanted to ask seriously and without mockery: What are you trying to achieve? Do you believe that you will be heard? That they don't laugh at you on Old Square [the offices of the Presidential Executive Office]?

As for me, I've just been using the advice of a psychologist for a long time. I live in the city of Moscow, in the country called Russia, according to the principle bequeathed to the victims of a rapist: I lie on my back, spread my legs, breathe deeply, and even try to enjoy it.

I know I'm wrong.

And you are trying to fight? And for what?[2]

It was the raving of a private person who understood that she lived in a brutal country and was trying to adapt to circumstances she had no power to change. She was a young, privileged mother of two children living in Moscow, and yet she didn't feel safe. That Lyubimova had resorted to a rape metaphor to explain what she saw as the best survival strategy was both jarring and telling.

One of the people who was apparently "hanging out at Jean-Jacques" was her husband, Zhenya Baranov. We saw more and more of him there, often accompanied by Anna Pavlova, and finally it dawned on us that the old love between them, something that always felt like unfinished business from their youth, had probably been rekindled. In May 2011 that became more or less public when Baranov made another documentary, this one about the United States and Osama bin Laden, who had been shot and killed in the US raid at his Abbottabad compound in Pakistan on May 2. At Jean-Jacques, Anna, who was there without Baranov when we saw her there shortly after the documentary's release, asked us what we thought about the documentary. The truth was that we felt Baranov's deep, persuasive voice as narrator couldn't disguise the fact that it was a crazy conspiracy-theory-driven film: Baranov had implied that bin Laden was "a link in the chain of monstrous staging operations of the American intelligence services," and either he had been killed two years previously, or he was never killed, and it was all a hoax by the Obama administration.[3] Andrei said as much to Anna, who later told us that Baranov had not been offended. It was clear that they were especially close.

In April, Petya Akopov's second daughter had been born. He was excited, but the joy of a newborn girl in his family was darkened by his career and financial problems. The previous summer, the *Political Journal*, the magazine where Petya had worked for many years, the last three as editor-in-chief, was shut down by the owner—a nationalist member of the Duma, who had found himself short of cash ever since the financial crisis of 2009.

In the months that followed, Petya could secure only a part-time job for an obscure pro-Kremlin website meant to resemble a grassroots project. Discussing the website's origins, he later told Irina that when he'd heard that *Political Journal* was closing, he had gone to a former TV journalist he knew, Ivan Demidov, who had once been a colleague of Baranov and Lyubimova, looking for a job. Demidov was then working in the internal policy department of the Kremlin, part of the Administration of the President, as deputy head of public organizations. As such, he dealt with the Russian Orthodox Church and youth organizations. "I came to him and said, 'I would like to work for ideology, for the state,'" Petya said. "At first, he was like—'ha ha.' And then—'Okay, help us first launch a website.'" So, Petya added, they "started making that website as a platform for discussions": "I invited the people from my magazine, we started doing everything, and in two months we launched a large website."

In this way Petya crossed over and began working directly for the state. But it didn't last long. "We launched it at a terrible pace, and I was kicked out immediately after the launch, a couple of weeks later," he admitted.

Petya's wife, Marina, with her bohemian lifestyle, was not known for her willingness to endure hardship. She was also not the most patient person on earth. When she got angry, everybody noticed. She had always thought it was Petya's duty to support her financially, especially since she was by now the mother of two small girls.

It was at that unfortunate moment that the Akopovs' neighbor Natalia Alexandrovna, the tiny intelligent elderly Crimean Greek woman who had rented two of the rooms in the apartment on Gogolevsky, died. That soon made the Akopovs' life in the apartment unbearable, as numerous relatives began to dispute the precious inheritance, worth the equivalent of $100,000 in US dollars. The Akopovs didn't have the money to buy out Natalia's two rooms so that the whole apartment could become theirs. Marina had long convinced herself that at some point in the future they would have the spacious apartment entirely to themselves, and they had arranged their life there in such a way that it almost felt it *was* theirs. They'd invested a lot in refurbishing the space, including the shared kitchen and facilities. Natalia had completely accepted their way of living, and Marina and Petya had hoped the pleasant arrangement would last for a very long time, until they had enough money to buy the rest of the apartment.

Suddenly, that dream was crushed.

Natalia's rooms were rented out to complete strangers, and Petya, Marina, and their daughters felt they had no choice but to move on.

Gogolevsky, the center of gravity for all the Akopovs' friends for more than ten years, was gone.

The Akopovs ended up living at Lyubimova's spare apartment on Kutuzovsky Prospekt, in southwest Moscow. They didn't find themselves on the streets, but the exodus from Gogolevsky didn't lift Petya's spirits.

Weeks passed, then months, without a decent job emerging on Petya's horizon. The winter before his second child was born, that uncertainty resulted in a heart attack, which deeply worried his friends, especially Baranov and Lyubimova. Petya survived the heart attack, but, without a place to publish his articles, he felt increasingly isolated. He began posting columns more often on Facebook as well as on his LiveJournal page.

Eventually, Petya issued a desperate call for help on Facebook—"I want to work like hell," he wrote. "I urgently need some kind of work, even a one-time thing." But it was to no avail.

He was getting more and more aggressive in his opinions, and the list of his perceived enemies was growing. In June 2011, he attacked gays on his blog. He got upset that RIA Novosti had fired a commentator who had written a column decrying a gay parade in Berlin. The commentator had said he didn't want such "freedom and democracy" in Russia and would rather the country had "a powerful bomb which could kill only gays."[4] To Petya, the commentator's firing was vile, a sign that the government agency had succumbed to the pressure of a gay lobby.[5]

Shortly thereafter, Petya openly insulted Medvedev, comparing him in terms of stupidity to Gorbachev.[6] He had long forgotten, apparently, that in his youth he had wholeheartedly supported Gorbachev's policies.

That same June, *Izvestia* lost its tenancy in the historic building on Pushkin Square. The paper had changed hands and had recently been taken over by the Rossiya Bank, controlled by Yuri Kovalchuk. Kovalchuk was one of Putin's oligarchs from St. Petersburg.

LOSING ONE'S SOUL

When Putin came to power, Kovalchuk's family was encouraged to buy up media assets that were politically important for the Kremlin. His National Media Group came to own several TV channels and had just acquired 25 percent of Channel One, where Lyubimova and Baranov worked. *Izvestia* was part of the media empire, and Kovalchuk's managers had very radical ideas for the newspaper. The most infamous editor of sensationalized media in the country was put in charge of running *Izvestia*, and his first decision was to move the editorial office out of the historic building the paper had occupied since 1926. It would now be farther from the city center in a much cheaper location. Only 38 of *Izvestia*'s 200 employees were taken to the new offices; the other 162 had all been laid off.[7]

That concluded the exodus of the media from Pushkin Square, where several top journals and newspapers had had their editorial offices since Soviet times.

Izvestia had survived the collapse of the Soviet Union and the wild capitalism of the 1990s. But apparently, Putin's friends' ideas of how to run mass media were a decisive blow. The newspaper changed beyond recognition.

On Saturday, September 24, Medvedev walked to the stage at Luzhniki, Moscow's vast sports arena, where he announced that he was endorsing Putin for a return to the Kremlin. The Russian establishment and top bureaucracy had gathered for the occasion. Putin, in turn, who was also present, promised to keep Medvedev as his prime minister after the election.

It was a terrible blow for liberal-minded people throughout the country. Angry posts flooded Facebook. "Well, the first twelve years went by fast," an editor of *Afisha* posted. "Some spent all their lives under Ivan the Terrible, or under Stalin, twenty-nine years . . . those who survived."

Petya was also angry, but for a different reason. In his eyes, Medvedev was still a dangerous liberal, even if he had given up his presidential ambitions. He feared that Putin would let Medvedev form a government entirely made up of liberals.

That day he posted an angry diatribe titled "How to Prevent Medvedev's Liberal Government," in which he advised his readers about what to do: "Well, in March—vote for Putin. In the hope that he will finally make the only possible choice and become an imperial nationalist. If he does not take this step to save the country (and himself, as a ruler who desires the greatness of his country), he will lose both power and country."

Petya continued to attack Medvedev over the next two days, calling him "a piece of SHIT."[8]

It was the first time we saw our friend identifying himself openly as an imperial nationalist. To us, it sounded disgusting, but we thought Petya was just playing his usual childish game of shocking his friends. Besides, we were too busy reporting from all the protest rallies in Moscow.

Angry Muscovites were not ready to give up without a fight. Thousands and thousands hit Moscow's streets in December; the rallies got bigger week by week. The authorities had no choice but to allow them: the rallies were organized as music festivals—with the stage, screens, and sound all paid for through crowdfunding. IT engineers, journalists, self-employed professionals, intelligentsia, teachers, and doctors were in the crowds, while TV personalities and well-known writers joined the opposition politicians on the stage.

Anna Pavlova, as always, was in the middle of the protests. Her Ej.ru became one of the organizational centers of the rallies. The protests attracted huge crowds, even in Moscow's freezing December temperatures. The Kremlin became furious and paranoid. For Putin, the Moscow protests were part of a bigger Western conspiracy that had started with the Arab Spring, facilitated by social media—Facebook and Twitter, American-made—and orchestrated by the US State Department. Putin was obsessed with the horrible death of Muammar al-Qaddafi, and so was Petya Akopov. In the eyes of Putin's defenders, the IT engineers, self-employed professionals, and intelligentsia who went to the streets with white ribbons—a symbol of the protests—were paving the way for bloody revolutionaries. But the revolutionaries were completely imaginary. They didn't exist.

The Kremlin propaganda attacked the protesters, but Baranov, contrary to our expectations, didn't take part in the vicious campaign against the liberals. Anna inevitably would have taken that personally, and he probably didn't want to risk his relationship with her by attacking her friends on TV.

The protests prompted Petya to get even more aggressive, however. On his Facebook page he attacked "non-Russian intellectuals, sitting in the warmth, who discuss the 'naivete and darkness' of the [Russian] people. As if they had anything to do with them [Russian people]."[9] Many thought he was hinting at Jews, an all-too-familiar echo of the antisemitic campaign of the Soviet era, when the dissident movement had been accused of being unpatriotic because there were Jews in their ranks. An angry friend pointed out to him that he was also a "non-Russian intellectual"—all his friends knew Petya had Italian and Armenian roots.

On December 24, 2011, the biggest protest rally yet took place on Sakharov Prospekt, named after the most famous Soviet dissident, Andrei Sakharov, a nuclear physicist and human rights activist. Despite the cold, more than 100,000 people came and stayed for hours, listening to Alexei Navalny, a rising star of the angry middle classes, and Boris Nemtsov, a former deputy prime minister turned opposition politician.

As usual, the bulk of the crowd was made up of the intelligentsia and urban middle class. But we also noticed a new kind of protester—middle-aged men in dark jackets, working-class people. There were also several oligarchs in the crowd, including Alexander Lebedev, owner of *Novaya Gazeta*, and Mikhail Prokhorov, a nickel tycoon and owner of the Brooklyn Nets. There were some new faces on the stage, too. One of the new people was Alexey Kudrin, a former finance minister and deputy prime minister who had resigned in September. Kudrin, from St. Petersburg, had once been very close to Putin.

Some optimists around us in the crowd suggested it could signify a crack in the system.

Navalny, in a black trench coat and gray scarf, provided the best headline when he called Putin a "small, cowardly jackal." From the stage, Navalny shouted, "I can see that there are enough people here to seize the Kremlin. We are a peaceful force and will not do it now." That sounded like a promise. And then he added, "We will take what belongs to us with our own hands. We are the power!"

Later that day, Petya posted a warning on Facebook that Navalny was becoming "very dangerous," reflecting on the options for dealing with him:

> To imprison him is impossible; leaving him in the wild for a long time is also dangerous (primarily because he will provoke "blood on the streets"—this is part of his program).
>
> The third option remains—remove him. And at the same time, blame it on the same Americans. . . . I think that, given all the costs, this is the best option. Not only for Putin, but also for the country. Better the blood of one than the blood of millions.[10]

Some of Petya's friends felt deeply shocked by this open call to kill Navalny. One commented on Facebook, "It is publicly calling for murder. But you have children, Petya. They need a dad not in prison, but at home. And not an embittered but a loving one. Maybe it's better to let it go?"

Another Facebook friend was more straightforward: "Petya, are you completely fucked up, or what?"

Lyubimova was also taken aback, saying, again on Facebook, "Akopov, why are you doing this? . . . [I]t is very difficult to understand what you want to say (I understand). But the brutality greatly distracts from the meaning."

Petya doubled down in response in another Facebook post:

> In the post itself, in my opinion, everything is clear—it is about what will happen to Navalny. And who exactly will kill him is not particularly important to me. Maybe the Jews themselves—what a howl they have after today's rally. But what I wanted to say about the situation in general—I have already written several times in recent weeks. And the tough stuff—well, before that I watched Navalny and what they [opposition politicians] said on Sakharov [Prospekt]. . . . If they talk tough—I talk tough.[11]

Lyubimova tried to calm the waters, writing, "I'm a little scared by the degree of reaction toward each other. . . . You've known Petya for many years. . . . He always thought that way." Evgeny Krutikov firmly stood by his friend: "First. My friend—and I know Petya better than anyone else here—has the right to his opinion."

It had taken less than a year since the spring of 2011—when the middle classes awoke to the challenge of Putin's return to the Kremlin—for our friend Petya, a soft, timid Moscow intellectual, a collector of books and political stamps, to become a man who called cold-heartedly for the killing of a political opponent.

CHAPTER 20

THE END OF OLD TIMES

January 2012 was as cold as December had been. As the New Year and Christmas holiday festivities wound down, a gloomy hungover feeling spread through Moscow. The rally on December 24, it turned out, would be the peak of the anti-Putin protests.

The opposition was trying to reinvigorate Muscovites by organizing new rallies, but the presidential election was looming, scheduled for March, and it became clear that the protesters had failed to build momentum. The rallies were not igniting a truly massive revolution, like the Arab Spring in the Middle East the year before. The protesters had also failed to produce a candidate capable of uniting the opposition or with any chance of winning the election. The mood changed. Thousands still returned to the freezing streets, but their excitement had ebbed. Putin remained the most popular politician in the country. He was going to return to the Kremlin, and there was nothing to be done about it.

Navalny set up his presidential election headquarters on the second floor of a former public bath, now the Masterskaya club, but since he was not allowed to take part in the elections, Masterskaya became a place where journalists and others in the opposition gathered the night of the election to watch Putin win.

Things changed for us, too, that January, on a more personal level.

By then it had been three years since we'd seen Petya Akopov in the dacha he rented for his family thirty miles from Moscow, a wooden house surrounded by white snowdrifts.

There, a Christmas tree had reached toward the ceiling of the airy living room. We had shared appetizers and a bottle of champagne; we drank, talked, and smoked cigarettes until the wee hours, just as we had done many times before. But even then we weren't having the fun we used to have. Something was missing, and we all knew it. We did not understand each other anymore.

Petya's cooperation with our website, Agentura, had come to an end many years before. After that we'd stopped seeing Petya and his family. We kept up with what was going on with him through Zhenya Baranov and Anna Pavlova.

Once when we saw Baranov in Jean-Jacques and shared a drink together, he told us that Petya and Marina were still living in his and Lyubimova's apartment. Baranov rented a villa in Montenegro on the seashore and was very proud of it—he had developed a habit of spending his holidays on the Adriatic coast, but surrounded by his Serbian friends.

Baranov told us he always invited the Akopovs to come to the villa with him, but Marina was no longer very enthusiastic. "You know, she prefers Normandy. She would very much like to go there instead of our place in Montenegro," Baranov shrugged, indicating his disapproval of Marina's high-society ambitions that Petya didn't have money to support.

We knew Petya had lost his job at *Political Journal*, but despite his vocal hatred of the protesters, we still took him for a harmless oddball. He had what we thought were some crazy political views, but they were too far from real life to be very threatening. We thought of Petya as someone who lived in a world that was as imaginary as the one depicted in the heroic-looking faces of his North Korean postage stamps.

Then in January, a long-forgotten story suddenly reemerged in Russian media and on social networks. It had to do with a 2006 Russian documentary, called *Shpioni* (The Spies), about British diplomats spying in Moscow.

That documentary had never resembled standard Kremlin propaganda. It relied on unique materials: a video taken by an FSB surveillance team of a British diplomat, identified as Marc Doe, walking past a gray rock along a Moscow street. The FSB claimed that the rock was fake, and that a sophisticated transmitter was hidden inside its hollow shell. Doe and other British diplomats, according to the account, using a palm computer, had downloaded classified data from it that had been supplied by an unnamed Russian official who had betrayed his country. The four large batteries and the radio device inside the "rock," tightly packed together, apparently provided proof of these espionage activities. The second part of the documentary then described Doe's ties with well-known Russian nongovernmental organizations (NGOs). The main point was clear: British spies were manipulating Russia's NGOs.

Shpioni was first aired at a time when Putin was starting a frontal attack on Russian NGOs, including imposing restrictions on their funding from abroad.[1] The film was supposed to prove that if NGOs were getting support from the West, they were effectively Western spies, simple as that.

There were several odd features of the documentary, though. For example, although the FSB claimed that it had caught the Russian who was communicating with Doe via the rock, this person was never named, let alone prosecuted. We had written about the discrepancies at the time.

Six years had passed since the documentary had first aired. The Medvedev era had come and gone, signifying nothing. Moscow had witnessed its biggest protests of the twenty-first century, and it looked as if the spy rock story was buried in the past. That is, until Jonathan Powell, former British prime minister Tony Blair's chief of staff, admitted in a BBC documentary that the spy rock was real. That confession got Kremlin propagandists excited. They picked up the spy rock story again and used it to attack the journalists who had questioned it six years before. Petya couldn't miss such a story, either.

Irina saw Petya's reaction first. "Andrei, come look at this. Petya has just put our names on the enemies' list!" Irina discovered that he'd written a post on LiveJournal with the title "How the Spy Stone Became a Tombstone for the 'Best People.'"[2] Below the title, he had posted a list of quotes about the spy rock documentary by prominent Russian journalists, compiled by a pro-Kremlin blogger. There were sixteen journalists and activists on the list in total, including us. Our quote was from our book, *The New Nobility*: "While [the documentary] was seen by many as transparent propaganda," we had written, "it nonetheless intimidated nongovernmental organizations, which feared they could be accused of harboring spies."[3]

"I have only one question," Petya continued. "What is the ratio among these 'heroes'? Half are just arrogant idiots (and therefore unconscious agents of influence) who believed in what they said, and the second half—just outright agents? Or do they have some other ratio? In any case, this rock will be the best tombstone for all this scum."

We looked at each other in disbelief, then back at the laptop.

It wasn't news that Petya supported the regime. But we never thought he'd attack us personally and in public by name. We'd always had different political views, and we'd argued incessantly about many things, but none of us had ever made it personal. It still seemed like a bad joke—that Petya would blacklist us and erect a tombstone to bury us.

But it was no joke. It was a new reality, one we still weren't ready to accept.

Petya did not stop at denouncing us as scum. In a second post that day he called the Moscow protests "an attempt at an anti-Putin coup d'état." The main cause of the crisis, according to Petya, was "an uprising of the small nation—Jewry and a part of the intelligentsia imbued with its cosmopolitan spirit.... Therefore, the conflict is banal—Jews against Putin," he went on, claiming that "they"—by which he meant Jews—"want to destroy [Putin]."[4] To solve the problem, Petya suggested starting a "second campaign to fight cosmopolitanism"—invoking the label Stalin had given to his own antisemitic campaign—in May, after Putin's inauguration.

The echoes were unmistakable: it was classical primitive antisemitism, worthy of a Stalinist purge or a tsarist pogrom. We knew such bile existed on obscure nationalist websites, or in the mouths of an occasional angry taxi driver, but it was rare among educated people like Petya. We had never heard him say anything like it. We certainly had never expected such a thing from a friend of Baranov's, who didn't hide the fact that he was a Jew.

How had Petya become so hateful? There was no real threat of the revolution he feared so much; the protests were petering out. Perhaps a year without a proper job and the loss of his beloved apartment on Gogolevsky Boulevard had played a part in his anger, but that couldn't be all of it. We believed that Petya, known for having a good gut feeling, sensed that the Kremlin was getting more vengeful. And that this was how he chose to express his readiness to play along.

On May 7, the authorities were laboriously readying Moscow's streets for a historical event. Putin had won the election and was planning to be driven from his suburban residence on Rublyovka to the Kremlin for a grand inauguration ceremony. Novy Arbat was cleansed of cars, and its wide, clean sidewalks were emptied of passersby to prevent any protesters from spoiling Putin's big day.

On its way to the Kremlin, Putin's motorcade was to ascend from the Moskva River on Novy Arbat and cross the Boulevard Ring. There, on the right side, stood the pride of the Russian military—the white rectangle of the neoclassical General Staff Building built at the peak of the Cold War—while on the left there was Nikitsky Boulevard, where Jean-Jacques's outdoor tables were filled with people. The usual Jean-Jacques crowd—journalists, artists, intelligentsia, most of them people who had participated in the winter protests—gathered there, planning to walk to Novy Arbat to protest along the route of the motorcade. One of the leaders of the protests, Boris Nemtsov, a tall, handsome man with an easy smile, was there surrounded by dozens of people listening to him talk to journalists and joke about the inauguration.

"The inaugurator fears his own people, guards himself with the anti-riot police, look, even with dogs," he pointed at the police and laughed. "Well, they are just cowards."

He spoke in his usual relaxed manner, which seemed to fit perfectly the mood of the people around him. A pro-Kremlin activist approached him and handed him a white, blue, and red ribbon, Russian colors, while her friends were filming, trying to provoke him to throw it away so he would look unpatriotic on camera. Nemtsov calmly took the ribbon and said to the young woman, "Look, this flag we erected on the Russian White House in 1991, when we fought the GKChP [a KGB-orchestrated coup-d'état attempt]. I was arrested for this flag, by your idol." He pointed out in the direction of Novy Arbat, where Putin's motorcade was to proceed, indicating that Putin, as a KGB officer, had not been on the side of democratic forces during perestroika.

In ordinary circumstances it would have been possible to see Putin's motorcade on Novy Arbat from Jean-Jacques, but police officers in helmets and anti-riot gear were lining up across the boulevard, effectively blocking the view.

Suddenly they moved toward Jean-Jacques. Nemtsov tried to calm the police down. "It's a restaurant, for God's sake," he said.

Several paddy wagons appeared. Orders were shouted, and police charged at the people standing around or sitting at the tables. The tiny Viennese chairs and round tables that famously made Jean-Jacques look like a French brasserie were crushed and turned over. Police began pulling people away from the tables and hauling them over to the buses. Batons rained down on those still seated. An editor of an opposition website, an imposing gray-headed man in his sixties, got his hand broken by a policeman while he was being dragged to a bus, and his friend, a famous avant-garde Russian poet, stood by helplessly, arguing with several policemen. The police turned and began pushing the rest toward the end of the boulevard, farther away from Novy Arbat.[5]

Then, suddenly, the police stopped, lined up in a column, and moved away. It was around midday, and it dawned on the remaining people that the motorcade must have already passed, and that Putin was safely in the Kremlin for his grand inauguration, celebrating his return.

CHAPTER 21

DREAMS OF RUSSIA

Thankfully, 2012 brought us a new home.

We finally bought our own apartment! Not that we'd earned enough money to buy it; there was no way two independent journalists could manage that. Alexey Soldatov had suddenly decided to help, offering us a sum large enough to buy a small one-bedroom in the neighborhood where Andrei had grown up—a fantastic gift, given Moscow's skyrocketing property values.

We found the apartment in a five-story edifice built in the late 1950s, with pointed rooftops over three elevator shafts that gave it the look of a typical Dutch house. Andrei had passed this building on his way to school every day as a boy, and we both loved it.

We painted the walls in one room—our living room—yellow, and we painted a second room red. The second room, where we placed a sofa bed, became a library as well as our bedroom.

We moved in and expected to live there happily ever after.

We installed bookshelves along the walls in the bedroom/library and filled them with our collection of old books, most of them nineteenth-century French and English volumes that had traveled with us through the many apartments we had rented in various Moscow neighborhoods.

Andrei had gotten obsessed with collecting spy books along with books once deemed subversive that were thus prohibited. The shelves were soon filled with an odd collection that included the Ashenden stories by W. Somerset Maugham, about a fictional World War I British spy; *Spycatcher* by Paul Greengrass and Peter Wright, a memoir of an actual British spy during the Cold War that was banned from being published in the United Kingdom; and an edition of Jean-Jacques Rousseau, printed with the royal decree declaring that it should be burned in France, included by the author as a preface—apparently to mock the eighteenth-century French authorities.

Andrei's favorites were the volumes of *Histoire Universelle* (*Universal History*), published from 1543 through 1607 by Jacques-Auguste de Thou—five huge books. De Thou was a sixteenth-century French politician and intellectual who had negotiated the Edict of Nantes that brought an end to the bloody religious wars between Catholics and Protestants. He had wanted to write an impartial history of those wars, but it became almost impossible under the Catholic Counter-Reformation. Still, he fulfilled his dream, taking just one precaution—he wrote his history in Latin. That didn't prevent the Vatican from adding the history to its Index of Forbidden Books. The 1740s edition we had was in French, the translation done in London, as the editors proudly stated in a foreword. We wondered if the edition was one of the subversive books intended to be smuggled to France from Britain. Evidence against this theory was the size of the volumes—they were massive, too big to be hidden.

Also among our books was one of the first editions of Alexandre Dumas's *The Three Musketeers* with engravings within, and Irina entertained our friends by comparing the figures of Athos, Porthos, and Aramis in the book with their images in modern movies.

Branches of a high poplar shaded the bedroom/library from the morning sun, and we could enjoy the sound of birds singing on summer days. But this idyll did not last long. Two weeks after we moved in, we smelled something burning. Clouds of dark smoke were belching out from a door on the floor below. We rang the bell, to no avail, then banged on the door until a white-haired old lady appeared out of the smoke.

"What do you want, young people?"

"You are on fire!"

"I didn't notice anything wrong; I am just cooking mushrooms in the kitchen."

When we stormed into her kitchen, we saw a frying pan burning on a gas stove. Irina turned off the gas, grabbed a bottle of water from the table, and poured it over the frying pan. It was a mistake—a gigantic flame flared up over the stove. We hardly could see through the smoke, so we took the old lady and pushed her out of the flat despite her resistance.

Several neighbors gathered near the door, agitated and nervous. One gave us the old lady's son's number and we asked him to come as soon as possible.

While we were waiting for the son to arrive, her neighbor told us that the old lady used to be a well-known Soviet theater critic.

Once we were back in our apartment, we googled her name. In the 1960s and 1970s she had worked for *Literaturnaya Gazeta* (Literary Gazette), one of the major Soviet publications. None of the reviews she'd written were posted on the internet, but we discovered many personal recollections of her by newspaper employees and journalists. According to them, our white-haired lady had been a very influential critic, and her reviews had once had the power to kill any play in Moscow—not because of her talent, but because of her connections with the KGB. When the KGB deemed a new play in a Moscow theater incompatible with Soviet ideology, they would send our neighbor to write a devastating review. After that, the show did not have much chance of survival.

That was not the last surprise our new apartment building had for us.

The following week, we were sitting in the kitchen when we heard the sound of a small waterfall coming from the library. Water was pouring down from the ceiling.

Andrei ran to the floor above ours, but no one opened the door. From a previous owner we knew that our neighbor upstairs was a priest at the Church of St. Tatiana at Moscow State University and that his name was Ivan, or, in Greek, "Ioann," the name he used in the church. We'd seen him once with his wife and children. A stocky man with a neat beard, in his mid-thirties, he looked pretty friendly, but we had not had a chance to really get to know him.

Fearing his books could be destroyed made Andrei frantic; he called the church urgently and in a minute the priest was found. Andrei didn't quite know how to address the priest, so he went clumsily with "Ahh, Ioann, I'm your neighbor; we have a problem."

"No worries, I'll nip round in a sec," the priest said.

Indeed, he arrived very quickly. The books were saved, but a dirty brownish spot remained on the previously pristine white ceiling. The priest looked genuinely upset. "We were away for a long time," the priest said. He then told us he had lived with his family in Switzerland, where he had served in the Russian church in Zurich, and only recently moved back to Moscow. "I am sorry, and I'd like to compensate you for all the inconvenience I caused."

We assumed he meant material compensation for renovating the ceiling, but he had a different idea: "I can bless your apartment!"

We exchanged glances and agreed to politely decline the offer. The priest shrugged his shoulders, looked a little uncomfortable, and glanced at the books. He passed by the leather spines of French novels and English history until his eyes alighted on the nonfiction titles about spies and intelligence services.

"This is an interesting collection!" he exclaimed. We explained that we were journalists and that this was our topic.

"Oh! Is this your book?" He pulled a copy of *The New Nobility* from the shelf. We nodded. "Can I have it? I am very interested in this topic."

We were momentarily stunned. It was a well-established fact that in Soviet times the KGB had penetrated the Russian Orthodox Church, and we knew that under Vladimir Putin the relationship between the Church and the security services had become even more cordial. And in front of us was a priest who had served in Zurich, a city famous for the activities of Russian spies since the 1930s. We had no choice but to give him the book.

A KGB-connected literary critic; a priest interested in spies—perhaps it came with the territory. It was not such a high price to pay for getting our own apartment in the center of Moscow.

We loved our neighborhood—for its history, for the carefree atmosphere created by the thousands of students at nearby Bauman Moscow State Technical University, and for the location just two stops by metro from the Kremlin.

The district was the first place in Moscow where foreigners from Europe had been allowed to settle, five centuries before, so its name—Nemetskaya Sloboda, or the German Quarter—reflected the largest group of incomers at the time. The Lefortovo Palace, the first European palace in Moscow, built for a Swiss associate of Peter the Great, François Le Fort (thus, Lefortovo), was around the corner. Wide and squat, the building did not look like a grandiose palace, but we liked it. By the time we moved to the neighborhood, the Lefortovo Palace housed the National Archives—where Petya Akopov and Anna Pavlova had once worked as young historians. For his Swiss friend, Peter the Great also built the first European park in Moscow on the opposite side of the river Yauza, and the neighborhood around the park became known as the Lefortovo district.

But five centuries later, Muscovites associated the district not with the park, but with the Lefortovo prison, where Stalin's executioners had tortured and killed people in the 1930s. The security service still had control over the prison—where we both had been repeatedly interrogated by the FSB—and the prison maintained its reputation. It was within walking distance of our apartment, as was a newcomer of the same sort—the massive, ugly high-rise of the Investigative Committee, a recently formed repressive body that "investigated" most of the politically motivated cases in the country, including those against protesters in Moscow.

The Investigative Committee had an insatiable appetite for more and more buildings in the district. We started noticing increasing numbers of short-haired young men in coffee shops, speaking in loud voices about the criminal cases and suspects they were working, while the committee's black Fords with red stripes on the side were speeding through the streets with sirens wailing—not because they were in a rush, but for fun, and because they could.

When we were feeling sour, we would mutter about how Putin's secret police appeared to be taking over the neighborhood, street by street, and the bitter irony that the district of Moscow where Westerners had first arrived to break through Russia's isolationism and open the country to new ideas and knowledge was now overrun by repressive security operatives.

That summer, we developed a pleasurable habit of dropping by to see Andrei's father, who worked at Moscow State University near the Kremlin, just two metro stops from our place. He had, as we saw it, the best office in Moscow—two big rooms on the second floor of the old MSU building with big windows and high ceilings, built at the end of the eighteenth century with a direct view on the Kremlin walls across Manezhnaya Square. Once we dropped by his office with our friend Marina Latysheva, on our way to the Kremlin, where in one of the palaces an exhibition of Latysheva's relative, a famous sculptor of gems, had just opened. We were having tea at

Soldatov Sr.'s office with the view on the Kremlin, and it all seemed very stylish.

Andrei's relationship with his father was never completely smooth, however. On another occasion, when Andrei dropped by to see his father alone, Soldatov Sr. asked him bluntly if he ever planned to have children. Andrei felt confused and frustrated that his father understood so little about the task of being a journalist in Russia and the risks it implied. Did he realize that for many years we felt we had been hanging onto our profession by our fingertips, always under threat of being pushed out of it? The conversation finished awkwardly and was never resolved. Andrei left it feeling a sense of disapproval from his father.

But, in general, things looked much better for us. We had a place to live, and we'd found a big new theme for our reporting: digital repression.

After the protests, the political landscape in Russia saw a dramatic change. Activists, journalists, and political opposition figures were increasingly relying on social media, and the Kremlin was fighting back. The government introduced blacklists of banned websites and updated the country's wiretapping system.

On the horizon were the Olympic Games in Sochi in February 2014. Activists of all kinds loved to use the Games as a stage because they guaranteed world attention. Putin invested his personal prestige in the Sochi Games, and we expected the Russian state to spare no effort to prevent protests. Nobody would be given a chance to embarrass Putin.

An international team of digital researchers and human rights lawyers from Toronto and London began to investigate the Russian surveillance the Kremlin was setting up in the Sochi area, and we joined the effort. It was a big project, and it felt good to work side by side with folks from other countries. Fighting digital mass surveillance had become a hot topic around the world, and we were on the front line. What else could we wish for?

The issue became very sensitive politically on April 15, 2013, almost a year before the Sochi Games, when two bombs detonated during the annual Boston Marathon. Three people were killed and more than 250 injured. When the culprits were identified as two brothers, Tamerlan and Dzhokhar Tsarnaev—Chechens from Dagestan, a republic in the North Caucasus—the forthcoming Sochi Games became a pressing security issue for the United States. Previously, it had been assumed that militants in the North Caucasus would not attack Westerners. The attack in Boston changed that. It suddenly dawned on US officials that in just a few months, thousands of Americans would fly to Sochi, which is 300 miles and a mountain range from the North Caucasus.

American officials of all sorts began to turn up in Moscow in droves. They needed to know what the security situation was, and wanted to hear from Russian journalists and experts as well as Russian bureaucrats. We were often invited to such meetings. It appeared to us that Western powers wanted to work with the FSB to improve the security of the Games and were ready to disregard the reputation of the FSB.

On June 23, 2013, Edward Snowden, the world's most famous chronicler of US mass surveillance programs, landed at Moscow's Sheremetyevo airport. All the major world news organizations sent their teams to cover his forty-day stay in the transit zone of the airport. Every debate about mass surveillance, Snowden, or WikiLeaks now inevitably included Russia.

Russians thoroughly enjoyed the attention! We felt it as well, when in October our investigation on Sochi's surveillance program was published on the front page of the *Guardian*.[1] The story was widely discussed, and TV crews and journalists from around the world called us asking for comments. Later, we would include that story in our second book, *The Red Web*, about the Kremlin's wars on the internet.

Russian society had developed a huge inferiority complex about being always on the outskirts of Europe. The story of Russian isolation was often one of the country feeling rejected or ignored by Western Europe. War was a crude form of reconnection, and it often left the West with their prejudices about the brutality of Russians reinforced.

But this time, it appeared as if Russia might be overcoming its isolation bloodlessly, through internet technologies and a global sporting event.

Still, in Putin's Russia, the country's autocrats always saw globalization as a threat to the regime. So Putin was as likely to approach the upcoming Olympics as a threat as he was to see it as an opportunity.

On February 7, 2014, the Olympic Games commenced in Sochi with a grand opening ceremony. The performance, titled "Dreams of Russia," was produced by the long-term head of Channel One, the suave and intelligent Konstantin Ernst—in essence, the chief propagandist of the political regime.

A spectacular show, it featured the key points of the Russian historical narrative according to Putin: a small girl dreamed of Russia, and each of her dreams became a play performed by actors and dancers. She listed the Russian alphabet, with each letter linked to a famous Russian writer or artist or Russian achievement—from Chagall and Dostoyevsky to Kandinsky, Malevich, and Tolstoy; or Lunokhod (the Soviet lunar rover) for L, or the Russian ballet for R. Remarkably, the letter I was associated with Empire (*Imperia* in Russian). Then the girl's dreams moved to Russian history, where every period offered the Russians something to be proud of—Peter the Great, who built St. Petersburg and the Russian army; Soviet industrialization; a Soviet sports parade on Red Square; a glossy version of the 1960s, with the inevitable Yuri Gagarin, the Soviet cosmonaut. The sketches told the story from medieval Rus to the Soviet period.

But there was no image of Russian achievement or accomplishment from after 1991, not a single sketch to depict anything that had happened after the collapse of the Soviet Union. Putin had memorably called the disintegration of the Soviet Union the biggest geopolitical catastrophe of the twentieth century, so perhaps he didn't think there was anything that Russians could be proud of in their modern, post-Communist history. The performance's title was "Dreams of Russia," but there were no dreams of Russia—only dreams of the Russian empire and the Soviet Union. The *New York Times* called the performance "Fanfare for a Reinvented Russia,"[2] but to us it looked like the creators had reinvented some other country, not the Russia that really existed.

The high point of the ceremony was the arrival of the Olympic flag, entrusted to eight flag bearers all carefully chosen. One of the eight was Nikita Mikhalkov, bristling his inevitable walrus mustache, the Soviet and Russian director with strong imperialist and Orthodox views who was Olga Lyubimova's patron.

The organization of the Games was praised on world television networks, and initial hesitancy and suspicion gave way to enthusiasm. And Russia's athletes kept winning, keeping Russia in contention to be the first-place team of the entire Games.

In those days, the Sochi Games became the only topic of conversation, and ordinary Muscovites in coffee shops and clubs, people on the streets, and our relatives in far regions reveled in their success. Irina's liberal-minded aunt from a small town 400 miles southeast of Moscow called to say, "I don't like Putin, but for the Olympics, I'm ready to thank him."

We, however, felt strangely disconnected, if not isolated, from the entire experience. For some reason, we couldn't be enthusiastic; we couldn't join the party.

On the third day of the Sochi Olympics, Anna's Ej.ru published a column by the famous Russian liberal satirist Viktor Shenderovich, once the author of the *Kukly* (puppet) show on NTV that had so angered Putin fourteen years before. The column was titled "Putin and a Girl on Skates."[3]

Shenderovich wrote about his mixed feelings and why he also didn't share the national excitement. Never afraid to raise the stakes, he put the name of the country's most beloved athlete, the fifteen-year-old figure skater Yulia Lipnitskaya, alongside that of Hans-Otto Woellke, a handsome German shot putter who had won a gold medal at the 1936 Summer Olympics in Nazi Germany. "Something, however, prevents us today from rejoicing at his victory," Shenderovich wrote. "Maybe it is the fact that we are aware of the final price of this sporting deed—a price that included Dachau, Coventry, Khatyn, and Leningrad. It was not Hans's fault, of course, but it so happened that he made his contribution."

The Shenderovich column caused outrage among the public, augmented by a wave of insults directed from the Kremlin. The leader of Putin's party in parliament called Shenderovich's piece "essentially fascist" and demanded he apologize. Shenderovich refused.

Three weeks after the sporting festival celebrating global community, Russian troops occupied Crimea. It was Putin's response to the pro-European Maidan Revolution in Kyiv. Always paranoid about democratic movements in neighboring countries—fearful that they might provoke revolution in Moscow—Putin had first sent a group of FSB advisers to the Ukrainian capital to help suppress the popular revolt, and when that failed, sent troops to the Ukrainian peninsula on the Black Sea. In a way, it was his message to all his neighbors: "If you like the idea of democratic change and getting close to the West, the price will be a piece of your land."

The West responded with sanctions. On March 18, Putin summoned both houses of the Russian parliament to the Kremlin to witness him sign a treaty on the "accession of Crimea," the Kremlin's chosen term for the annexation. He gave an emotional speech in which he sounded like a tin-pot dictator, hurling accusations against the West, the fifth column, and "this disparate bunch of national traitors."

The same month, Anna's Ej.ru was blocked by the authorities. Russian internet censors also blocked Alexei Navalny's blog and several other liberal sites. Petya Akopov praised the decision, calling it, bizarrely, "psychotherapeutic," while insisting that it was not censorship.[4]

Petya then wrote a column expressing his happiness at the fact that Russia was turning away from Europe, toward the East. Russia's problems historically had been caused "by the separation of part of the elite from its national roots that began in the 18th century, its Westernization—and in the late Soviet years it was these people who came to power," he explained. "They were attracted not only by Western culture and economics, not only by their way of life—they thought that what was good for Europe, was good for Russia. They thought of themselves as the lost 'tribe of Israel'—as part of European civilization. The price of these misconceptions was a liberal experiment in recoding the Russian national code and way of life."[5]

That time had come to an end, Petya wrote. And for once, he had a point.

PART IV

CHAPTER 22

UKRAINE

Throughout history, Russian xenophobes considered many peoples to be their enemies, but Ukrainians never occupied first or even second place on their hate list.

Jews were very often at the top, a tradition promulgated by the tsars and successfully pursued and encouraged by Stalin and his Soviet successors. In the late Soviet period, second place on these hatred charts was a tie between the Georgians and the Armenians, who, according to the stereotype, showed a suspiciously entrepreneurial spirit.

In the 1990s, as Mikhail Gorbachev and Boris Yeltsin put an end to government-promoted antisemitism, the Jews were replaced as objects of fear and loathing by the Chechens and other peoples of the North Caucasus, because of the bloody wars in Chechnya. In the 2000s, a Central Asian workforce came to Russia, inflating anti-immigrant feelings toward Tajiks and Uzbeks. And the Chinese, who were suspected of plotting to take over and populate Russia's Far East, were always seen as a threat.

Xenophobia toward the Ukrainians usually manifested itself in offensive anecdotes, most of which made fun of the thrift and greed supposedly typical of Ukrainians. Those jokes were focused on "salo," cured slabs of pork fat that were a staple of Ukrainian cuisine. One such joke:

> *The Ukrainian night is quiet,*
> *but the salo must be rehidden.*

The first line is borrowed from Alexander Pushkin's poem "Poltava," which praises the beauty of Ukrainian nature; the second refers to the supposedly greedy nature of Ukrainian farmers.

To Irina, who in childhood regularly visited relatives in a village in the Odessa region, those jokes suggested envy of Ukraine's rich black soil, which provided a huge harvest. Russian peasants worked in much less fertile Russian lands. While the jokes were clearly insulting, they didn't reflect aggression or fear—the feelings Russian xenophobes had toward Central Asians and North Caucasians.

The Maidan Revolution in 2013–2014 changed that. Fear and aggression emerged, and Ukraine became a target. That aggression became directed not only at Ukrainians, but Ukraine as a country. All of a sudden, ordinary Muscovites were talking dismissively of Ukraine as a failed state that had no history and was full of Nazis.

This change was not exactly spontaneous. It was the consequence of an extensive campaign orchestrated by the Kremlin, and many Russian journalists were recruited to make it work. In fact, nearly all of our old *Izvestia* friends answered the Kremlin's call.

The Maidan Revolution had been good for Zhenya Baranov's career. He'd worked for television's Channel One, a Kremlin propaganda flagship that broadcast throughout Russia, and did his stories for its most popular Sunday night political show. To cover the crisis in Kyiv, he adopted a very aggressive style: rapid speech; dramatic and frightening footage; and facts, opinions, analysis, and predictions all thrown in indiscriminately. It became his signature style. It was all slightly manic.

The stories varied—the Maidan Revolution, the situation in Crimea on the eve of Russian annexation, European and US policy toward Russia. But almost every story was an occasion for Baranov to issue a terrifying reminder that if Russia didn't stand strong against the West—the United States, NATO, and the European Union—it could end up like Serbia, humiliated and "partly occupied" as a result of NATO bombings and a Western-sponsored coup d'état. Another obligatory element of Baranov's newscasts was to profess admiration for Vladimir Putin's strength and political will. Baranov's straightforward and brutal style would become typical of TV propaganda generally, but Baranov was obsessed with Serbia much more than his peers were.

At the beginning of March 2014, Baranov reported that the Russian parliament had authorized Putin to use the Russian armed forces in Ukraine. He warned the West that Russia was going to protect Russians in Crimea and that those who had bombed Belgrade (i.e., the Americans) couldn't challenge him this time. Baranov framed events in Ukraine in the context of what he saw as an unstoppable twenty-year offensive by the West. In his mind it had started with Serbia.

As he was broadcasting his story, Russian troops were taking control of Crimea.

At that time, Evgeny Krutikov and Petya Akopov, now in their mid-forties, found themselves once again working at the same media outlet, the online publication Vzglyad, set up by Kremlin spin-doctors in the mid-2000s, which had become infamous for its particularly nasty attacks on the opposition. It was Vzglyad that had attacked the March of Dissenters in the late 2000s, portraying protesters as clowns at a circus, stupidly entertaining themselves as they sold out their Motherland.

Petya had been writing for Vzglyad since 2013. "This is the organ of the Administration of the President [AP], and not just the AP, but the department of internal politics," he later told us. "The AP wanted something from them [the editorial office], but the guys themselves didn't understand what was needed of them—some kind of patriotism, some kind of greatness, and then they remembered me from the early 2000s from *Izvestia*," he said. "They called me, and at first, they wanted me to manage something, then they realized that too much energy was spent on leadership. And I began just writing but called myself deputy editor-in-chief. It was easy to write, and I worked like that for seven years. And the AP were very pleased, they were just like that—let's have more Akopov!" He sounded genuinely thrilled to be writing blatant state propaganda.

Krutikov had joined in early 2014, after a long period without steady employment. Both got their jobs thanks to a former *Izvestia* colleague who had become the head of Vzglyad. The Maidan Revolution in Ukraine deeply troubled Putin, and it looked as if the Kremlin wanted to recruit every available writer with appropriate views to its massive media manipulation effort.

Krutikov's very first column in Vzglyad, in March 2014, was about Ukraine, and it contained all the Kremlin's favorite buzzwords and stock phrases: "the Kyiv junta," "well-armed pubescents with swastikas on their flags," "ideology of radical nationalism," and so on and so forth.[1]

Petya, meanwhile, wrote in praise of Putin's decision to send Russian troops to Crimea. To him it represented the end of the post-Soviet period and the unipolar world, and he exuberantly insisted that this was how Russia would restore its position as "one of the global centers of power."[2]

A few months later, when Russian-backed separatists started a war in Eastern Ukraine in the Donbass region, Krutikov responded with wild enthusiasm, though he loved to pose as a coolheaded geopolitical analyst.

When, later, Andrei asked Krutikov the reason for his warmongering glee, his justification was personal. "Some of my relatives lived in Donbass," he said. "And I needed to get them out from there to Rostov [a city in Russia], to the refugee camp, in March 2014. I know Donbass. I've been there. I know all these towns, I know these people."

He'd convinced himself that the Donbass population had its own identity, a "sub-ethnos," or sub-ethnic group—meaning a community of people living in close proximity to each other who belong to a larger ethnic group, but who differ from that group culturally and linguistically, who geographically became a part of that group later than the others in it, and who are aware of that difference. This "sub-ethnos," according to Krutikov, was deeply and fiercely rooted in the Donbass land. In his view of the world, the Ukrainians were sending death squads to Donbass to either kill the locals or forcibly Ukraine-ize them, and the "sub-ethnos" were bravely fighting back against this invasion.

This version of reality didn't address the presence of Russian troops and Russian tanks in Eastern Ukraine, nor did it account for Russia's mobile surface-to-air defense missile system (BUK), which on July 17, 2014, shot down Malaysia Airlines Flight MH17 bound from Amsterdam to Kuala Lumpur, killing 298 people.

So, ten days after that tragedy, Krutikov wrote in Vzglyad claiming that "the plane was shot down by Ukrainians; shot down by accident. There will be no investigation; no one needs it."[3] Such blatant misdirection was about as far from genuine reporting as any onetime journalist could go. But Krutikov went further.

In the same piece, he radically switched his language and his arguments. According to him, the leaders of Georgia and Ukraine were talking in "monkey English," and this was why they were loved by the West; Ukrainian antiaircraft gunners were "monkeys with a grenade" who "were taken by drink."[4] He also rehashed xenophobic, derogatory anecdotes that emphasized how helpless the Ukrainians were, portraying them as peasant simpletons with military equipment. That was a new narrative: it contrasted the allegedly advanced sophistication of Russia with the supposedly narrow-minded and uneducated peasants of Ukraine.

This language was soon being echoed across Moscow. Pro-Kremlin newspapers swiftly adopted it for their stories about Ukraine, and TV talk-show hosts shocked their viewers with it, speaking aggressively and loudly, even breaking into screams.

Sensing the change in the political atmosphere, Krutikov went full Imperial. He offered a new, and newly arranged, analysis of the collapse of the Soviet Union: the independence movements had been based in the ideology of Russophobia, which, according to Krutikov, was an attempt in those countries to compensate for their lack of ancient history and culture. He suggested that countries such as Estonia, Lithuania, and Latvia should have been grateful to be incorporated into the superior Russian world, rather than wishing to live on their own.

Sounding very Soviet, and very Stalin-like, Krutikov also promoted the return of state ideology to Russian foreign policy. He began reminiscing in his columns about his grandfather, the deputy prime minister under Stalin, perhaps to remind readers in high places of his pedigree.[5] Oddly, his expectations of a big Soviet return were accompanied by an increasing feeling of impending doom.

Later, Krutikov would admit he'd had a strong feeling in 2014 that the global order was collapsing. All the old, long-established rules had failed, and he felt that a big war was coming. It was a very dark view.

Sveta Babayeva was back in Moscow. She was still the same tiny, fit, agile blonde she had been in 2000, now sporting fashionably short hair. RIA Novosti, the Kremlin news agency she had worked for in Washington, had experienced a traumatic purge at the end of 2013 when the Kremlin demanded it take a more aggressive stance on Ukraine.

By then Babayeva had moved to lead Gazeta, a big online media organization. Gazeta enjoyed some limited freedom, and Babayeva's main backer in the Kremlin, Sergei Ivanov, was head of Putin's presidential administration. Babayeva got back into the habit of regularly dropping by his office in the Kremlin, seeking his advice, and also his protection. And Ivanov protected her, including from his fierce deputy Vyacheslav Volodin.

Babayeva had big plans for Gazeta and recruited young journalists and some experienced former colleagues from *Izvestia* to build her team. She tried to remain professional, insofar as that was possible given the Kremlin's tight control over the media.

And, surprisingly, unlike our other friends from *Izvestia*, she didn't share the enthusiasm about Crimea being absorbed into Russia. Two months after Crimea's annexation, she described Russia's high emotions about Crimea as a "crazy energetic exaltation" that could open something in the nation, deep down, adding that from those depths, something terrible could emerge.[6]

In the summer of 2014, she wrote a column observing that, unlike the West, Russia always lacked an alternative:

> Those who travel to the decaying West, bursting with all the vices, know: all the doors of hotels, shops, stadiums, theaters, if they exist, are open. Even a building that seems completely asleep often gives the option to enter it and get out of it. Especially if the lobby is used as a public space—say, as a passage from one street to another or as a place for a fair on the weekend.
> Not so in Russia.
> Have you ever noticed how doors are arranged in our country? Of the five provided by the project, only one is operational. The rest, at best, are marked with an arrow to the open

one; at worst, they are found closed by poking their nose and forehead into them.

In essence, this is a good picture of life: neither enter nor exit.[7]

She went on, expressing her concerns: that the authorities were banning protests out of fear of extremism; that they were prohibiting public debate about the annexation of Crimea out of fear that it could lead people to question Kremlin policy; and that they were imposing stifling restrictions on the internet in the same interests.

In post-Crimea Moscow, where the test of a writer's patriotism was obligatory condemnation of the West, her column did not seem especially patriotic.

Two years later, we saw Babayeva at a grand July 4 reception in the garden of Spaso House, the yellow neoclassical residence of the US ambassador in Moscow with its legendary colonnaded veranda.

In the 2010s in Moscow, the parties hosted by Western embassies became a sort of a "water truce" area (a term coined by Rudyard Kipling referring to how, during the dry season in the jungle, predators and prey didn't attack each other around the watering hole). At the embassies, one could meet in a garden and share a drink with a pro-Kremlin priest, an oligarch, or propagandists as well as opposition politicians and journalists very critical of Putin. The embassy fences provided an illusion of protection from the world outside.

Babayeva rushed to hug us, something she never would have done in the old days. Her manner was unexpectedly open and friendly as she showed off the new tattoos on her arm. She spoke about the young journalists she worked with and their outbursts against Kremlin pressure, and she said how she'd tried to prevent them from leaving because "there are not a lot of jobs for journalists these days." She talked about how her longtime protector, Ivanov, continued to back her.

Later that month she was forced to resign from Gazeta. The month after that, in August 2016, Ivanov lost his position as head of Putin's presidential administration. Ivanov was known for his obsession with leopards,[8] so Putin made him the president's special representative on environmental issues, keeping him on the Security Council.

It was a huge blow, but Babayeva had spent too much time around the Kremlin to be thrown out completely. As a consolation she was given a position as adviser to the head of *Russia Today*, a state propaganda monster that included the TV channel broadcasting abroad and the former RIA Novosti—the agency that had deployed Babayeva to London and Washington in the past.

The media behemoth was now fully engaged in promoting the Kremlin's increasingly belligerent message about Ukraine and the West.

In March 2014, over 50,000 people gathered in the center of Moscow for an antiwar rally, many more than the Kremlin managed to gather for a prowar rally the same day.

Many from the Moscow intelligentsia were among them. Boris Nemtsov was ecstatic: "False propaganda from morning to evening washed our brains that there are bandits in Kyiv, that there is the fifth column over here. They shitted themselves! So many people are here today!" he shouted from the stage. He then attacked Putin. "He is a sick man. . . . No, he is not just a sick man. He is also a cynical and vile person. Using this operation to occupy Crimea, he is going to rule forever!"[9]

A year later, in March 2015, on a gloomy, sunless Sunday morning, thousands of Muscovites were marching, again, in the streets of central Moscow. There were no shouts this time, but there were many handmade banners, many of them with the words "I'm not afraid" or "No political assassinations!" and portraits of Nemtsov. The crowd around us was talking in low voices. We were marching in honor of Nemtsov, an energetic, always cheerful, larger-than-life man, who had been shot dead by assassins just two days before, when he was walking with his girlfriend over the Bolshoy Moskvoretsky Bridge near the red-brick Kremlin Wall. The sense of shock was overwhelming, visible on the faces of young professionals, journalists, and the members of the Moscow intelligentsia who were walking along with us. Marching along the wall, looking at Nemtsov's portraits in the crowd, we couldn't believe he was dead. Not him. He had always emanated such a huge, endless stream of positive energy that he drew people to him. He was protesting Russia's immoral war in Ukraine to the day he died.

Nemtsov had started his career as a talented physicist and had been elected governor and become a deputy prime minister before reaching the age of forty. In the 1990s Putin had seen his star rising from his obscure position at St. Petersburg's city hall.

The killing of Nemtsov was shocking, and his loss was irreplaceable. It was almost certainly his opposition that got him killed. The security cameras that covered the bridge were mysteriously shut off for "maintenance" that day, so Nemtsov died in the shadows. But very few in Russia had any doubts about where the decision to kill him had originated.

One of the pillars of the Russian propaganda narrative about the war in Ukraine was Putin's highly revisionist account of the Great Patriotic War, or World War II, as the West knows it.

In Putin's view, most of the events of World War II were just backstage episodes in the drama of the Eastern Front. It was the Soviet Union that had saved the world from Hitler, period. The West was either defeated (France, and Britain, almost) or hesitant (the United States). The Ukrainians had a special role in this narrative: they had been treacherous during the war, and now their descendants, supported by the West, had become Nazis, the modern successors of

Hitler. Thus, they left Russia no choice but to get back to the fight where they had left it in 1945.

Some crucial ammunition for that narrative was supplied by Olga Lyubimova.

By 2014 Lyubimova was a successful screenwriter of documentaries, many of them about the Russian Orthodox Church. In the spring of 2014, she was the coauthor of a six-episode series called *The War and the Myths* on a very different theme: it set out to dismantle "Western" myths about the Great Patriotic War. Lyubimova's coauthor was Vladimir Medinsky, the minister of culture, who had written a series of highly popular revisionist books about Russian history.

The series, which aired on Channel One, promoted the Kremlin's version of the war. It alleged, for instance, that Soviet leaders had had to make an enormous effort "to force the Americans and British to enter the war," and that Western help to the Red Army via the Lend-Lease Act was negligible.[10] In this version of history, Stalin emerged as a wise and responsible world leader—just as he was portrayed during the Cold War in the Soviet Union.

By November 2015, Lyubimova had been rewarded for her patriotism by being made adviser to the head of the cinematography department of the Ministry of Culture—the department that provided generous government funding for documentaries. The culture minister, Medinsky, created the position especially for her.

That same year, independent online media was feeling greater pressure than ever, much of it blocked since the annexation of Crimea in 2014, including Ej.ru. After more than a year of putting up a desperate fight, the website gave up its editorial offices—Ej.ru moved out from the top floor on Nikitsky Boulevard, to nowhere. But the site maintained a presence online.

The liberal geography of Moscow was shrinking. Not only were editorial offices shutting down, so were the clubs where liberal-minded intelligentsia used to hang out. The Paperny family's Masterskaya—the huge club/theater space in the former public baths a stone's throw from Lubyanka, where Alexei Navalny had set up his headquarters during the presidential election—was closed, for good, in April 2015. "Soon after the sanctions imposed on Russia, prices for food and alcohol rose sharply at all suppliers. Property owners increase rent as it pleases them, and there is no way to resist that," the owners explained.[11]

Only the brasserie Jean-Jacques, with its red walls and mirrors on Nikitsky Boulevard, miraculously survived.

The spring of 2016 finally shattered our belief that Russian reporters were part of the international journalistic community. In early 2016, the Panama Papers became a big scandal. This involved the publication of a huge trove of documents of offshore Panamanian firms that government officials and oligarchs all over the world had used for fraud, tax evasion, and evasion of sanctions. Several teams of investigative journalists from different countries had worked on the documents, including our colleagues in Moscow. Russian journalists, our friends, discovered in the trove multimillion-dollar accounts owned by a cellist, Sergei Roldugin, a close personal friend of Vladimir Putin's. The millions were believed to be Putin's.

Putin, understandably, was angered and attacked the journalists. So did, to our astonishment, the team at WikiLeaks. WikiLeaks' Twitter account accused the Russian journalists of being "no model for integrity" and claimed that the organization they worked for—the Organized Crime and Corruption Reporting Project—was "funded by USAID & Soros."[12]

The WikiLeaks tweet essentially accused the Russian journalists of being paid agents or useful fools of the US government. A few days later, Putin happily picked up those charges, saying, "We now know from WikiLeaks that officials and state agencies in the United States are behind all this!"[13]

As it happened, the next day we were both at the International Journalism Festival in Perugia, where Sarah Harrison, the head of the WikiLeaks investigative team, was about to give a talk about WikiLeaks and Edward Snowden.

We went to her talk along with Ewen MacAskill, a veteran journalist of the *Guardian*. Ewen had famously interviewed Snowden in Hong Kong.

During the question-and-answer session, Andrei stood up and asked Harrison about WikiLeaks' response to the Panama Papers and Putin's reaction. Andrei also said that the journalists who took part in the Panama Papers investigation were correspondents of *Novaya Gazeta*, a newspaper that had lost several journalists who had been mysteriously killed.

Harrison snapped back, "Please, do not make me responsible for what Putin says!" And then she went on the offensive, claiming that the story was used as an attack on Putin, and stressing that the funding for the journalists, she believed, came from the US government, and that explained the "cherry-picking with a clear anti-Russian agenda."

We were outraged—we knew too well the risks that Russian journalists had to live under, and now the head of the investigative team of WikiLeaks, our colleague, was providing ammunition for the Kremlin.

At that moment, Ewen MacAskill, who was sitting next to Irina, stood up. He spoke about the role the *Guardian* had played in Snowden's story, and then added, "My initial response when I heard about what WikiLeaks and Sarah had done was to think it was a mistake—that Snowden ended up in Moscow. He was heading for Latin America; it was a complete fiasco. I now realize that WikiLeaks and Sarah did exactly the right thing. It might not have been the end that they wanted, but it's exactly the right outcome. Russia is the only country in the world where Edward Snowden would be safe."[14] It was amazing, and very wrong.

When the session ended, we hastened from the venue, avoiding MacAskill.

Once outside, on the astonishingly beautiful medieval street of Perugia, we argued furiously—all this talk about camaraderie among journalists, of us being in the same business, facing the same challenges, was it just for show? Did it mean there were different standards for journalists in different countries? Where was their loyalty to Russian reporters doing dangerous investigative work—or were Russian journalists just acceptable collateral damage?

During our careers, essentially all our adult lives, we had firmly believed that we were part of something bigger—a global community of journalists, where there were no borders or nationalities, and where we all shared clear professional ethics.

That warm and lively evening in Perugia was the moment we felt the lowest about the path we had chosen. It was a very lonely feeling.

The fortunes of our former colleagues at *Izvestia*, in the meantime, were changing for the better. Petya Akopov's financial situation had much improved, and he took his family—Marina and two daughters—on a tour across Europe, including Paris and Rome, something Marina and Petya had wanted to do for a long time. Their chances of getting back to Gogolevsky Boulevard didn't look to him as desperate as they once had—the Akopovs started saving money to purchase the two rooms that would complete the apartment.

The following year, Olga Lyubimova was made deputy director of the Directorate of Social and Journalistic Programs at Channel One, where her husband, Zhenya Baranov, also worked. She came to oversee both the production of all the documentaries for Channel One, and, as adviser to the Culture Ministry's department, the government funding for them.

At that time, Channel One produced an ambitious documentary series called *Myths About Russia* based on the writings of Minister

Vladimir Medinsky, Lyubimova's old coauthor. The main objective of the series was to dismantle "black myths" about Russia (and more "black myths" were created about Russia than about any other country, claimed the authors).

"We are not going to prove that 'we are all in white,' no. But for centuries we've been told that we've been the worst of all," declared the authors of the project, funded by the Ministry of Culture. Each episode dealt with one supposedly negative stereotype that was applied to Russia: the myth of Russian cruelty; of unwashed and always drunk Russia; of the obedience of the Russian people; of Russia's backwardness; of the Russian threat; and finally, of Russia as the "prison of nations," a phrase that had been invented by a nineteenth-century French writer, Astolphe de Custine, and was picked up by Lenin as a damning description of the way the Russians kept the nations of its vast empire together. The fifty-minute-long "prison of nations" episode was narrated by a journalist walking the grand halls of the Kremlin's palaces to make it sound like he was making grand statements. The narrator blamed the British for having slaves in the colonies, the Americans for mistreatment of the Indigenous people, etc., and assured the watchers that Russia was never like that. "We have never been white colonists in pith helmets!" said the narrator, insisting that the myth had been invented simply to belittle the great Russian civilization.[15] According to the authors, the fact that Russia had successfully fought off the invasions of Napoleon and Hitler was proof positive that all the people of Russia wanted to stay in and fight for Russia.

It was probably the most revanchist project ever shown on Russian TV.

Two years later, Lyubimova shed any pretense of impartiality and became a government official when she was appointed head of the cinematography department of the Culture Ministry. Now she controlled the production not only of documentaries but also of fictional films made with government support. From that point on, the flow of propaganda films attacking the West and Ukraine became an industry unto itself.

In the meantime, Sveta Babayeva was getting desperate. As adviser to the head of the RIA agency, she had no real job. She started to look for adventure, turning to sports. She constantly raised the stakes: first, it was horse racing, followed by shooting all kinds of weapons on a shooting range, then knife fighting and full-scale special forces training.

She began sending her friends photos of herself posing in military fatigues and participating in drills with special forces soldiers.

In 2019 she accepted a position as head of the RIA bureau in occupied Crimea at the headquarters in Simferopol—a dusty provincial town in the middle of the peninsula with a population of roughly 300,000—and moved there. Her new job was to tell Russians how great life had become in the annexed peninsula. Her office was in a squat, Stalin-era trade union building on the corner of Simferopol's main square, where a statue of Lenin still stood, next to a neglected street of unsightly and unkempt Soviet-era apartment blocks and typical nineteenth-century wooden houses. It must have made, for Babayeva, a striking contrast to South Kensington and Dupont Circle, where she had been working so recently.

Once she moved to Crimea, however, she firmly closed the door on the West—and on the respect she had developed for it during her postings in London and Washington, DC. After a posting as a head of the Kremlin propaganda outlet in Crimea illegally torn away from Ukraine, she knew she would never get any position in Europe or in the United States. We weren't sure whether this patriotic turn was at her own initiative—a way to get herself back in the game—or whether it was the price someone else told her she had to pay if she wanted to be a player in the new Russia.

In the meantime, that new Russia was getting even more autocratic. In January 2020, Putin announced he would change the constitution.

His amendments would eventually make it legally possible that he could be elected to two more terms—in 2024 and 2030—for another twelve years in total. Essentially, he made himself irreplaceable, arrogating to himself powers very reminiscent of those once possessed by the tsar.

That same month, he appointed Lyubimova as the minister of culture.

CHAPTER 23

FAREWELL PARTY

Just two months earlier, in November 2019, we returned to Moscow after a promotional tour for our third book, *The Compatriots*.

It was an exciting trip after a very exhausting year, as *The Compatriots* had proved to be a difficult book to write. It focused on the Kremlin's efforts to subdue or exploit Russians who had emigrated abroad. It was a fascinating topic with a very long, dramatic, and bloody history, but it was hard to do the necessary research. The authorities were closing access even to those archives that had been accidentally opened in the 1990s, and inside sources in the Russian intelligence and security services were getting less enthusiastic about talking to us. The climate in Moscow had changed dramatically over the course of the decade.

We had felt a little self-conscious taking on such a topic, because nobody from our immediate families had ever had the experience of having to emigrate. We asked ourselves what actual Russian emigrants and their descendants would say about what we had written. We were sufficiently anxious about this—that people would ask us why on earth they should read a book about émigrés and exiles by writers who had never gone through such a wrenching experience themselves—that we decided to add a brief disclaimer in the introduction, acknowledging that we had "never lived abroad for more than a few months."

But contrary to our expectations, nobody attacked us. At book events across the United States, people with very different backgrounds came forward to share dramatic and amazing stories about their ancestors who had emigrated from Russia, some involving interactions with the murky world of Soviet espionage.

Back in our Moscow apartment, we were looking forward to the publication of the Russian version of the book. It had become sort of an established routine that our Russian publisher would wait for the English-language book to come out, then buy the rights to publish the book in Russian, a procedure allowing them to maintain that they hadn't initiated publication of the book; they were just issuing a translation. This routine was a precaution we all hoped would protect the Russian publisher from possible problems with the authorities.

The translation and editing usually took several months, time during which we began thinking about what kinds of promotional events we should do. We didn't know that the next few months would be our last in Russia.

In mid-November 2019, *New York Times* Moscow bureau chief Neil MacFarquhar held a farewell party in his spacious apartment on Sadovaya-Samotechnaya on the Garden Ring in central Moscow—his assignment there had come to an end. A very distinguished crowd had gathered to say goodbye. There were foreign correspondents, a famous actress who had starred in many Russian movies, a respected publisher who was also an oligarch's older sister, and a Black female TV personality who had hosted the first show in Russia about sexual issues.

Very late in the evening, when most of the guests had gone home, we found ourselves talking with Arcady, a tall, cheerful, and charming man in his late fifties who worked as a film producer on Russian TV. As often happens at parties, we soon found we had many friends in common, and the conversation whirled around them.

At some point Arcady mentioned Olga Lyubimova. He had known Lyubimova since her childhood; her father had been his professor at the theatrical arts school. Arcady remained grateful to Lyubimova's father, because he had supported him once when he ran into trouble with the Soviet system.

When we mentioned Zhenya Baranov, Arcady got gloomy. He said he knew a little about Baranov, and the only thing he'd noticed about him was his beautiful deep voice. But, he added, it didn't matter anymore, since Lyubimova had left Baranov. This was astonishing news to us: they had seemed to have a durable marriage even though we knew about Baranov's long affair with Anna, our friend at Ej.ru.

"What happened?" Irina asked, incredulous.

Arcady's explanation had nothing to do with extramarital affairs, however. "Baranov got obsessed with his crazy anti-Western ideas too much," Arcady said. "As a result, he got involved somehow in a failed coup d'état in Montenegro. Long story short, he's been banned from entering Europe."

This was also news, though not completely unexpected. Baranov was hardly the first in our circle of former journalists to get mixed up in Russian intelligence operations abroad. Two years before, Krutikov's closest friend, Dmitry Medoyev, the one he had danced with on the streets of Moscow after the war with Georgia, had visited Barcelona as the de facto foreign minister of separatist South Ossetia on the eve of the referendum on Catalonia's secession from Spain. The Spanish suspected him of helping stir up trouble by encouraging Catalonia's independence movement and leaked this information to the media.[1] In London it was believed the operation in Spain had been supervised by Russian military intelligence.[2]

The coup in Montenegro was reportedly organized by a group of alleged Russian intelligence agents and pro-Serbian politicians to prevent Montenegro from joining NATO.[3] We remembered Baranov's reporting on Channel One in May 2016, when he had essentially openly warned Montenegro of a possible civil war if the country voted to split from Serbia. The attempted coup d'état came four months after his warning.

Arcady insisted that Lyubimova didn't approve of Baranov's participation in the events in Montenegro and that this was why she'd decided to break up with him.

But we'd followed the Montenegro story closely, and Baranov's name had never been mentioned in connection with the scandal around Russian spy exploits in that country. Arcady's version of events, taken obviously from Lyubimova, that she had broken up with Baranov ostensibly because she disapproved of him mixing with Russian intelligence activities, didn't sound very convincing to us.

Irina could hardly contain her astonishment. She texted Anna the next day, asking whether she knew that Lyubimova had left Baranov because of his supposed involvement in a failed coup d'état in Montenegro.

"Well, he lives with me now," responded Anna, "but it probably had nothing to do with Montenegro." It turned out that after a long and dramatic affair with Anna, Baranov had left Lyubimova for her, for good.

The old friends—Baranov, Petya Akopov, and Anna—became even closer as a result. "Those two, Petya and Baranov, sit in my kitchen almost every day, and talk all night!" Anna exclaimed, in understandable desperation, a few days later, at the nonfiction book award ceremony called "Enlightener" held in the School of Modern Drama theater, where we bumped into each other. The award was sponsored by the Liberal Mission Foundation, and it was usually an occasion for liberal-minded people to gather.

When we moved away from the crowd with Anna to a nearby bar to talk, it became clear that she still believed in the illusion of life as usual at the virtual Ej.ru. New articles were being published, if not very regularly, and she was updating and keeping the site going on her own as best she could, even though the funding for the project had dried up. She was making a living by tutoring students for a history exam.

And now Baranov and Petya had effectively turned her tiny kitchen in the two-room apartment in Moscow's suburbs into a new place for their eternal, endless debates—a sort of a substitute for the apartment on Gogolevsky Boulevard until Petya saved enough for his family's return.

The allure of an old college flame had prevailed, and an old university friendship had endured, despite the gaping differences in political views between Anna and the two men she hosted in her kitchen.

On December 6, 2019, we got hit from a completely unexpected direction. That day, the Russian daily *Kommersant* ran a story directly attacking Andrei's father.[4] He was accused of transferring a pool of national IP addresses out of Russia to the Czech Republic.

As the internet pioneer who had set up the very first internet service provider in the Soviet Union, Alexey Soldatov had played a crucial role in building up Russia's national internet infrastructure. That had consisted of many things, including the national registry of IP addresses assigned to Russia by the international internet governance bodies.

For several years, the Kremlin had been on a crusade to put more and more elements of the Russian internet infrastructure under government control, but Alexey had refused to cooperate when it came to control of the IP address registry. Apparently, he hadn't appreciated how much things had changed since he had brought the internet to the country thirty years before.

Kommersant's story deeply worried us. For many years we had believed that Soldatov Sr., thanks to his background and his status of the father of the Russian internet, had a way to fix his problems with the Kremlin. The story was a clear sign that the tension had become public and that the Kremlin was preparing the ground for something much more sinister. Andrei was concerned that his father's health had been deteriorating; he'd been in and out of the hospital for the past four years, including a recent stay that lasted for months, though he was still teaching at the university.

On December 25, Andrei got a call from a friend, a journalist with the independent news website Meduza. "Andrei, I don't know how to put this.... Are you aware that your father was arrested?"

Alexey Soldatov had been detained at the airport, handcuffed, and brought to the main Moscow police station, where he had been thrown into a cell. He had spent a night in jail. The next day, the court had placed him under house arrest.

The arrest of the internet pioneer and a former deputy minister was all over the news. We jumped into a car and drove to see him, but, as we approached his house, Irina had to stay outside in the freezing cold: the conditions of his house arrest stipulated that only close relatives could see Alexey Soldatov, and that included only Andrei.

In the house, Andrei saw that his father's wife was completely terrified and that his father was confused, visibly shaken after the night in jail. The criminal charges brought against him were daunting: he was accused of large-scale embezzlement, punishable by up to ten years in prison.[5] Large-scale embezzlement was the most popular charge the authorities used against businessmen, and Russian courts acquitted fewer than 1 percent of all defendants.[6]

The report to the police denouncing him was signed by Andrei Lipov, head of the Putin administration's department in charge of regulating the Russian segment of the internet.[7] It confirmed our worst suspicions: the attack on Andrei's dad had been launched from the Kremlin.

Now Soldatov Sr. had no choice but to abandon his regular life, get used to being locked up, and wait for his case to be sent to court.

Spring didn't bring any changes for the better to Soldatov Sr. When the stipulated three months assigned for the investigation expired, he was taken to court so that the investigation could be prolonged for another three months.

As journalists, we had spent a lot of time in Moscow's courts. It was always the same: a prosecutor would read a prepared text without looking up; the defendant would smile to his friends and colleagues, putting on a brave face; a lawyer would point out the mistakes in the investigation, knowing deep down that it was all hopeless; and, finally, a judge would quickly mumble a decision that had already been made elsewhere. The routine almost never varied. But this time it was personal.

Andrei's father sat in a small courtroom with a large Russian coat of arms above the judge's chair. From our bench we watched in despair as Soldatov Sr., in a sweater and slacks, in stark contrast to his usual suit, tried to address the judge. But he was speaking to a blank, empty face. He had suffered from a stutter all his life, but after his forties he had almost overcome it by incorporating it into his manner of speaking. Only rarely would there be pauses in unusual places. Now, before the judge, he started to stammer again. The judge approved the prolongation of the investigation, a routine that would be repeated many times in the coming months.

In the meantime, Andrei Lipov, the Kremlin official who had initiated Alexey's persecution, got a new job. Lipov became the head of the Russian media and internet censorship agency Roskomnadzor.

Andrei's father remained under house arrest, surrounded by surveillance cameras and listening devices that had been installed by police in his home. When Andrei visited him, they always went out to the balcony to talk in hushed voices.

Soldatov Sr.'s isolation was suddenly and unexpectedly shared by most Russians when COVID-19 hit the country, followed by a lockdown.

Spring bloomed unstoppably in Moscow, but the city government introduced harsh measures to keep Muscovites inside. The city's vast surveillance and face recognition system was deployed to identify those who broke the lockdown rules. It was surprisingly efficient: anyone who transgressed was identified and fined. The government had made enormous progress since we'd investigated the Russian "Big Brother" set up in Sochi for the 2014 Olympic Games.

We were working on editing the Russian translation of *The Compatriots* when Andrei was told to check the status of the media license for our website, Agentura.

In Russia, every media outlet required a license issued by Roskomnadzor; Agentura had had one since the early 2000s. But when Andrei checked the list of media licenses on the Roskomnadzor website, Agentura's license appeared to have been recently revoked.

Curious, we sought out the reason. Usually, if a license had been pulled, it was ostensibly because of some bureaucratic issue. But that was not the case this time. Agentura's media license had been canceled, according to the government agency, because of "the death of the physical person."[8]

We looked at each other, stupefied. Andrei was the only person listed on the license, as Agentura editor, and Andrei was, by all indications, quite alive. But the government agency, led by the official who had put Andrei's father under house arrest, had declared that he was dead. It didn't require much imagination to see that as a threat.

Throughout centuries of authoritarian rule, Russian bureaucracy has perfected the art of sending "signals." In the Soviet Union, officials would use the phrase "there is an opinion" to indicate what a Soviet citizen was expected to do and not do. There was an opinion that a scientist should not accept a job offer from abroad, or publish an article on the "wrong" topic with the "wrong" coauthors; there was an opinion that an actor should not accept a role in the "wrong" film or play; there was an opinion that an editor of a journal should not publish the "wrong" author; and so on. And when a Soviet dissident crossed a line, he or she was sometimes told, always calmly, that there was an opinion that the time had come to leave the country. Assuming the dissident had not immediately been sent to jail.

Nobody knew to whom exactly that "opinion" belonged, but everybody had a pretty good idea where it came from, and what the consequences of disobeying it would be. Under Putin, the Kremlin's signaling became more complicated, but essentially it was left to repressive agencies—the police, the FSB, the Investigative Committee—to hint to the victim what the authorities expected of him or her. As part of this signaling system, criminal cases would be opened, raids of apartments conducted, problems with taxes suddenly revealed, until it dawned on the victim: it was time to change one's behavior, or else.

It was new for Roskomnadzor, the official Russian internet censorship agency, a Kremlin department, but not a security service or a law enforcement agency, to take part in the signaling game—in our case, by announcing that someone was "dead." We had never come across it before, so we weren't sure what it signified. We reached out to our contacts in different agencies to ask about it. Was this a bureaucratic glitch, or a hint? And if a hint, then a hint to do what, exactly?

By the end of the summer, it became clear we had no choice but to find a way to go, at least for a year, probably as soon as possible. But leaving Russia was not easy at the height of the COVID pandemic. Russia was essentially closed to Europe. Foreign embassies had shut their doors and weren't issuing visas. But inside them, diplomats were still working, and we asked our friends and colleagues in different European embassies for help.

By the end of August 2020, a plan had emerged: as Russian citizens we could fly only to Switzerland, provided we had Swiss laissez-passers. The Swiss diplomats kindly helped us to obtain them.

FAREWELL PARTY

We decided against having a farewell party, for security reasons. In our conversations, we pretended that we were leaving for a month or two.

On Saturday, September 5, we went to Sheremetyevo airport with two suitcases—a large black one and a small red one—all that we could take with us. After officials carefully checked our documents, we were allowed to board an Aeroflot plane bound for Geneva.

Three months later, our book about emigration and the Kremlin's spies was published in Moscow. The Moscow Book Fair held a discussion about the book, and the room was full—as far as we could make out, watching the event on Zoom from a small flat we rented in Bloomsbury, London. The building in which we were renting, we found out later, was situated between the houses where two Russian dissident exiles—Alexander Herzen and Vladimir Lenin—had once lived. Herzen had edited the famous nineteenth-century *Kolokol* (Bell) newspaper from exile, read even by the tsar, next door to our place.

CHAPTER 24

FOREBODING

All autumn, squirrels and kids scurried across the large park on tree-lined Russell Square, a stone's throw from the British Museum, where we came to walk almost every day. Then winter arrived, but, strangely, to us, not a lot changed in the mild British weather. There were the same trees, green lawn, and squirrels, but fewer kids. COVID lockdown hit the United Kingdom just weeks after we moved to London and began settling into our new life as exiles.

Of course we had considered the possibility that we might someday have to leave Russia. Everyone in our generation—at least among our friends, university-educated Muscovites—asked themselves at some point the same question. Not because the country was bad, but because we were the first generation of Russians that had grown up with a *right* to leave. After all, we'd come of age right after the Soviet Union collapsed, and all Soviet travel restrictions had vanished with it.

In Moscow in the 1990s, many things had remained very much as they were in the Soviet era: people went to work in brutalist offices via the Soviet-era metro, and at the end of the day came home to Soviet-era high-rise apartment buildings. But Moscow was full of opportunities.

And along with the new businesses of all sorts, the clubs, and the newspapers, there was the opportunity to leave, to travel to the world outside. Andrei had a university classmate, a handsome guy and a master in martial arts, who wanted to go to Hollywood. He moved to the United States in the mid-1990s, ended up acting in movies alongside Angelina Jolie and Keanu Reeves, and became quite famous among martial arts practitioners.[1] Two of Irina's neighbors from her hometown—a father and daughter—had also moved to America, and they became very successful there financially.

As young reporters we had never wanted to leave the country: in journalism you stay close to your story, as close and as long as is physically possible, and Russia was a fascinating story of constant political turmoil, wars, and a never-ending crisis on the back of globalization. Besides, the practice of journalism was universal—the standards, the understandings of what constituted achievements and failures in that profession, were the same in Moscow as in New York, or at least that was what we believed.

In the 2000s, and then the 2010s, as pressure from the Kremlin was constantly rising, we had still believed we could remain in Moscow, and we didn't want to leave. Until the summer of 2020, we believed we still had time for one more book.

Now we found ourselves suddenly in London, in a very different world from what we knew in Moscow, one made stranger by the fact that our "ground-floor" flat was in fact a basement in an Edwardian building with windows half below ground level. The front door had a letter slot where a postmaster pushed mail every day with a terrible clatter, reminiscent of the first Harry Potter movie.

When the British government introduced the COVID lockdown, all our activities moved online. That included endless Zoom meetings conducted in front of our semibasement window to let in some light; more than once our interlocutors became distracted by the view of human legs or a dog in the window above us. London felt very foreign and different. Foxes were walking the deserted streets as if they were dogs. Birds started singing after midnight, and we wondered if the lockdown had affected them or if that was just normal for England.

From London, we watched the Kremlin ratchet up pressure on Russian society. The Kremlin had censored mass media and social media for years, but the rules for theaters, books, and movies had remained relatively loose. Now that began to change. In December, Putin called publicly for limits on "some out-of-the-ordinary content" on television.[2]

From then on, all Western films and sitcoms, along with popular Russian TV shows and movies, were to be censored. That task fell to the Ministry of Culture, and to the new minister of culture—Olga Lyubimova.

During the two years when she was still head of the ministry's cinematography department, Lyubimova had banned the Anglo-French film *The Death of Stalin*, a black comedy that depicted the struggle for political power among Soviet dignitaries following Stalin's sudden death. Russian conservatives, led by Lyubimova's patron Nikita Mikhalkov, whose father had written lyrics for the Soviet anthem praising Stalin, were outraged by the movie. Mikhalkov predictably accused it of smearing "our history" and demanded that it be banned.[3] Lyubimova didn't let her patron down. She promptly withdrew the film's license, citing "appeals from groups of citizens" that the ministry couldn't ignore.[4]

That expression had been very popular in Stalin times—in the 1930s, Soviet newspapers had printed, on a daily basis, the "appeals from groups of workers" calling for Trotskyists and other enemies of the people to be punished with death. When asked about her opinion of the film by an interviewer from TASS, the state-run news agency, Lyubimova said, "I am less concerned about the figure of Joseph Vissarionovich [Stalin] and top politicians in the film. The only thing that I personally, as a viewer, took very painfully was the incredible irony, sarcasm, and cynicism with which the victims of Stalin's repressions were shown."[5] Her pious opinion was nonsense.

Lyubimova's first year as minister was marked by a huge scandal. Never before had the appointment of a minister sparked such enthusiasm in social media. "An uncultured person appointed a minister of culture!" "Sex, drugs, rock-n-roll!" "The new minister of culture doesn't like museums, and she swears!" Bloggers and journalists rediscovered Lyubimova's old blog on LiveJournal, the one that had attracted such attention ten years before, thanks to her post about Dmitry Medvedev's urinals.

The blog became a treasure trove for journalists. She had been amazingly open about her personal and sexual life, her relationship with Zhenya Baranov, and her fierce quarrels with neighbors. Her language had been very colorful.

In a vain attempt to mitigate the harm, Lyubimova took her blog down, but it didn't help—the juiciest posts were copied and posted everywhere.

But the stream of jokes and memes in social media didn't hurt her career. Most important of all, her patron, Mikhalkov, remained close to Putin. That was all that mattered.

In her official photos, taken in her old-fashioned office at the ministry, sitting at a massive wooden desk adorned with a green lamp and a collection of Soviet-like desk phones to communicate with the Kremlin, Lyubimova looked confident, certain of a bright future ahead.

A week and a half after Putin called for the censorship of films and television, Channel One aired a new story by Baranov. His subject was the new US president, Joe Biden.

Baranov told the Russian audience that Biden's administration was sure to increase pressure on Russia "on all fronts," and followed up by showing footage of new Russian weapons, including missiles being launched and the Russian navy engaged in maneuvering—aggressive militaristic porn, North Korea style. The story concluded with a warning: "Illusions about the possibility of overtaking us in the new arms race that has already begun are doomed in advance."[6]

Shortly before that, Baranov had presented another big story on Channel One that concerned the poisoning of Alexei Navalny with the nerve agent Novichok in Siberia. Baranov denied the Kremlin's involvement, claiming that Navalny had "allowed himself to be turned into a sacred sacrifice in the struggle between Western intelligence services and the Kremlin."[7] He accused Germany, where Navalny went to recover, of nefarious interference in Russian affairs. As always, Baranov brought up the Balkans as a warning. This time he compared Navalny's poisoning with the killing of Archduke Franz Ferdinand in Sarajevo, Bosnia, in 1914, hinting that NATO was seeking a casus belli with Russia. Not for the first time, Baranov sounded as if he was almost looking forward to this colossal clash with the West.

Soon Baranov left Russian journalism entirely: in February 2021 he was appointed head of the Russian House in Belgrade, Serbia, part of the government-funded "soft power" network abroad that operated under the auspices of Rossotrudnichestvo, a behemoth Kremlin agency that helped support Russian émigré organizations loyal to the Kremlin and Russian-speaking media.

Baranov had been part of a "soft power" network in Serbia for several years already. His new job coincided with the arrival of Rossotrudnichestvo's new head—Evgeny Primakov Jr. Primakov was a TV journalist, but, most importantly, he was a grandson of the Soviet diplomat who in the 1990s under Boris Yeltsin had risen from the directorship of the Russian intelligence agency to become foreign minister and then prime minister.

The Russians mostly remembered Primakov Sr. for two things: first, for his personal friendship with Saddam Hussein, and second, for "Primakov's Loop." In March 1999, Primakov was flying to Washington for an official visit when he learned that NATO had started bombing Serbia. Furious, he ordered his plane to turn around over the Atlantic Ocean, hence the loop, and returned to Moscow. In a nutshell, Primakov was a top-level bureaucrat of the Soviet imperial school. Putin admired him as a living monument to the glorious days of Soviet power.

Primakov Jr. shared his grandfather's worldview. So did Baranov. Once Primakov Jr. settled in as the new boss of Rossotrudnichestvo, Baranov moved to a yellow four-story building with a colonnaded entrance in the center of Belgrade, the headquarters of the Russian House. It had been built in the 1930s with funds collected among Russian emigrants, remains of the White Army that settled in Serbia after their defeat by the Bolsheviks. The impressive building had once housed a theater, a library, a church, an elementary school, and a secondary school, along with two museums—one on the last tsar, and the other on the Russian cavalry. But these days, the Russian House was part of the Kremlin's network of propaganda and influence operations.

Shortly after he installed himself in Belgrade, Baranov granted an interview to RIA Novosti focusing on the 1999 bombings of Belgrade. It was headlined "The Bombing of Yugoslavia Killed Faith in the West." Baranov expressed a view that was no doubt expected of him:

> I often say that the first bomb that fell on Belgrade hit me right in the head, once and for all. In part, I may even regret it, because from now on, I see everything that is happening in international relations through the prism that has stuck like a splinter in my head. I can't look at this cynicism differently, at those double standards, I don't know how many layers of standards there are for lies, for lies in the face, "set-ups," provocations. The main thing is the incredible feeling that their radiant smiling world can suddenly turn into this face with an evil grin.[8]

Baranov had become a top-level Russian government official, allocated a key role in the Kremlin's information wars, just like his estranged wife, and both were utterly convinced of the rightness of their cause.

To take the position, he was forced to make some sacrifices, though. Some years before, he had obtained citizenship in Abkhazia because he had wanted to buy a house there. Now, as a Russian government official, he was forced to give up his Abkhazian citizenship. It had become really difficult to navigate through the crazy and sudden changes in Russian rules, caused by the annexation and recognition of breakout regions, even for someone like Baranov who had always toed the Kremlin line.

Anna Pavlova followed Baranov to Belgrade, which came as a big surprise to all her friends.

Of our original group in the 1990s, four of us were now living abroad, although for very different reasons. Evgeny Krutikov and Petya Akopov remained in Moscow, both working for Kremlin propaganda media, while Sveta Babayeva continued to oversee Russian information operations on the Crimean Peninsula.

We had spent less than six months in exile when other Russian journalists began fleeing the country—in many cases, en masse. The Kremlin's direct attack against independent media started in April 2021, when FSB officers came to raid editorial offices. It quickly turned into a massive campaign. Police broke into journalists' apartments, Roskomnadzor blocked media websites, and the Kremlin added first more media outlets, and then individual journalists, to its list of "foreign agents."

Those who found themselves on the Kremlin's list were required—under threat of fine and criminal prosecution—to add to their every article and video a disclaimer, in large print, saying that it had been made by a foreign agent. Journalists on that list also had to report to the authorities not only every ruble they made, but every ruble they spent, including on trivial things like toothpaste and medications. They began leaving the country in droves.

In the fall of 2021, the pressure became unbearable. It looked as if the Kremlin was deliberately pushing journalists out of the country. The journalism community, those who had left and those who remained in the country, felt a need to meet and talk about the disaster that had overtaken our profession and our lives. We all needed to get together to think about what to do next. For several frantic weeks, journalists looked for a safe place to meet up and talk. Western Europe was ruled out: not everyone could get a visa, and Europe didn't consider Russia's Sputnik COVID vaccine certificates valid for entry. We also didn't want to meet in a country where the regime was on friendly terms with the Kremlin, or where Russian agencies could play games. We finally chose the Bosnian capital, Sarajevo.

In late October, dozens of Russian journalists flew to Sarajevo, including us. It was freezing, and the city, locked in a valley along the river Miljacka, smelled of tobacco, coffee, and smoke from the fireplaces that heated many of the city's homes.

A grand classic Austro-Hungarian hotel in the city center became home for Russian journalists for a few days. In its enormous lobby with huge windows, burly Bosnian waiters in stale white shirts smelling of sweat took their time bringing tiny cups of Turkish coffee, while mustached men at tables were smoking, observing us. We felt as if we were in a film noir set just before the Great War. The street corner where the Austrian archduke Franz Ferdinand had been killed was just around the corner.

We had much to discuss, and we didn't have much time. Journalists needed to figure out how to keep working when they and some of their colleagues had already left their editorial offices in Russia and others remained in the country. What could they do about all the legal problems that came with being proclaimed a foreign agent? Which countries would take Russian journalists? There was also a question about the audience for our reporting: What if Roskomnadzor blocked all the websites? And what if social media was completely banned, including YouTube?

After a day surveying the dismal state of the profession, when night fell, we moved to a bar nearby with the intention of getting drunk. For some, including the two of us, it was an occasion to be with our friends, and we knew such an opportunity would be rare in the years to come. The Balkan way of drinking—nonstop bottles of rakia (fruit brandy)—perfectly suited the group's fatalistic mood at a time when it seemed things could hardly get worse.

And as if to prove the Balkan stereotype true, when we finally headed back to the hotel in the early hours, we bumped into a wounded local guy lying just around the corner, stabbed with a knife, his friends and policemen standing around, chatting with the wounded. The assailant's weapon was lying in a pool of blood.

Four months later, the Russian army invaded Ukraine.

CHAPTER 25

THE WAR

The night of February 24, 2022, the night of invasion, we didn't sleep. We were constantly checking the news and social media, fearing that Ukraine would collapse under the attack of the Russian army. We both have families in Moscow and also Ukraine—Irina's lives in the Odessa region on the Black Sea coast, and Andrei's is spread across several villages in Zaporizhzhia.

It was a difficult night, one of many to come, but a week later it became clear that the Russian army had been unable to capture Kyiv. Putin's initial plan of attack had collapsed.

Those first weeks felt as if our world had just flipped upside down. It looked like many in Russia supported Putin's war. Most of our friends, in Moscow and abroad, began questioning how far Putin had succeeded in corrupting Russian society. Had we reached the point of no return? Could our society ever be cured of the aggressive militarism and brutality Putin had infected it with?

We went to the protest rally in support of Ukraine in Trafalgar Square. It was full of people and Ukrainian flags. Andrei put some money in a donation box, but when a Ukrainian man in charge of the box thanked us, Andrei couldn't hold back his tears. Embarrassed that he couldn't control his emotions, he hurried away.

The world we once knew had been completely destroyed.

That was not how Petya Akopov felt. Finally, the moment he'd anticipated for so long had arrived. On the third day of the invasion, RIA Novosti published an ecstatic column he had written titled "The Advent of Russia and the Coming of the New World."[1] Its tone was triumphal. The text was written by someone who believed that Russia had already won the war. Even though lines of Russian tanks were stuck on the way to Kyiv, Petya wrote that "Russia is restoring its historical fullness, gathering the Russian world, the Russian people together—in its entirety of Great Russians, Belarusians, and Little Russians. . . . There will be no more Ukraine as anti-Russia." His joy was unrestrained. He praised Putin for taking "historical responsibility" because he had chosen "not to leave the solution of the Ukrainian question to future generations."

Petya's column went viral on social media. Many were shocked by its shameless tone, and some saw a clear parallel between his invocation of "the solution of the Ukrainian question" and the "final solution of the Jewish question," the euphemism for the mass annihilation of European Jews used by Nazi leaders during the Holocaust.

The next day, the column disappeared from the news agency website without explanation, which caused an even bigger scandal. World media, including the BBC and Sky News, ran stories about its removal.[2] Petya was now a global phenomenon.

There were various theories about why the article on "the Ukrainian question" had been taken down. Some believed that Petya had gone too far in attacking Ukraine and Ukrainians. We doubted that. Since the annexation of Crimea in 2014, Russian propagandists had indulged in all sorts of excessive insults, denying that Ukraine had the right to exist, denying that Ukrainians had their own language and constituted their own nationality. Putin himself led the way with his articles on the history of Ukraine. We thought it was more likely that because Petya's op-ed had proclaimed Russia's victory prematurely, it had become an embarrassment to the Kremlin, because the military situation was so fraught.

The war was not to be won quickly, as Putin had planned, so in Moscow, the entire intellectual and propagandist workforce was mobilized to help promote it. A week after the start of the invasion, Evgeny Krutikov launched his Telegram channel—a tool for broadcasting public messages to large audiences on a social media platform that was widely popular in Russia.

His first, rather laconic post—"Any Russian soldier who is outside Russia defends its independence. In Kabul, in Damascus, in Kyiv, in Belgrade"—implied, essentially, that a Russian soldier should be prepared to fight anywhere in the world, because everywhere he went, no matter how far it was from Russia's borders, he was just protecting the Motherland. It was a preapproval for any Russian military intervention worldwide, full stop.

Three days later, Krutikov posted his article "How the Ukrainian Army Will Be Defeated" on the Vzglyad news media website. There, he defended the Kremlin's strategic vision in Ukraine. "Some Western sources even began to question the very existence of this plan," he wrote. "Meanwhile, this plan exists, it works—and its result will be the complete military defeat of Ukraine."[3]

Like Petya, Krutikov was completely supportive of the invasion, and he was equally delusional. From then on, the two of them would work for the Kremlin war propaganda machine.

In the first weeks after the invasion, our instinctive reaction was to treat the disastrous war as professionals. That was the attitude that had always helped us to remain sane in the past while covering Russia's horrors, whether they were terrorist attacks, military conflicts, or natural disasters.

We reached out to our sources in Russia, and to our surprise, many of them agreed to keep talking to us, despite the fact that we had made our position against the war public immediately after the invasion. This was in part the result of many years building mutual trust, but it also betrayed confusion and perplexity among the military and intelligence agencies about the lack of success of the "special military operation," as the Kremlin ludicrously insisted on calling the war with Ukraine.

Our sources told us that two weeks after the invasion, Putin launched another attack, this time much closer to home, on his beloved agency, the FSB. Inside the FSB, the Kremlin secret police, there is a special department called the Fifth Service that is tasked with conducting operations in the former Soviet Republics, including Ukraine, that split from Russia in 1991. We had been writing about this particular department of the FSB since the early 2000s, when we broke the first story of its existence.

We now had sources at the Fifth Service who confirmed Putin's attack on it. They told us it was the Fifth Service that had been responsible for briefing Putin on political developments in Ukraine on the eve of the invasion. The gist of those reports was that Ukraine was essentially a failed state and would quickly collapse under the attack.

Those FSB reports had reflected a desire to please Putin. That had become something FSB generals had had to keep in mind since the annexation of Crimea, when Putin had started selective repressions against his beloved security service to remind them who was boss. But the reports also reflected a very dark vision that the FSB, as a direct successor of the Soviet KGB, had developed toward elites in former Communist countries. The Russian security services had convinced themselves that those elites were by definition prone to corruption, weak and unreliable. In Russia, such people could be kept under control only via repression; in Ukraine, they were expected to collapse and desert after the first attack.

That dark vision of human nature—shared by Putin, who had the same KGB training—not only completely disregarded the differences between Russia and Ukraine but ignored a vibrant Ukrainian society. The Soviet KGB never trusted Soviet citizens: they were unreliable, and thus needed to be kept under control. The Soviet KGB officers were trained to think that every person was driven only by base, inferior motives. When the Soviet Union was collapsing, and even the KGB generals did nothing to save it, the rank and file of the KGB saw proof that they were correct in their darkest assumptions about human nature in general and their superiors in particular.

And then those rank-and-file members became Putin's generals.

In a way, Putin and his FSB generals fell victim to the traumatic legacy of the collapsed Soviet Union, from which they learned completely the wrong lessons. And now that misbegotten legacy was killing Ukrainians and Russians alike.

Two weeks into the war, it finally dawned on Putin that he had simply been misled. Furious, he had the leadership of the Fifth Service placed under house arrest. It was a good story, and we published it on March 11. That didn't go unnoticed in Moscow, in the FSB building on Lubyanka Square.

In early June, Russian independent journalists gathered together again, this time in a small resort town in Montenegro.

In the first months of the war, Russian censors had blocked Facebook and Twitter and introduced censorship on reporting about military operations. Roskomnadzor started banning independent media outlets en masse. Hundreds of journalists urgently left the country, heading to the Baltics, to Armenia and Georgia, to Germany and Israel, to the Czech Republic and France.

We spent two days in a conference hall in a seaside hotel, talking and arguing about the best way forward or if there even was such a thing. It was another difficult conversation, for sure, yet it was not utterly depressing. Most of the media found a way to keep operating, even if journalists were on the move and facing all kinds of problems, from getting European visas to establishing bank accounts abroad. There was a great sense of collective determination: we saw that those Russians who were not brainwashed by the Kremlin still trusted the voices of the exiles. They were the only voices they came to trust. Millions of Russians watched Russian journalists in exile on YouTube every day, and that spring, the numbers of followers of Russian media on social media skyrocketed.

In the early morning of the last day of the conference, Andrei's phone started flashing. Dozens of text messages from a VTB Bank in Moscow he still had accounts with were pouring in. All of them told the same story—that his accounts were blocked.

Each account now showed an enormous deficit—the equivalent of $80,000 in different currencies. It looked like a phishing attack, until another text from Uralsib Bank arrived saying that Andrei was a suspect in a criminal investigation.

A colleague who happened to be nearby suggested we check the "wanted list" on the Russian Interior Ministry's website. Andrei typed in his name. Below the headline *Attention. Wanted!* was Andrei's photograph, taken from his passport file. He had been charged with "spreading fake news about the war," an offense punishable by up to ten years in prison.

The deficit of $80,000, or 5 million rubles, had been added to each of Andrei's accounts to freeze his assets in the country.

As a rule, before the war, almost every customer of a Russian bank had accounts in rubles—debit and credit—but also accounts in US dollars and euros, even if the last two were empty. The accounts in dollars and euros were a legacy of the turbulent 1990s, when Russian citizens learned the hard way that it was good to keep some of their savings in a currency that was more stable than the seesawing ruble. Andrei had four accounts in two banks, most of them empty except for $200 he still had in one account since before we had left the country. The authorities had added a debt of 5 million rubles to every account, so that overall Andrei suddenly "owed" the enormous sum of 40 million rubles—around $438,000 in US dollars.

To add comedic insult to financial injury, our twenty-year-old Opel was impounded. Our apartment with the rooms painted red and yellow would have been seized, too, if we hadn't already sold it.

Suddenly, it didn't feel very safe to stay in Montenegro. The beautiful mountainous country on the Adriatic Sea had a huge Russian population of all sorts, from small business owners and oligarchs to government officials and their families: Russian nationals owned 19,000 properties in Montenegro by 2022.[4] The small country had also received a huge influx of Russians after the invasion, and we guessed that among them would be people working for Moscow. But that was not our main security concern.

Our hotel was just over 300 miles from Belgrade in neighboring Serbia, a 7.5-hour drive. Serbia was known to be deeply penetrated by Russian agents. Russia's attack on Ukraine had prompted massive expulsions of Russian spies from Europe, and many of them had landed in Serbia. According to the European Union's rules, a diplomat expelled from one European country is banned for life from being posted again not only in that country, but in any other European country.

This rule could not be violated, but Serbia was not in the European Union—yet. Though it had applied in 2009, it didn't comply with EU rules in 2022, and as a result, it became the only European country to welcome expelled Russian diplomats after the start of the war.[5]

That made the Serbian capital a key Russian spy center in Central Europe. Our journalist colleagues would discover the names of FSB officers expelled from Europe resurfacing in the Russian embassy in Belgrade.[6]

Belgrade was also, of course, where Zhenya Baranov, now the head of the local Russian House, lived, along with Anna, but, understandably, we never thought of dropping by to see our old friends.

On our way back to London via Vienna, we felt nervous. There was a big question in the air: What did Andrei's new status mean? Could Russian authorities add his name to the Interpol wanted list? And if so, could Andrei be arrested at the Vienna airport and extradited to Russia?

Back in London—we made it through Vienna without issue—we turned to our contacts in Moscow for information. They obtained and sent us a copy of the criminal file. It appeared that the criminal investigation had been launched following a report by the FSB. The report was dated two days after we had published our story about the Fifth Service of the FSB in Ukraine. In the file, Irina was described as Andrei's "criminal accomplice." It proved that the FSB had started the attack.

We also learned that Putin had returned the leader of the Fifth Service to his position—a highly unusual move, reminiscent of Stalin's tactics—intending to show that there was no problem with Putin's plan in Ukraine, thus no need to punish his beloved FSB. For us, the implications of all this information were serious.

Soon, the British police paid us a visit and promised to inform us if Interpol got involved. Then several Russian human rights organizations contacted us with a more reassuring message—that Interpol headquarters had a list of people wanted by the Kremlin for political reasons, and in accordance with the organization's constitution it would not "undertake any interventions or activities of a political . . . character."

Even so, from that time on, we understood that we had to become more cautious in our travels. We also realized we needed to find a way to live as Russian outlaws, probably for years.

A few months later, the Russian Ministry of Justice added Andrei to the already very long list of foreign agents. That immediately affected the status of our books in Russia. Initially, the publisher had been forced to hide the cover with an opaque paper wrapper emblazoned with the words "FOREIGN AGENT," and to add a warning on the Russian equivalent of Amazon that the books were only for adults, as if they were some sort of porn. Apparently, Russian censors were not satisfied with such half-measures, and soon all our books disappeared from bookstore shelves entirely and became unavailable for order in Russian online bookstores.

Given the fact that we'd collected prohibited books as a hobby, the suppression of our own was a sad and ironic twist. But that was not the end of the story. Some months after the invasion started, we were contacted by readers who discovered that our book about the FSB had suddenly reappeared in some Russian online stores.

We checked the link: *The New Nobility* was indeed available, but it had a different cover. It was beautifully designed, in bright colors, but it was not the one our Russian publisher had created. It took us some effort, but finally we got a copy. The book's contents were ours—there was no alteration but for the cover—and there was no information on the book to indicate who had published it.

We realized that it was a brand-new edition, created by a mysterious group of dissenters who wanted to republish the book and make it available again for the Russian audience. Of course, we weren't getting royalties from the sales, but to us, those responsible were not pirates, but partisans, who made sure the book was on sale in defiance of the censors. We still don't know whom to thank for the beautiful new cover design!

The prowar hysteria, heavily promoted by the Kremlin media, including by Akopov and Krutikov, hit Moscow, and then a quiet panic invaded in the city's biggest corporations when an epidemic of mysterious deaths began taking out top managers of the Russian oil companies and banks, one by one.

The series of suspicious deaths started in April 2022, when a former manager at the Russian gas giant Novatek was found hanged and his wife and daughter stabbed in a villa in a resort town near Barcelona. In the months to come, the oligarchs and their managers kept falling out of windows or were just found dead with their families in their luxury homes, but one company was hit particularly hard: Lukoil, Russia's largest private oil company.

First, the body of a former manager at Lukoil was found in a basement of a cottage in a Moscow suburb, supposedly after an attempt to relieve a hangover had gone wrong.[7] A few months later, Lukoil's chairman fell from the sixth-floor window of a hospital in Moscow: the official version declared that he had "taken his life," but a press release issued by Lukoil the same day said he "passed away following a severe illness."[8] His successor died the next year at the age of sixty-six—from acute heart failure, according to an official version.[9] In March 2024, another top manager at Lukoil, its fifty-three-year-old vice president, died suddenly. There were rumors that he hanged himself in his office.[10]

Four deaths in Lukoil's leadership in two years felt like too much of a coincidence, even by Russian standards.

Lukoil had been under US sanctions since 2014 but had avoided European sanctions, although Vagit Alekperov, the company's founder and president, resigned in April 2022, after being personally sanctioned by Australia and the United Kingdom over the invasion of Ukraine.[11]

Russian oil and gas funds were the major source of funding for the Kremlin for its war in Ukraine despite the sanctions, and we wondered if that had something to do with the dramatic changes in the leadership of Russian oil companies.

Alekperov was one of the two oligarchs who had funded *Izvestia* in 2000. Vladimir Potanin, the second oligarch who had funded *Izvestia*, had become Russia's second-richest man by 2022, and he was also placed under UK sanctions after the invasion. That happened in June 2022, and US sanctions followed in December.[12]

We seriously doubted that either Alekperov or Potanin could have imagined that the support they had provided to Putin in the crucial early years of his reign would cost them so much twenty-four years later.

In the first months of the war, a significant number of prominent Russian artists, actors, and writers left the country and began speaking openly of their disgust at the war. That became a problem for Putin's minister of culture, Olga Lyubimova.

In April, she admitted this in a long interview on Russian state television. "Yes, indeed, several conductors left us, several artists left us," she said. "Some were forced, but others, I'm afraid, were not forced. Some just wanted to become famous on their social media." She suggested that just a few had left compared to the thousands of artists that had rushed to help wounded Russian soldiers in military hospitals—a line of patriotic defiance that sounded very scripted. But then something weird happened. When an interviewer asked whether there was a chance for the antiwar artists to return to Russia, Lyubimova became emotional:

> Imagine if a person abandoned his orchestra, 110 artists, turned his back on them and said goodbye, I'm flying out of here, I have business. What do you think? Even without the Ministry of Culture, how would those 110 artists react? It

is, you know, as if a husband tells his wife: you are sick, it's not fun anymore to be with you, I'm flying out! Well, when could one accept such a husband back? I don't know, I don't know.... To me, such a thing is just impossible.[13]

Was she talking about the antiwar artists, or her former husband, Baranov, who was far away, in Belgrade, with Anna?

In the summer, Lyubimova launched a full-scale offensive against dissenters, attacking those who had left Russia and the countries that hosted them.[14] She claimed that the host countries—and she meant the Baltics—had no culture, nothing comparable to the greatness of Russian culture. She set out to be insulting.

Her imperious tone was reminiscent of Krutikov's, when he'd argued that the independence movements in the Soviet Union, including in the Baltics, had been built on an ideology of Russophobia to compensate for their lack of ancient history and culture.

On September 30, in the Grand Kremlin Palace, Putin signed "accession treaties" concluding the annexation of four occupied regions in Ukraine: Luhansk, Donetsk, Kherson, and Zaporizhzhia—the region where Andrei's Ukrainian relatives lived. The Kremlin wanted the new regions, where fighting was still going on between the Russian troops and the Ukrainians, to be fully integrated and absorbed into Russia—not only politically, but also culturally. That job fell to Lyubimova's ministry.

Four days later, Lyubimova dutifully reported to Putin directly that her ministry had organized a "cultural exchange" with Luhansk and Donetsk.[15] In a month, she launched a new national project: broadcasting documentaries about the war in Ukraine in cinemas across the country.[16] It was a pure propaganda campaign, reminiscent of those once undertaken in Stalin's era.

Putin appreciated her efforts. In November, he sang Lyubimova's praises as "a woman of patriotic convictions, views, a very active young woman."[17]

The next month, the European Union added Lyubimova to its list of Russian officials sanctioned because of the invasion of Ukraine: "Under [Lyubimova's] responsibility, the [Russian Culture] Ministry has extended both financial resources and programme support to the so-called 'Donetsk People's Republic' and 'Luhansk People's Republic.'"[18]

This could hardly come as a shock to Lyubimova. Her friend Petya Akopov had been under European sanctions since June. The European Union had called him a central figure in Russian government propaganda, "responsible for, supporting or implementing actions or policies which undermine or threaten the territorial integrity, sovereignty and independence of Ukraine, or stability or security in Ukraine."[19] In July, he was sanctioned by Canada.[20]

The following February, marking the one-year anniversary of the invasion, Olga Lyubimova was placed on the US Department of Treasury's list of high-profile Russians sanctioned due to Russia's ongoing war on Ukraine.

When the invasion started, Sveta Babayeva was living in Crimea. She was about to turn fifty, which was difficult to believe, given how fit, tanned, and energetic she seemed. For three years she had been in charge of Kremlin propaganda in the annexed Crimea as head of *Russia Today*'s Crimean office in the former trade union building in Simferopol, and on the surface she was doing well. She had bought a flat in Crimea, where she lived with her husband, and her chauffeur drove her to the meetings that she loved to arrange, either in palaces built by Russian aristocrats at the Black Sea coast or in luxury hotels.

But the mild climate and sunshine of the occupied peninsula couldn't soften the bitterness of her exclusion from Moscow. The Crimean assignment would have been good enough for someone without ambitions, but she had never been such a person.

The adrenaline rush and sense of power Babayeva had once gotten through her closeness to Putin she now sought in demanding sports training. She started with rock climbing, then moved on to horseback riding. But this was not enough.

She was never afraid of physical pain: in her mid-twenties she had lost a child in childbirth, and when she soon got back to work, no one among her colleagues heard her complaining or saw her depressed. Much later, when she was running to a meeting with then president Dmitry Medvedev, she stumbled on the stairs and felt a severe pain in her leg but said nothing about it through three hours of conversation. When she finally went to see a doctor, he told her it was broken. She flew from Moscow to Washington with her leg in a cast.

Since the intensity and pace of her life in Moscow, London, and Washington was impossible to replicate in Crimea, Babayeva turned to special forces training. She had always been fascinated by the power accompanied by violence emanating from the Kremlin, so she sought out power in the most straightforward place—among special forces instructors. She crawled through snow, she shot targets and did martial arts, she climbed rocks, and she began training in knife fighting with men who were twice her size. She became a firearms instructor and took part in the selection of special forces soldiers for the crimson beret—awarded to a Russian spetsnaz soldier only after he has gone through a grueling test that includes a brutal twelve-minute sparring session with three soldiers. On her Facebook page, Babayeva posted photos of herself wearing camouflage, standing with a gun in the middle of a group of men, alongside the photos of her with Kremlin officials.

The whole performance was camouflage of a different sort: her career was becalmed. She was in a kind of limbo. Her main patron, Sergei Ivanov, couldn't help her get back, and Babayeva's contract with the Russian propaganda behemoth was soon to expire.

It seemed that she had no idea what she was going to do next. Her friends in Moscow heard her talking about starting a new career—leading a private security company, maybe—but then she said she felt too old for that.

When the invasion started, it offered a chance for desperate people.

Babayeva told her friends she wanted to go to war. She was thinking of becoming a *voenkor*—a pro-Kremlin military correspondent embedded with the troops. To her husband she admitted she had begun to think about joining the army—as a soldier, with a weapon in her hands.

In late August 2022, she texted Mikhail Kozhokin, her former editor at *Izvestia*, that she couldn't find any meaning in her life.

In October, when she texted him again, she sounded desperate and asked for advice. "You're smart . . . Not urgent. Text me (SB)."

They never had a chance to speak. Ten days later, the news broke that Sveta Babayeva was dead, killed in what was described as an accidental shooting at a Crimean shooting range.

Her death shocked the establishment in Moscow and Crimea. Condolences were sent by the Russian foreign minister, Sergei Lavrov; by the head of Crimea, Sergey Aksyonov; by Putin's spokesperson Dmitry Peskov; by the editor-in-chief of *Russia Today*, Margarita Simonyan; and by former president Medvedev, who at that moment was deputy head of the Security Council, and who called her life "an example of high professionalism, great talent, and sincere love for the Motherland."[21]

How she died was never properly reported. Some suggested she was shot by a ricochet; others that she killed herself by mistake. Her husband and her friends insisted on an investigation, and in May 2024, an arms instructor at the shooting range admitted to the court in Crimea that he was guilty of involuntary manslaughter in her death.[22]

At least she did not kill anyone in Ukraine.

Sveta Babayeva had been a key player in Putin's propaganda machine, from his advent to power to the start of the war in Ukraine. In the end it was Putin's system, built on reckless violence, that claimed her life.

EPILOGUE

In September 2023, our third autumn in exile began in London. The hopes of the previous year that the war would end soon had dissipated, replaced by an ever-present combination of anger and anxiety. The Kremlin's spy agencies, it appeared, had regrouped after the failures at the start of the invasion and turned to attacking political opposition abroad. Russian journalists in exile were exchanging news about recent poisonings, smartphone hackings, and threats.

In London, we felt relatively safer than our colleagues who had taken refuge in Georgia, Armenia, or the Baltics, but only to a degree. We started avoiding places frequented by Russians in London after we had a worrisome experience at Zima, a popular Russian restaurant in Soho. We had invited a friend of ours there and made the mistake of booking a table by providing a false name and phone number but using a real email account. We were seated at the table next to the window, and through that window we saw a group of young, bearded Chechens who had positioned themselves strategically at the entrance of the restaurant, and who watched us the entire time we were there. It seemed the booking website had been compromised.

Two constables of the counterterrorism branch within London's police department paid a visit to our apartment in Bloomsbury and told us they would check on us from then on. When Irina asked them which exiles from which countries they were watching, the answer was Iranians and Russians. That didn't sound very comforting.

Next came news from Germany, where a Russian businessman, Alexey Kozlov, had suddenly filed a lawsuit against our book publisher. Kozlov had complained about the way we had described his relationship with Russian intelligence in *The Compatriots*, our third book, and his lawyer had gone to the Hamburg district court and secured a ban on German sales of the audiobook and ebook versions. Kozlov was a scion of a prominent family of Soviet spies—his step-great-grandfather was Nahum Eitingon, who had organized Trotsky's murder in Mexico on Stalin's orders. He was very proud of his spy ancestry. In the early 2000s, he had sponsored a stipend named after another relative for graduates of the Russian intelligence academy—his great-grandfather, a head of the Soviet spy station in New York during World War II.

Kozlov had moved to Berlin, and he launched his lawsuit four years after the book's publication. We think it didn't make any sense for him as a businessman newly established in Germany to raise a complaint, so many years later, about his relations with Russian spy agencies, and we couldn't help but think that he was not acting on his own initiative. But he was suing us, and his lawyer sent Andrei a friend request on Facebook—a classic fishing expedition for information. The German lawsuit ate up our time as we prepared for court. We couldn't help but wonder how many graduates of the Russian foreign intelligence academy, recipients of Kozlov's stipend, were now stationed as Russian spies across Europe, and we became very careful about our trips to Germany. In the meantime, in Moscow, the criminal investigation against Andrei was regularly prolonged, in order to keep us feeling on edge.

On top of this personal bad news, the war left us in a state of psychological shock, recovery from which was slow. Not all our friends in Moscow felt that way. Our former chief of the department at the newspaper *Segodnya*, who had always been liberal and made a career in the media independent of the Kremlin, and who was also a talented guitarist, toured the occupied territories singing his songs to the Russian soldiers invading a neighboring country. Another, a doctor, who treated drug-addicted teenagers after he himself had recovered from alcoholism in the early 1990s, thanks to Alcoholics Anonymous, also vocally supported the war. Irina's former boyfriend, a successful lawyer, praised the Russian special forces' attack on Kyiv's airport.

And then there was Petya Akopov, whose op-ed on the Russian government news agency website in the first week of the invasion called for "the solution of the Ukrainian question."

Although we had not spoken with Petya for a decade and a half and did not really follow his writing, we thought we had a pretty good idea of his political views. But his allusion to the Nazi's final solution of the Jewish question, we thought, was too much even for him. We knew that he was very pro-Kremlin and anti-Western, but we couldn't imagine that he had become more radical than Putin. After that op-ed we began to follow his writing and saw that there was apparently nothing, including killings of civilians, that would temper his support for the war.

How could that have happened? He had grown up in an intelligent family in a friendly environment, had gotten a good education, and had married a woman he loved. His family was blessed with two daughters. How had he become so bloodthirsty?

We also kept tabs on what happened to the other people we used to drink with at Petya's apartment on Gogolevsky. Many of them chose to stay on Putin's side or overtly supported the war. The deaths of civilians in Kyiv or Odessa didn't bother them. They couldn't feel deceived or misinformed by the Kremlin's propaganda, because they were themselves part—and a willing part—of the deception. What had happened to the intelligent, well-informed, thoughtful people who used to be our friends?

The answer to that question was not obvious, and we felt that it had to be found. That was when we decided to write this book.

And, to write the book, we needed to talk to them. We had our reservations about reaching out to them. We didn't know what their reaction would be, and we didn't know how it might affect us. And we couldn't just go and sit with them. After all, we were in London, on the Kremlin's wanted list; they were in Moscow, on the opposite side of the wall.

We also understood that such a book would make sense only as a story of real people, using their real names, so we needed to tell our former friends that we were writing it.

We would try to understand them—that was the only promise we could offer. Our common past, and all we had been through together, were the only credentials we had to persuade them that we wanted to listen, not argue; to report honestly, not to attack or undermine them.

In the fall of 2023, we began reaching out to them in Moscow. For several days we'd been discussing our strategies for talking with them. We decided to begin our conversations by asking questions about the circumstances of the events of twenty years ago. We didn't want to start with a head-on collision over Putin and the war, which could end the contact abruptly.

First, Irina texted Petya Akopov.

At some level she hoped he wouldn't talk to her. She wished he would just call her a traitor and tell her to go to hell. When we'd last seen Petya in the country house he rented, in the living room lit by the Christmas tree garland, his twelve-month-old daughter was sleeping in a nursery. Now she was sixteen years old.

But Petya didn't call Irina a traitor and didn't tell her to go to hell. He texted back and enthusiastically agreed to talk. When Irina called him via Telegram, he sounded sincerely happy to hear her voice. His husky voice instantly took Irina back to Moscow, where she hadn't been for three years. His appearance hadn't changed much—the same thin, bearded face, the dark hair now a little salt and pepper.

"Petya, as you possibly know, Andrei and I moved to London," Irina started. "Now we are going to write a new book about what happened to Russian people, who are divided now not only by their views, but also by the borders. How could it have happened to us? We worked together, we spent a lot of time together, we had different ideas about politics, but it did not affect our friendship back then. Now we can't even live in one country, not to mention other things. I don't understand that. Do you agree to talk to me about all this stuff?"

During the first conversation, Petya sounded upset about our flight from Russia and was genuinely regretful that we had ceased to see each other so many years ago. In the months to come Petya and Irina talked for hours on Telegram. During their lengthy conversations, he spoke openly about his life, his career, and his interactions with the Administration of the President. He told Irina just how hard it had been for him emotionally to leave the apartment on Gogolevsky Boulevard.

We also wanted to talk to Zhenya Baranov, and Irina texted him in Belgrade. She sent him a message on Telegram almost identical to the one she had sent to Petya.

His response came almost immediately: "Hi, Irina! It's not you and me, it's you who found yourself on the other side of the border." That sounded quite aggressive, as if he was counterattacking what he took as aggression from Irina.

The rest of his reply was bureaucratic and slightly officious: "In accordance with Russian legislation, I, as a government official, should not give interviews to authors recognized as foreign agents. Sorry. [Write your book] without me. Say hi to Andrei."

Irina had nothing to add but to thank him for replying. Baranov answered, "We will always remain Russian people, and nothing can cancel the fact that we know each other. This means [your] request cannot remain unanswered." He clearly wanted to end the conversation and have the last word on a note that made him look noble, to show that he honored the old friendship by getting back to someone who had crossed over to the other side.

We also tried to reach out to Olga Lyubimova, using her private number. We received a response, purportedly from her secretariat, advising us to send a formal request to the Culture Ministry's press office.

Andrei decided to reach out to Evgeny Krutikov as well. We thought it would be better for Andrei to talk to him because they'd had a very emotional relationship, even if it had been many years ago. Besides, we knew that Krutikov was following what we were doing—and that his interest hadn't disappeared after we left Moscow. Once, in mid-January, Andrei was giving a long interview on Alexei Navalny's organization's YouTube news show from our small apartment in Bloomsbury when he saw a comment that said, "For God's sake, put some decorations on your Christmas tree, it looks pathetic." It was signed "Krutikov."

Andrei reached out to Krutikov by text and after just a short delay, he agreed to talk.

When Andrei called him on Telegram, Krutikov at once requested a video chat. Always curious, he wanted to see the circumstances of our life in exile. Andrei didn't want to show him everything and placed the camera so as to reveal as little as possible about the flat and its location. We weren't sure how close Krutikov was to the Russian security and intelligence agencies.

Once Andrei's laptop showed Krutikov on the screen, Andrei gave him a cheerful greeting. Krutikov immediately snapped, "I'm ruining my karma by talking to you, you understand that, don't you?" Andrei said he did and followed up with some questions about our time at *Izvestia*. Krutikov switched gears and began offering explanations and justifications. He sounded a bit tense and bitter, but his voice, his sardonic manner, was almost the same as ever.

Physically, Krutikov had changed a lot. He looked much older, thinner, and weaker. Andrei talked in an intentionally modest, unpretentious manner, using more words than needed to give Krutikov time to respond, which he seemed to need.

EPILOGUE

Sveta Babayeva had been killed a year earlier, and Andrei and Krutikov started talking about her and the times when they had all worked together. "At that time, humanity saw the president through the eyes of a few excited women, and one of them was Babayeva," Krutikov recalled. He remembered how, at Putin's press conference about the *Kursk* submarine in Sochi, Babayeva had stood up and given Putin advice on what kind of tie he should wear. "She sincerely believed, as they were all there, that they were making history, helping the president," he added acidly.

But he denied that there was any political agenda behind the attacks on the media and journalists in the early 2000s. According to Kruitikov, all those blows had been caused by the activities of the oligarch-owners of the media, which interfered in Kremlin business. Journalists, in his opinion, were just soldiers acting on the orders of the oligarchs. In other words, they had it coming.

His lack of sympathy for fellow reporters was astonishing. "I'm telling you again; I don't associate myself with journalism on a personal level," he said. He also attacked liberal-minded journalists of the 1990s:

> Throughout the second half of the '90s, these people considered themselves the kings of the world. They defined ideology, they believed that they ran the country—in all seriousness. And partly that was true. They controlled the audience, they considered themselves very important persons, they kicked open doors to ministers and in the Kremlin. And it seems to me that the actions of these people now [when they became opponents of the government] are determined not by the fact that they think differently, but by the fact that they suddenly lost their positions. They were everything, they were the elite, and then Putin came and deprived them of it. It was an elite, a closed caste, into which it was impossible to enter.

From the tone of his voice, it was clear that Krutikov still held a grudge that he had not been let into that "closed caste," though he'd tried hard and worked for the liberal newspaper *Segodnya*—the newspaper where we all had met in the late 1990s.

Krutikov's voice rose when he said, "What is happening now is not their fight for a happy, free Russia—it is an attempt to get back [to power]. This is stupid revenge. And that is why I hate them, although I am not an emotional person, as you remember."

But Krutikov did get emotional, and Andrei couldn't help but ask whether he thought that the access those liberal journalists used to enjoy to ministers and inside the Kremlin was now lost to the entire profession, even for those who were on the Kremlin's side. Andrei tried to go with what Krutikov cared most about: status and place in the hierarchy.

"There is a certain truth in your words," Krutikov responded. He admitted to the existence of "a filter in the form of the Presidential Administration," but he blamed the liberals of the 1990s for Putin's decision to degrade the role of journalists in the 2000s and 2010s and make them obedient servants of the propaganda machine.

In the months to come, Krutikov and Andrei spoke for hours, and Krutikov seemed to enjoy those conversations. It was not that easy for Andrei. On the screen he saw his old friend, but that same Krutikov kept writing war propaganda praising Russian troops fighting in Ukraine.

Krutikov admitted that the country was experiencing a significant level of repression. He continued to insist that all the assassinations and attacks on liberal politicians and journalists before 2022 were "isolated cases," and that before the war there had been no "big tank crushing everyone, no totalitarian machine [of repression]." But he did see that tank crushing people's lives after 2022.

He also admitted that Russian security and intelligence services had become more Stalin-like in their methods.

EPILOGUE

Petya and Irina talked regularly. Winter came and almost went when on February 16, 2024, the Russian prison service admitted to the sudden death of Alexei Navalny, Putin's main political opponent, who had been in jail since 2021.

It came as a total shock. Navalny, the same age as us, always optimistic and cheerful, had been killed by an aging dictator whose regime was claiming more and more lives—in Russia and abroad.

Navalny's supporters had no doubts Navalny had been killed. Neither did we. The day of his death, we posted on our Agentura Telegram channel:

> Of course, Navalny's death is a murder committed under aggravating circumstances.
>
> Every time Putin's opponent—a journalist, politician, activist—is killed, the Kremlin responds with the same thing: the victim was so insignificant that Putin "didn't need to do it."
>
> In fact, Putin's more than twenty years in power have shown that political murders have a very practical meaning for Putin—and each time, not only the victim, but also the method of murder, is carefully thought out.
>
> Slowly killing Navalny, taking him through all the circles of hell of the Russian prison system, ultimately sending him to the Arctic Circle, made complete practical sense: The memory of Stalin's Gulag is embedded in Russian genes, and what was done to Navalny after his return [to Russia in January 2021, after his treatment in Germany from poisoning] is meant to awaken precisely those memories.

A month later, Irina spoke to Petya again. She wanted him to explain why he had become so aggressive since 2011–2012. Back then he had justified his aggression by fear of a bloody revolution. But did he really believe that? she asked.

"Yes," Petya confirmed. "I opposed all those rallies because their goal was to provoke the authorities into bloodshed."

"The protesters were not armed, no one fought, there were no military or security forces on their side," Irina countered. "We didn't beat anyone there; it was the police who beat us all the time!"

"Right," Petya said. "Navalny counted on that brutality of the [police] dispersal of protest rallies, with beatings, so that it would result in repressions. I saw the whole picture, everything exactly in such a way as to lead all these demonstrations, that there would be dispersal [by police forces], blood, this would cause indignation of the people, the people would take to the streets and storm the Kremlin. [This was the plan] which, in principle, he himself [Navalny] did not particularly hide."

It was paranoid, circular reasoning: the protests were so reasonable and responsible because that way they would provoke unreasonable and irresponsible violence, which would lead to revolution.

The hardest question for Irina was why he had personally and publicly placed us on his "enemies list." She believed personal attacks between us were off limits, despite the differences in our views.

It turned out that Petya didn't remember doing so. Apparently, he'd just blocked that episode in his memory. But he saw no need to apologize.

Petya admitted that he had praised the blocking of Ej.ru, where his friend Anna Pavlova had worked. He had approved of the ban on liberal media because he himself had been banned from writing for the mainstream media in the 1990s. "The 1990s I spent under liberal censorship!" he exclaimed.

Irina reminded him that he had worked for a mainstream newspaper in the 1990s and that there were several other nationalist papers in Moscow he could have worked for that had not been banned by the authorities. "Yes, but there were very few people who worked there!" he responded. There was nothing that reflected his views on television, nothing in the big media, Petya claimed bitterly. For him, the liberal domination of the media of the 1990s was high on his personal list of grievances against liberals. He sounded a lot like Krutikov.

Finally, Irina reminded Petya of his 2011 column calling for Navalny to be killed: "You wrote then that he should be eliminated."

"Yes, yes. Because sometimes the blood of one person saves hundreds of thousands of people later."

"And now they've killed him."

"I don't think he was killed."

"Okay, they tortured him to death," said Irina.

"The fact that they undermined his health in prison—yes, I agree. But the fact that this death is accidental in this understanding of the word—a blood clot just came off, this could happen to anyone." Petya still wouldn't admit the assassination.

"But there was a chain of events—poisoning, imprisonment, then terrible conditions in jail, don't you think?"

"He chose to go to jail by himself, because his return was an attempt to put before the authorities the choice: either you don't touch me and close the criminal investigation, or you imprison me. It was recklessness, and by and large it was a gamble. He played all-in; apparently, he was that confident in his charisma."

It was the same paranoid logic he used to justify the police violence during the protests—Navalny provoked the Kremlin to imprison and kill him because he returned to Moscow.

"And how do you feel now—that's it, Navalny is gone?" Irina asked.

"And what is it to me? For me he was not interesting after 2014. It didn't matter. He was dangerous only at the time of 2011, 2013; that's when he was dangerous for the country. Not for Putin, but for the country. After that, after Crimea, it was finished. He could try to harm Putin, bite, expose him, but there was no longer any chance of causing any kind of mess. I think he would have been swapped in a year, or year and a half, if he agreed."

Petya kept talking:

But now I don't have any feelings for him. . . . This whole story with his poisoning in recent years, I perceived it as some sort of farce on both sides. When I worked at Vzglyad, they [the Administration of the President] issued all sorts of instructions—whether to attack him or not. I never particularly approved of that, because I believed that one should simply ignore him. . . . After 2014, I believed that he should simply be ignored. Let anyone write, but the authorities and the progovernment media should have ignored him. . . . But I didn't determine the policy.

And I always had this attitude, I always told them: Why are you inflating all this, refuting it [Navalny's investigations of Kremlin corruption]? It's all unnecessary. He is stubborn, he has a goal, he is going toward it, and any game with him in the propaganda field is doomed to failure. Yes, of course, he was a stubborn guy, yes.

Petya displayed astonishing sangfroid, and he sounded brutal. Like Krutikov, he appeared to just accept that zero tolerance of any opposition, coupled with extreme violence, had become commonplace in Putin's Russia. Many generations of Russians had lived as if they were the dwellers of a tiny village clinging to the cliff on the shores of the mighty ocean in the Middle Ages—a victim of storms and hurricanes one could only accept, but never challenge. Now Putin just turned those hurricanes into the perfect storm.

Akopov, Baranov, Krutikov, students of Russian history by training, all of them perfectly understood that. Just like those villagers, they firmly believed nothing could be done about the reason for that storm—the country was doomed to be run by a dictator, in one form or another. The only difference one could make was to choose whether to stay outside the regime—doomed to be a loser, a victim of inevitable repression—or try to stay inside and play a role. And all of them, ever ambitious, chose to stay in and play.

EPILOGUE

During the first year of the war, we forbade ourselves from feeling sad about our own situation or thinking about our chances of ever getting back to Moscow. The war, the sufferings of the Ukrainians, made that seem self-indulgent. Now, after three years of living as émigrés, it is clear that some things are irreversible: Andrei's grandparents both died after we left, and we could not be there to say farewell. That can never be undone.

The wall between Russia and the rest of the world became a very poignant, real thing in the spring of 2024, when Andrei's father's trial finally started. On July 22, Alexey Soldatov, terminally ill and seventy-two years old, having spent much of his life building Russia's internet, essentially to connect the country with the world, was sentenced to two years in a labor colony on charges of "abuse of power" in an organization where he had no position. Given his health, two years in Russian prison means an almost certain death sentence.

The last time Andrei and his dad spoke was the night before the verdict, mostly about Alexey's new interest in AI. He also told Andrei a story of a meeting with some top Kremlin figures years back when they were all talking about the need to remove "negative things" from the internet, and how he raised his hand and suggested building something good on the internet instead. He didn't find a lot of support.

The last time we saw Andrei's father was in the summer of 2020, days before we left Moscow. When he was imprisoned, all contact with him was severed: Andrei couldn't call him and couldn't send him a letter, being on the Russian wanted list himself. The man who constructed Russia's portal to the global world was sealed away from all that he loved. It didn't require "an opinion" to work out what it meant for Russia.

The Russian state, vindictive and increasingly violent, threw him in jail, a perfect illustration of how Russia treats the people who helped contribute to the modernization and globalization of the country.

EPILOGUE

The war didn't get Putin the victory he wanted. The historical moment for turning Russia into a modern combination of the Russian empire and the Soviet Union never happened.

But the war did lead to a historical change. It resulted in the isolation of the country. This isolation is not something abstract. It is very real, with tangible results, which all of us who were once friends in Moscow felt. Petya and Lyubimova couldn't travel to the West because they were under sanctions; Baranov is stuck in Serbia; Krutikov appeared to have given up any hope of visiting his beloved England; and we, in London, living under police protection, don't know when we will be able to come home to Moscow.

The wall between us and the isolation it caused has already deeply affected everyone—not just us and our friends but the entire society. Part of it is about access to all sorts of consumer goods. BMWs and Volkswagens are being replaced with Chinese cars on the streets of Moscow, and Zara and other global brands are gone from the city's shopping malls. Moscow itself also changed. Jean-Jacques on Nikitsky, the last remaining place we used to go to see like-minded people, went through a complete renovation in November 2023. The team and the design both changed: the red walls were painted white, as if to whitewash all that had happened within those walls over twenty years.

But it's not only about consumerism. It's also about cultural exchange with Europe and the United States, which has become almost impossible for ordinary Russians. Muscovites can't expect art exhibitions from Paris or New York to come to the city anytime soon; they'll have no chance to see works by Andy Warhol or Louise Bourgeois. Taylor Swift is not performing for the Russians; there's no *Vogue* or *Elle* in Russian anymore, and there were no Russian athletes at the Paris 2024 Olympics.

The war established new rules for Russian society. Those rules consist of the acceptance of unrestrained and arbitrary violence from the state—"a big tank crushing everyone," to use Krutikov's expression—and accepting the loss of basic freedoms—of speech, of association, and of the right to have a different opinion.

The new restrictions, constantly updated and expanded, are understood very clearly by those inside but are getting more incomprehensible to outsiders. And that is separating the country from neighboring Europe more definitively than the war.

Russia has experienced that division before in its history. The Soviet Union was once an isolated island surrounded by a barbed wire fence. But unlike Soviet citizens, who'd been taught over decades to live in the closed box, with most of the population never traveling abroad or seeing any foreigner, our generation, on both sides of the ideological divide, knows exactly what we lost.

Our friends in Moscow felt very emotional about it.

Petya wrote after the annexation of Crimea that he was happy about the country turning away from the West. But, he told Irina, "when I wrote that, I didn't call for Russia to build a fortress and fence it off. I wrote about the perception of our elites, that they were part of a global club of elites. This was what I didn't like. And the fact that things would come to a complete break, as now, is just the course of history."

Irina reminded him that he had traveled to Paris and to Spain and had liked it there. "I liked the culture and didn't like the Western orientation. And I also like China and India. And I do like the Middle East. Yes, of course, there are French museums and English ones, but I did not like the orientation of the elite toward the West. For me there is no contradiction here."

"But didn't you travel to China with your family?"

"I did travel to China. But the girls, they like Europe. Marina doesn't like China."

"But Petya, we don't have any cultural ties with China. We don't know anything about it. We know European literature, music, movies. But with Chinese—no one knows anything. And what about your children?"

"They know K-pop, they know the TV series—*Squid Game*—they know manga."

"Petya, but manga is Japanese, and K-pop and *Squid Game* are from South Korea."

"Of course, we know the East and the Arab world not so well. We've been closely tied to the West over three centuries. And this is now such a historical moment. . . . My view of the history of Russia is that during the time of Peter the Great we took too big a step toward Europe, we got too carried away into European affairs—through marriages, through wars."

Wasn't he a bit angry that his daughters and wife couldn't go to Paris? Irina wondered.

"Why can't they? They can. They were already there!" Petya exclaimed, suddenly getting emotional. "I took them to Paris and Rome, and we managed to visit Vienna and Budapest; we just didn't have time to see Prague. Besides, I don't think that such a conflict will last thirty years. By the end of the 2020s, I think by 2030, it will come to a certain resolution. There will be no friendship, but contacts will be resumed. Tourist ones at least. But the world is so diverse, you can see Latin America and the Arab world."

Krutikov, apparently, also felt divided about the isolation. On the one hand he denied it: "Maybe this isolation is visible from London, but from the center of Moscow I don't see any isolation." But when Andrei asked him about the breakup with Europe, Krutikov went into more detail:

> We can't escape European culture, simply by the fact that we exist. You will always have a cultural gap with an Indian, but you can still come to an agreement with a European. . . . I agree with you that there is a certain group, numerous, that has already been integrated into European structures. For whom a trip to Europe or life in Europe was part of their existence; my first wife, the mother of my son, lives in Nice, and for a long time. They bought an apartment in the 1990s. And they live there and are fully integrated.

But there are people who cannot integrate.... For example, I've been to a lot of places, but I'm not integrated in a foreign culture. I can understand foreign culture, I can even think like some European peoples, but to consider it to be my own... it's a little difficult for me.

Most of our friends in Moscow had very close and emotional relations with Europe—Baranov, happy that people drank to his health in Paris and Jerusalem when his son was born; Petya, who loved European culture and whose wife adored Paris; Krutikov, whose former wife lived in Nice. And yet they insisted that they hated the West, and they disparaged European values. We wondered if that closeness to Europe was what made them so emotional, and angry, for not being let into Europe, for real, on their conditions.

In response, they helped Putin isolate the country.

ACKNOWLEDGMENTS

Writing this book proved to be a very emotional journey for us. At times we felt happy to relive some of the best moments of our life in Moscow in the 2000s; at other times, we felt sad and very angry—at our friends, and about what happened to them and to our country.

Often, we felt very uncomfortable—as reporters, we had been trained to stay out of the story, but this one is a special kind of story, one in which we are an integral part. This is also the first book we wrote in exile—with no physical access to the places in Russia where the story unfolded. Sources' safety is always a priority for journalists, but with this book, it became paramount. For those who remain in Russia, we are very dangerous people to be in touch with: wanted criminals, foreign agents—in other words, troublemakers.

This is why, unlike in our previous books, in this one those who cannot be named now include not only our contacts in the security services and in government agencies, but some of our friends. You know who you are, and you know how grateful we are to you.

We would like to thank our friends beyond Russia's borders—Marina Latysheva, who has always been supportive of us, along with Lev Danilkin, Grisha and Dina, and Alexey and Alla Akradyevna, for making our lives a bit better.

We would also like to thank Alina Polyakova and Geysha González, at the Center for European Policy Analysis (CEPA) in Washington, for their unwavering support. We are indebted as well

ACKNOWLEDGMENTS

to Daniela Richterová, Michael Goodman, and David Gioe at King's Centre for the Study of Intelligence in London for taking us on board and giving us a place to write. Guys, you've been just amazing. In Vienna, Ivan Krastev, Dessy Gavrilova, and Clemena Antonova have been always supportive of our ideas.

We are very grateful to Lucy Ash and John Kampfner for their friendship, and for the blankets they brought us on the first day we came to the apartment in London. Fiona and Laurie Bristow gave us something incredible—they made us feel at home in Britain. Luke Harding has been the friend we could always count on all those years, first in Moscow, now in London.

This book would have been impossible without Clive Priddle at PublicAffairs, who always supported our ideas, from our first book proposal in 2009. Clive, we wish you the best of luck in your new endeavor, wherever it takes you! We are also immensely grateful to Lara Heimert for believing in the project and making the transition from Clive as smooth as possible, and to Lisa Kaufman, our editor, who has now worked on two of our books. Your help and advice have been priceless.

And, as always, we thank Robert Guinsler at Sterling Lord Literistic for being our agent, and most importantly, our friend, for more than sixteen years.

NOTES

CHAPTER 1: WELCOME TO *IZVESTIA*

1. "Vagit Alekperov," *Forbes*, accessed September 2, 2024, www.forbes.com/profile/vagit-alekperov.

2. Tatyana Plotnikova and Oksana Tyrtychnaya, "Akcioneri Izvestiy ishut zolotuyu aktciyu" (*Izvestia*'s shareholders are searching for a golden share), *Kommersant*, June 5, 1997, www.kommersant.ru/doc/178878.

3. Dmitry Pavlov, "Vzyali Vladimira Gusinskogo" (Gusinsky is caught), *Kommersant*, June 13, 2000, www.kommersant.ru/doc/17059.

4. Viktor Shenderovich and Alexander Arkhandelsky, "Zhit v aktsionernom obshestve i bit svobodnym ot nego" (To live in a joint-stock company and be free of it), *Izvestia*, July 21, 2000. The July 29 issue has the second part of the conversation.

CHAPTER 2: THE APARTMENT ON GOGOLEVSKY BOULEVARD

1. Vladimir Gelman, "Russia's Communists: The Paper Tigers of the Opposition," Open Democracy, November 7, 2011, www.opendemocracy.net/en/odr/russias-communists-paper-tigers-of-opposition.

2. Kremlin, "Interview gazete *Izvestia*" (Interview to *Izvestia*), July 14, 2000, http://kremlin.ru/events/president/transcripts/24171.

CHAPTER 3: RING OF SPIES

1. "Steven Aftergood," Federation of American Scientists, accessed September 3, 2024, https://fas.org/expert/steven-aftergood; Steven Aftergood, "Project on Government Secrecy (1991–2021)," Federation of American Scientists, February 12, 2014, https://fas.org/initiative/government-secrecy.

2. "Spooks—Shortwave Spy Numbers Stations," list subscriber page, accessed September 3, 2024, http://mailman.qth.net/mailman/listinfo/spooks. Juvenal posed this question in "Satire VI," written in the late first or early second century AD.

3. Andrei Soldatov, "Viktor Zakharov: Toptatsya na meste pozvoleno ne budet" (Viktor Zakharov: Standing by will not be allowed), *Izvestia*, August 3, 2000, accessed on the website of the FSB, www.fsb.ru/fsb/smi/interview/single.htm%21id%3D10342786%40fsbSmi.html.

CHAPTER 6: LANGUISHING IN LIMBO

1. "A Web Site That Came in from the Cold to Unveil Russian Secrets," *New York Times*, December 14, 2000, www.nytimes.com/2000/12/14/technology/a-web-site-that-came-in-from-the-cold-to-unveil-russian-secrets.html.

CHAPTER 7: PLAYING WITH THE SPIES

1. Yuri Borodin, "Vasily K," *Ogonyok*, no. 52 (January 2001).

2. Harry Schwartz, "High Soviet Aid Ousted by Party," *New York Times*, September 18, 1954, www.nytimes.com/1954/09/18/archives/high-soviet-aide-ousted-by-party-a-d-krutikov-once-a-deputy-premier.html.

3. CIA, *Central Intelligence Bulletin*, September 21, 1954, archived in the CIA Historical Collections at www.cia.gov/readingroom/document/cia-rdp79t00975a001700320001-7.

4. Vash Tainy Sovetnik, "V ottepel lager byl pochti sanatoriem" (During the thaw the camp was almost a sanatorium), June 30, 2008.

5. Kristie Macrakis, Thomas Wegener Friis, and Helmut Müller-Enbergs, eds., *East German Foreign Intelligence: Myth, Reality and Controversy* (London: Routledge, 2010).

6. Nigel West, *Historical Dictionary of Cold War Counterintelligence* (Lanham, MD: Scarecrow Press, 2007), 186–187 (in this book, Felix Krutikov is mistakenly identified as Vladimir Krutikov).

7. "Kenneth Cohen," Le Plan Sussex 1944, accessed September 4, 2024, www.plan-sussex-1944.net/anglais/biography/cohen.htm.

8. Keith Jeffery, *MI6: The History of the Secret Intelligence Service, 1909–1949* (London: Bloomsbury, 2010), 632.

CHAPTER 9: NEW BEGINNINGS

1. Bill Keller, "Home from Afghanistan: Russia's Divisive War," *New York Times*, February 14, 1988, www.nytimes.com/1988/02/14/magazine/home-from-afghanistan-russia-s-divisive-war.html.

2. Andrei Soldatov, "Maskirovka" (Camouflage), *Versia*, May 27, 2022, available at Agentura, https://archive.agentura.ru/dossier/russia/people/soldatov/maskirovka.

3. Elena Rykovtseva, "Nikita Mikhalkov: Geroy truda i rab lubvi" (Nikita Mikhalkov: A hero of labor and a slave of love), Radio Svoboda, October 22, 2020, www.svoboda.org/a/30906878.html.

NOTES

4. Oliver Burkeman, "'Russian Mafia Kingpin' Accused of Fixing Olympic Skating Result," *Guardian*, August 1, 2002, www.theguardian.com/world/2002/aug/01/russia.sport.

CHAPTER 10: COMRADES IN ARMS

1. Robert Coalson, "Russian Town Marks 10th Anniversary of Terrorist Raid," Radio Liberty, June 14, 2005, www.rferl.org/a/1059256.html.

2. Giulietto Chiesa, "Da Mosca due giornalisti testimoni dell'attacco: 'La versione ufficiale non corrisponde ai fatti.' L'attacco deciso prima dell'esecuzione degli ostaggi" (From Moscow two journalists testify about the attack: 'The official version doesn't correspond with the facts.' The decision to storm was made before the execution of hostages), *La Stampa*, October 28, 2002.

3. Civic Initiative, "Nord-Ost, Neokonchennoe Rassledovanie" (Nord-Ost, an Unfinished Investigation), available on Pandia, accessed October 8, 2024, https://pandiaonline.ru/text/77/160/10645-6.php.

CHAPTER 11: BESLAN

1. Web archive of *Izvestia*, 2011, https://web.archive.org/web/20131015160518/http://izvestia.ru/news/292578.

2. Ksenia Solyanskaya, "Kostin za Govoruna" (Kostin for Govorun), Gazeta.ru, September 12, 2011, www.gazeta.ru/politics/2011/09/12_a_3764905.shtml; "Svyato mesto" (Sacred place), Kasparov.ru, September 13, 2011, www.kasparov.ru/material.php?id=4E6F9D96D53C7.

3. See the copy on our Agentura website, https://archive.agentura.ru/dossier/russia/ideology.

4. Putin's speech, September 4, 2004, translation on the Kremlin website, http://en.kremlin.ru/events/president/news/31681.

5. Olga Shkurenko, "Razoblachitelnoe Televidenie" (Revelatory television), *Kommersant-Vlast*, July 12, 2010, www.kommersant.ru/doc/1408632.

6. Arina Borodina, "Govorit, chto NTV sposobno byt oppositsionnim, prosto smeshno" (To say that NTV could be in opposition is absurd), *Kommersant-Vlast*, October 25, 2004, www.kommersant.ru/doc/519015.

CHAPTER 13: BARANOV ON THE EDGE

1. "Religious Belief and National Belonging in Central and Eastern Europe," Pew Research Center, May 10, 2017, www.pewresearch.org/religion/2017/05/10/religious-belief-and-national-belonging-in-central-and-eastern-europe.

2. Konstantin Simonov, "Kill Him!," July 1942, online at RuVerses, https://ruverses.com/konstantin-simonov/kill-him.

3. Olga Knyshevskaya, "Russkaya Pravoslavnaya Tserkov v godi voini" (Russian Orthodox Church during the war), *Zhivaya Istoria*, December 6, 2017, https://

lhistory.ru/statyi/russkaya-pravoslavnaya-cerkov-v-gody-velikoj-otechestvennoj-vojny.

4. Anna Danilova, "Olga Lyubimova: Zhizn i smert Pravoslavnogo TV" (Olga Lyubimova: Life and death of the Orthodox TV), Pravmir, February 24, 2011, www.pravmir.ru/olga-lyubimova.

5. Danilova, "Olga Lyubimova."

6. "Nikita Mikhalkov peredal Aleksiyu II fragment ikonostasa pokhodnoy cerkvi XVIII veka" (Nikita Mikhalkov gave Alexy II a fragment of the iconostasis of a field church, 18th century), Newsru.com, December 21, 2017, www.newsru.com/religy/21dec2001/patr_cercov.html.

7. Baranov's story on the referendum in Montenegro ran on Channel One, May 21, 2006, www.1tv.ru/news/2006-05-21/221281-zakanchivaetsya_referendum_o_statuse_chernogorii.

CHAPTER 14: THE ARRANGEMENT

1. "V. Putin: Ubistvo Politkovskoy napravleno protiv deystvuyushey vlasti" (V. Putin: Assassination of Politkovskaya directed against the authorities), RBC, October 10, 2006, www.rbc.ru/politics/10/10/2006/5703bcd09a7947afa08cadae.

2. "Putin Criticized over Journalist Remarks," Al Jazeera, October 11, 2006, www.aljazeera.com/news/2006/10/11/putin-criticised-over-journalist-remarks.

CHAPTER 15: TO THE STREETS

1. "Samie massovie aktsii protesta v Moskve s 1990 goda" (Most massive protest rallies in Moscow since 1990), *Kommersant*, December 11, 2011, www.kommersant.ru/doc/1836086.

2. "11 Marta 1991 proizoshel, vozmozhno, samy massovy oppositsionny miting v istorii Rossii" (On March 11, 1991, probably the most massive opposition protest rally in Russian history took place), Meduza, March 10, 2021, https://meduza.io/feature/2021/03/10/10-marta-1991-goda-proshel-vozmozhno-samyy-massovyy-oppozitsionnyy-miting-v-istorii-rossii.

3. "Chem zapomnilsa Yegor Gaidar" (How Yegor Gaidar is remembered), *Kommersant*, December 17, 2009, www.kommersant.ru/doc/1293944.

4. Pavel Danilin, "Nastoyashee predatelstvo" (A real treason), Vzglyad, April 11, 2007, https://vz.ru/columns/2007/4/11/76801.html.

5. "V Moskve proidet neskolko ulichnikh aktsiy" (There will be several street protest actions in Moscow), Vzglyad, April 14, 2007, https://vz.ru/news/2007/4/14/77350.html.

6. His name was Naoya Sugio. See "Rabotodatel izbitogo na Marche Nesoglasnykh yaponskogo zhurnalista zayavil protest MIDu" (An employer of a beaten-up Japanese journalist filed a protest to the Foreign Ministry), Grani.ru, April 17, 2007, https://graniru.org/Society/m.120847.html.

NOTES

CHAPTER 16: THE GAME OF SUCCESSION

1. "Zamistitelem glavi Minsvyazi stal osnovolopozhnik Runeta" (A founder of the Runet became a deputy head of the Ministry of Communications), *Rossiyskaya Gazeta*, July 2, 2008, https://rg.ru/2008/07/02/naznacheniya-anons.html.

2. Svetlana Babayeva, "Svoboda ot morali, Chto cenit sovremennaya Rossia" (Freedom from morality, what contemporary Russia values), Rossia v globalnoy politike, August 2007, https://globalaffairs.ru/articles/svoboda-ot-morali-chto-czenit-sovremennaya-rossiya.

3. A report from the news conference, RIA Novosti, August 5, 2008, https://ria.ru/20080805/150108956.html.

4. "Yuzhnaya Osetia mojet nachat relsovuyu voinu" (South Ossetia could start a rail war), Regnum, August 5, 2008, https://regnum.ru/news/1036622.

CHAPTER 17: RETURN OF THE EMPIRE

1. Kimberly St. Julian-Varnon, "Navalny's Future Russia Did Not Include Everyone," *New Lines Magazine*, March 1, 2024, https://newlinesmag.com/spotlight/navalnys-future-russia-did-not-include-everyone.

2. "V Peterburge vyshla kniga Nikolaya i Mariny Svadindze o Medvedeve" (A book of Nikolai and Marina Svanidze about Medvedev published in St. Petersburg), Leninzdat, August 21, 2008, https://lenizdat.ru/articles/1065817.

3. Indigo, accessed on October 8, 2024, https://indigo-studio.ru/#/showreel.

4. "Georgia: Russian Cluster Bombs Kill Civilians," Human Rights Watch, August 15, 2008, www.hrw.org/news/2008/08/15/georgia-russian-cluster-bombs-kill-civilians.

5. Alexei Levinson, "Putin May Have High Ratings—but Russians Are Terrified Too," *Guardian*, May 9, 2022, www.theguardian.com/commentisfree/2022/may/09/putin-may-have-high-ratings-but-russians-are-terrified-too.

CHAPTER 18: THE URINALS IN OSTANKINO

1. Andrei Soldatov and Irina Borogan, "Chto znaet podpolkovnik" (What the lieutenant colonel knows), *Novaya Gazeta*, October 6, 2008, https://novayagazeta.ru/articles/2008/10/06/36345-chto-znaet-podpolkovnik.

2. Soldatov and Borogan, "Chto znaet podpolkovnik."

3. "V poryadke prokurorskoko nadzora" (In the limits of the prosecutor's oversight), *Kommersant*, February 23, 2009, www.kommersant.ru/doc/1122353.

4. Interview of Medvedev to *Novaya Gazeta*, April 15, 2009, https://novayagazeta.ru/articles/2009/04/15/43159-deklaratsiya-medvedeva-god-2009.

5. Interview of Sergei Ivanov to *Vesti*, May 18, 2010, accessed on Smotrim.ru, https://smotrim.ru/article/2069236.

6. "The Political Skirmish Behind the 'Moskovskie Novosti' Newspaper: An Insider's View," August 9, 2006. The cable was published as part of the US

NOTES

State Department cables leaked by WikiLeaks, https://wikileaks.org/plusd/cables/06MOSCOW8507_a.html.

7. "Medvedev: Managing a Foreign Policy Novice," February 5, 2008, WikiLeaks, https://wikileaks.org/plusd/cables/08MOSCOW288_a.html.

8. Andrew Clark, "Dmitry Medvedev Picks Silicon Valley's Brains," *Guardian*, June 23, 2010, www.theguardian.com/business/2010/jun/23/dmitry-medvedev-silicon-valley-visit.

9. Andrew Clark, "Anna Chapman's Call to Father Led to FBI Spy Arrests," *Guardian*, July 12, 2010, www.theguardian.com/world/2010/jul/12/anna-chapman-call-father-fbi-spy-arrests.

10. "Suburban Spies from Russia," WBUR, June 30, 2010, www.wbur.org/onpoint/2010/06/30/spies-russia.

11. Baranov's story about the spy scandal on Channel One, July 11, 2010, www.1tv.ru/news/2010-07-11/140471-razvyazka_shpionskogo_skandala_mezhdu_rossiey_i_ssha_neizvestnye_podrobnosti_nashumevshego_dela.

12. Baranov's story, Channel One, July 11, 2010.

13. "Biden Tells Jay Leno US Got Good Deal in Spy Swap," NBC, July 10, 2010, accessed on Daily Motion, www.dailymotion.com/video/xdzh3t.

14. Gordon Corera, *Russians Among Us: Sleeper Cells, Ghost Stories, and the Hunt for Putin's Spies* (New York: William Morrow, 2020).

15. The post itself was deleted, but extracts are available elsewhere. See "Radi Medvedeva v Ostankino opustili pissuari" (For Medvedev Ostankino lowered the urinals), News2, December 21, 2010, www.news2.ru/story/286022; "Live: Pervy Kanal dlya Medvedeva opustil pissuari na 10 sm" (Live: Channel One lowered the urinals for Medvedev by 10 cm), Obozrevatel, December 23, 2010, www.obozrevatel.com/news/2010/12/22/411582.htm; "Pissuari opustili" (The urinals lowered), Media Port, December 21, 2010, https://mediaport.ua/pissuaryi_opustili.

CHAPTER 19: LOSING ONE'S SOUL

1. Petr Akopov's LiveJournal page, https://petr-akopov.livejournal.com/3063.html.

2. Archive of Olga Lyubimova's LiveJournal page, December 21, 2010, http://web.archive.org/web/20190118203549/http://kropalik.livejournal.com. The manifesto was cited in full by Alexey Navalny on January 22, 2020, on his Telegram channel, https://t.me/navalny/1596; see also "Navalny pripomnil ministru Lyibimovoy ee postydny manifest" [Navalny reminded Minister Lyubimova of her shameful manifesto], January 22, 2020, Rusmonitor, https://rusmonitor.com/navalnyj-pripomnil-novomu-ministru-lyubimovoj-eyo-postydnyj-manifest.html.

3. Baranov's story about bin Laden on Channel One, May 15, 2011, www.1tv.ru/news/2011-05-15/121847-chto_sluchilos_s_ben_ladenom_vse_versii_likvidatsii_terrorista_nomer_odin.

NOTES

4. The news about the firing of the RIA Novosti journalist for the antigay post, Newsru.com, June 30, 2011, www.newsru.com/russia/30jun2011/troitsky.html.

5. Akopov's LiveJournal page, June 30, 2011, https://petr-akopov.livejournal.com/?skip=190.

6. Akopov's LiveJournal page, June 29, 2011, https://petr-akopov.livejournal.com/18025.html.

7. Olga Tanas, "*Izvestia* poteryali redactsiu" (*Izvestia* lost its office), Gazeta.ru, June 6, 2011, www.gazeta.ru/business/2011/06/06/3654621.shtml.

8. Akopov's LiveJournal page, November 26, 2011, https://petr-akopov.livejournal.com/?skip=160.

9. Akopov's Facebook post, November 24, 2011, www.facebook.com/pakopov/posts/pfbid02dW21kWwcogSFYAGHcToChr64Kqh72rxfkvMHLyqn4zisX2TMxu6XtcMcMLHwUS3pl.

10. Akopov's Facebook post, December 24, 2011, www.facebook.com/pakopov/posts/pfbid0g4ysvwfGhDsUNqbWBwGtJP5ViLBW5gMXTeRnfzkT8agubQjKGe49GEj9AnX29vGKl.

11. Akopov's Facebook post, December 24, 2011.

CHAPTER 20: THE END OF OLD TIMES

1. "An Uncivil Approach to Civil Society: Continuing State Curbs on Independent NGOs and Activists in Russia," Human Rights Watch, June 17, 2009, www.hrw.org/report/2009/06/17/uncivil-approach-civil-society/continuing-state-curbs-independent-ngos-and.

2. Petr Akopov's LiveJournal page, January 19, 2012, https://petr-akopov.livejournal.com/43978.html.

3. Andrei Soldatov and Irina Borogan, *The New Nobility: The Restoration of Russia's Security State and the Enduring Legacy of the KGB* (New York: PublicAffairs, 2010).

4. Akopov's LiveJournal page, January 19, 2012, https://petr-akopov.livejournal.com/44228.html.

5. Natalya Zotova, "Bely gorod razognali" (White town dispersed), *Novaya Gazeta*, May 7, 2012, https://novayagazeta.ru/articles/2012/05/07/49582-171-belyy-gorod-187-razognali-pomahat-kortezhu-putina-belymi-lentami-grazhdanam-ne-udalos.

CHAPTER 21: DREAMS OF RUSSIA

1. Shaun Walker, "Russia to Monitor 'All Communications' at Winter Olympics in Sochi," *Guardian*, October 6, 2013, www.theguardian.com/world/2013/oct/06/russia-monitor-communications-sochi-winter-olympics.

2. David M. Herszenhorn, "Olympics Opening Ceremony Offers Fanfare for a Reinvented Russia," *New York Times*, February 7, 2014, www.nytimes.com/2014

NOTES

/02/08/sports/olympics/russia-opens-sochi-games-with-pageantry-and-pride.html.

3. Viktor Shenderovich, "Putin and a Girl on Skates," archived on his website, www.shender.ru/paper/text/?.file=814.

4. Petr Akopov, "Internirovannie v internete" (Interned in the internet), Vzglyad, March 14, 2014, https://vz.ru/columns/2014/3/14/677143.html.

5. Petr Akopov, "Rossia razvorachivaetsa" (Russia is turning around), Vzglyad, March 28, 2014, https://vz.ru/columns/2014/3/28/679483.html.

CHAPTER 22: UKRAINE

1. Evgeny Krutikov, "Udavi i kroliki" (Boas and rabbits), Vzglyad, March 9, 2014, https://vz.ru/columns/2014/3/9/676104.html.

2. Petr Akopov, "Vozvrashenie" (The return), Vzglyad, March 2, 2014, https://vz.ru/politics/2014/3/2/675068.html.

3. Evgeny Krutikov, "Posledny shans" (The last chance), Vzglyad, July 28, 2014, https://vz.ru/columns/2014/7/28/697354.html.

4. Krutikov, "Posledny shans."

5. Evgeny Krutikov, "Ekzamen dlya diplomatii" (Exam for diplomacy), Vzglyad, July 3, 2014, https://vz.ru/columns/2014/7/3/694007.html.

6. Svetlana Babayeva, "Polet betona" (Flight of concrete), Gazeta.ru, April 29, 2014, www.gazeta.ru/comments/column/babaeva/6012369.shtml.

7. Svetlana Babayeva, "Ni voiti, ni vyti" (No entry, no exit), Gazeta.ru, June 12, 2014, www.gazeta.ru/comments/column/babaeva/6065501.shtml.

8. Interview of Ivanov to Babayeva at Gazeta.ru, October 1, 2013, www.gazeta.ru/politics/2013/09/30_a_5675153.shtml.

9. "Marsh mira v Moskver sobral desyatki tisyach uchastnikov" (March of Peace in Moscow gathered tens of thousands), BBC Russian Service, March 15, 2014, www.bbc.com/russian/international/2014/03/140315_ukraine_moscow_rallies.

10. The page of the TV series is on the Kinopoisk website, www.kinopoisk.ru/series/839215.

11. "V Moskve zarkyvaetsa kafe i teatr Masterskaya" (In Moscow the café and theater Masterskaya is closing down), Moskva24, April 10, 2015, www.m24.ru/articles/eda/10042015/70880.

12. "WikiLeaks: Panama Leak Is Attack on Putin by U.S. and Soros," *Moscow Times*, April 6, 2016, www.themoscowtimes.com/2016/04/06/wikileaks-panama-leak-is-attack-on-putin-by-us-and-soros-a52416; Matthew Rozsa, "WikiLeaks Alleges Someone in the White House Is Leaking Things, and That's Making Them Mad," Salon, January 6, 2017, www.salon.com/2017/01/06/wikileaks-alleges-someone-in-the-white-house-is-leaking-things-and-thats-making-them-mad.

13. Truth and Justice, regional and local media forum, Putin's speech transcript, Kremlin.ru, April 7, 2016, http://en.kremlin.ru/events/president/news/51685.

NOTES

14. A video of the talk appears on the website of the International Journalism Festival at www.journalismfestival.com/programme/2016/from-wikileaks-to-snowden-protecting-high-value-sources-in-the-age-of-mass-surveillance, and also on YouTube at www.youtube.com/watch?v=_MpkOW3FDJU.

15. The documentary is posted on YouTube at www.youtube.com/watch?v=9VQn-uFD4tY.

CHAPTER 23: FAREWELL PARTY

1. David Alandete, "Putin Encourages Independence Movement via Envoy to Catalonia," *El Pais*, October 26, 2017, https://english.elpais.com/elpais/2017/10/26/inenglish/1509011964_600939.html.

2. Isambard Wilkinson, "Russian Spies Visited Catalonia at Height of Independence Bid," *The Times* (London), February 12, 2024, www.thetimes.com/world/russia-ukraine-war/article/russian-spies-visited-catalonia-at-height-of-independence-bid-mkkkhwxsh.

3. Shaun Walker, "Alleged Russian Spies Sentenced to Jail over Montenegro 'Coup Plot,'" *Guardian*, May 9, 2019, www.theguardian.com/world/2019/may/09/montenegro-convicts-pro-russia-politicians-of-coup-plot.

4. Dmitry Shestoperov, "Adres vybil v neizvestnom napravlenii" (Address is gone), *Kommersant*, December 6, 2019, www.kommersant.ru/doc/4181814.

5. Maria Kolomychenko, "Soviet Internet Sovereignty," Meduza, December 31, 2019, https://meduza.io/en/feature/2019/12/31/soviet-internet-sovereignty.

6. US State Department, "2020 Country Reports on Human Rights Practices: Russia," 2020, www.state.gov/reports/2020-country-reports-on-human-rights-practices/russia.

7. Kolomychenko, "Soviet Internet Sovereignty."

8. Agentura's page on Roskomnadzor site, https://rkn.gov.ru/mass-communications/reestr/media/?id=198567.

CHAPTER 24: FOREBODING

1. The films were *Salt* (2010) and *John Wick* (2014).

2. "Putin obyavil ob ispitivaemoi im otoropi pri prosmotre televisora" (Putin said he is shocked when he watches TV), RBC, December 11, 2020, www.rbc.ru/rbcfreenews/5fd394c09a79474c429feafd.

3. Profile of Mikhalkov on Lenta, January 26, 2018, https://lenta.ru/news/2018/01/26/mihalkov.

4. "Minkulturi otozvalo prokatnoe udostovereinie u filma Smert Stalina" (Ministry of Culture cancels *Death of Stalin*), *Novaya Gazeta*, January 23, 2018, https://novayagazeta.ru/articles/2018/01/23/138869-minkultury-otozvalo-prokatnoe-udostoverenie-u-filma-smert-stalina.

5. Ministry of Culture's statement on *Death of Stalin*, TASS, February 7, 2018, https://tass.ru/kultura/4936830.

NOTES

6. Baranov's story about Joe Biden, Channel One, December 20, 2020, www.1tv.ru/news/2020-12-20/398801-mesyats_do_prihoda_v_belyy_dom_dzho_baydena_i_ego_komandy.

7. Baranov on Navalny's poisoning, Channel One, September 6, 2020, www.1tv.ru/news/2020-09-06/392793-istoriya_alekseya_navalnogo_razvivaetsya_po_znakomomu_stsenariyu.

8. Baranov's interview to RIA Novosti, March 24, 2021, https://ria.ru/20210324/yugoslaviya-1602561411.html.

CHAPTER 25: THE WAR

1. Petr Akopov's "Natuplenie Rossii I Novogo mira" (The advent of Russia and the coming of the new world), RIA Novosti, February 26, 2022, archived at https://web.archive.org/web/20220226051154/https://ria.ru/20220226/rossiya-1775162336.html.

2. "Ukraine Invasion: Russian State Media Article Deleted After Suggesting Russia Victory Achieved," Sky News, February 28, 2022, https://news.sky.com/story/ukraine-invasion-russian-state-media-article-deleted-after-suggesting-russia-victory-achieved-12553977; "Ukraine Crisis: Russian News Agency Deletes Victory Editorial," BBC, February 28, 2022, www.bbc.co.uk/news/technology-60562240.

3. Evgeny Krutikov, "Kak budet razbita Ukrainskaya armia" (How the Ukrainian army will be crushed), Vzglyad, March 9, 2022, https://m.vz.ru/society/2022/3/9/1147736.html.

4. Milos Rudovic, "Montenegro Told the EU It Had Frozen Assets of Blacklisted Russians, but It Wasn't True," Radio Liberty, November 11, 2023, www.rferl.org/a/montenegro-sanctions-blacklisted-russians-frozen-assets/32680495.html.

5. As of mid-2024, its membership is still pending.

6. Maja Zivanovic, Sonja Gocanin, Riin Aljas, Mark Krutov, and Sergei Dobrynin, "Exclusive: Expelled Russian Diplomats with Spy Links Resurface in Serbia," Radio Liberty, March 13, 2023, www.rferl.org/a/russia-serbia-home-spies-expelled-diplomats/32310285.html.

7. "Another Russian Tycoon Dies Under Strange Circumstances," Radio Liberty, May 9, 2022, www.rferl.org/a/lukoil-subbotin-dead-oligarchs/31841615.html.

8. Paul Kirby, "Ravil Maganov: Russian Lukoil Chief Dies in 'Fall from Hospital Window,'" BBC, September 1, 2022, www.bbc.co.uk/news/world-europe-62750584.

9. "Chairman of Russia's Oil Major Lukoil Dies Suddenly Aged 66," Reuters, October 24, 2023, www.reuters.com/world/europe/chairman-russias-oil-major-lukoil-dies-suddenly-aged-66-2023-10-24.

10. "Umer Vice-President Lukoil" (Vice president of Lukoil died), RBC, March 13, 2024, www.rbc.ru/business/13/03/2024/65f1c4ca9a79470a924ac61f.

NOTES

11. Rob Davies, "Putin Ally Alekperov Resigns as President of Russia's Lukoil," *Guardian*, April 21, 2022, www.theguardian.com/business/2022/apr/21/alekperov-resigns-president-russia-lukoil-putin-oil-eu-uk-sanctions.

12. "UK Sanctions Russia's Second Richest Man," press release, June 29, 2022, www.gov.uk/government/news/uk-sanctions-russias-second-richest-man.

13. Lyubimova's interview, April 13, 2022, is posted on YouTube at www.youtube.com/watch?v=pgQWRyvMICM.

14. Lyubimova's interview to *Komsomolskaya Pravda*, June 19, 2022, www.kp.ru/daily/70.5/4604897. She made the same points in an interview to Interfax a day before: "How can an artist continue to live in a country where there is no art, where there are no scenes like in Russia, not to mention the fact that there are no fees like here? There will not be such a legendary troupe there, this troupe will not perform in the Baltic country, you will not have such partners on stage." Interfax, www.interfax.ru/interview/846837.

15. Channel One news about Lyubimova and Putin meeting, October 3, 2022, www.1tv.ru/news/2022-10-03/438888-vladimir_putin_provel_rabochuyu_vstrechu_s_ministrom_kultury_rf_olgoy_lyubimovoy.

16. Alexander Lisitsa, "V kinoteatrakh pokazhut dokumentalnoye kino o specoperatsii" (Documentaries on special military operation to show in cinemas), Gazeta.ru, November 16, 2022, www.gazeta.ru/culture/news/2022/11/16/19049965.shtml.

17. Account on Putin's meeting with soldiers' mothers, Kremlin.ru, November 25, 2022, http://kremlin.ru/events/president/news/69935.

18. Legislation, L 322 I, vol. 65, December 16, 2022, *Official Journal of the European Union*, December 16, 2022, https://eur-lex.europa.eu/legal-content/EN/TXT/PDF/?uri=OJ:L:2022:322I:FULL&from=EN. She was placed under US sanctions in February 2023. See Sophia Kishkovsky, "US Imposes Sanctions on Russian Culture Minister," *Art Newspaper*, February 24, 2023, www.theartnewspaper.com/2023/02/24/russia-culture-minister-olga-lyubimova-us-sanctions.

19. Legislation, L 153, vol. 65, June 3, 2022, *Official Journal of the European Union*, June 3, 2022, https://eur-lex.europa.eu/legal-content/EN/TXT/PDF/?uri=OJ:L:2022:153:FULL.

20. Marie Woolf, "New Sanctions Hit Russian TV, Media in Crackdown on Disinformation," *Canada's National Observer*, July 8, 2022, www.nationalobserver.com/2022/07/08/news/new-sanctions-hit-russian-tv-media-crackdown-disinformation.

21. "Medvedev nazval gibel Svetlani Babayevoy nevospolnimoy utratoy dlya zhurnalistiki" (Medvedev called the death of Svetlana Babayeva an irreparable loss for journalism), TASS, October 28, 2022, https://tass.ru/obschestvo/16190875.

22. "Obvinayemoi v gibeli jurnalistki Babayevoy prisnal vinu" (Accused of the death of Babayeva, admitted his guilt), *Vedomosti*, May 15, 2024, www.vedomosti.ru/strana/southern/news/2024/05/15/1037342-obvinyaemii-gibeli-zhurnalistki.

INDEX

Abkhazia, 48, 169, 254
activists, social media and, 213
Administration of the President (AP), 224
Afghanistan, 81, 86
Afisha (magazine), 188, 195
Africa, Soviet Union and, 77–78, 83
Aftergood, Steven, 27
Agentura
   Akopov, Petya, and, 31, 83, 201
   Borogan and, 41, 57–59, 85, 97–98, 138–140, 143, 167–168, 245, 281
   FSB and, 73, 76–138
   genesis of, 25–32
   Izvestia and, 30–31
   Kozlov and, 73, 75, 98
   Krutikov, Evgeny, and, 83
   Latysheva and, 28, 41, 84
   New York Times and, 58, 59
   revocation of media license of, 245
   Russian security services and, 26, 28–32, 40–41, 85, 138
   Soldatov, Alexey, and, 29, 30, 73, 138–139, 155
   Soldatov, Andrei, and, 26–31, 40, 41, 57–59, 73, 85, 97–98, 138–140, 143, 167–168, 245, 281
   Versia and, 84–85
Akopov, Marina, 16
   Akopov, Petya, and, 193, 201, 234
   Baranov, Zhenya, and, 19, 78, 124, 201
   Borogan and, 59–61, 79, 80, 124, 201
   children of, 192, 194, 234
   Gogolevsky Boulevard apartment of, 20–21, 42–43, 59, 117, 124, 131, 193–194, 234, 275, 277
   hardships of, 193–194
   Lyubimova and, 194, 201
   overview, 20–21
   Soldatov, Andrei, and, 59–61, 79, 80, 124, 201
   Somalia and, 78–79
Akopov, Petya, x, 123, 289
   Agentura and, 31, 83, 201
   Akopov, Marina, and, 193, 201, 234
   antisemitism and, 204
   Baranov, Zhenya, and, 19, 78, 88, 89, 106, 194, 201, 241, 242
   Borogan and, 59–62, 79, 80, 121, 201–204, 275–277, 281–284, 287–288
   children of, 192, 194, 234
   Duma club and, 60–62
   Gogolevsky Boulevard apartment of, 20–21, 42–43, 59, 117, 124, 131, 193–194, 234, 275, 277
   hardships of, 192–194
   Izvestia and, 16, 60, 78, 79, 108, 190
   Kremlin and, 192–193, 204
   Krutikov, Evgeny, and, 16, 199
   liberal media and, 282–283
   Lyubimova and, 194, 199, 201, 269
   Medvedev and, 194, 196

INDEX

Akopov, Petya *(continued)*
   Moscow protests and, 197, 199, 204
   on Muscovites' 2011 political
      awakening, 190
   Navalny and, 198–199, 283–284
   parents of, 77, 78
   Pavlova and, 241, 242
   Political Journal and, 121, 141, 192, 201
   politics of, 16–17
   RIA Novosti op-ed on Ukraine war
      by, 258–259, 275
   on Russian breakup with West,
      287–288
   Russian Orthodox Church and,
      129–130
   Russian propaganda and, 269
   sanctions on, 269, 286
   Soldatov, Andrei, and, 59–62, 79, 80,
      121, 201–204, 275–277
   Somalia and, 78–79, 83
   Ukraine-Russia war and, 258–259,
      269, 275, 286
   Vzglyad and, 224
   on Westernization of Russia, 218
Albats, Evgenia, 121
Alekperov, Vagit, 8–9, 266, 267
Alekseenko, Vladimir, 75–76, 82
Alekseev, Sergey, 107
All-Russia Broadcasting Company, 154
Americans, Russians and, 81
Andropov, Yuri, 122
antisemitism, 204, 221
AP. *See* Administration of the President
Arifdjanov, Rustam, 84–85, 98, 99,
   104, 105

Babayeva, Sveta
   Borogan and, 228
   Crimea and, 227–228, 236, 269, 271
   death, 271, 279
   Gazeta and, 227, 228
   Ivanov and, 156–157, 178, 227, 228
   Izvestia and, 38–40, 52, 60, 156,
      227, 271
   Kremlin propaganda and, 269,
      270, 272
   Putin's press pool and, x, 10, 18, 39,
      40, 52, 60, 156, 279
   RIA Novosti and, 157, 158–159, 178,
      180, 226, 228, 236
   Russia Today and, 229
   Soldatov, Andrei, and, 228
   special forces training and, 270
   SVR undercover agents and, 181
   on traditional values, 157–158
   Ukraine-Russia war and, 271, 272
   US diplomats and, 179
Balkan wars, 136, 171
Baranov, Zhenya, 21, 289
   Abkhazia and, 169, 254
   Akopov, Marina, and, 19, 78, 124, 201
   Akopov, Petya, and, 19, 78, 88, 89,
      106, 194, 201, 241, 242
   Belgrade Russian House appointment,
      252, 253–254, 264
   Beslan terrorist incident and,
      109–110, 114–116
   Biden story by, 251–252
   bin Laden documentary by, 191–192
   Borogan, Irina, and, 80, 88, 93,
      124–126, 131, 132, 134–137,
      184–185, 191–192, 201, 277
   Channel One and, 130, 170–171,
      172, 181–183, 195, 222, 234, 241,
      251–252
   Kremlin propaganda and, 116, 136,
      252, 253–254
   Krutikov, Evgeny, and, 19
   Lyubimova and, x, 88–89, 90, 123,
      131–132, 135, 169–170, 184–185,
      191, 201, 234, 240, 241, 251
   Maidan Revolution and, 222–223
   Misha and, 116
   Montenegro coup attempt and, 240, 241
   Moskovia TV channel and, 95, 98
   Navalny poisoning story by, 252
   Order of Courage and, 81
   Pavlova and, 22, 23–24, 123–125,
      153, 176, 191–192, 197, 240, 241,
      242, 254
   Russian military intelligence and,
      240, 241

INDEX

Russian nationalism and, 131
Russian Orthodox Church and, 124–126, 129–131, 135–136
Soldatov, Andrei, and, 88, 93, 109–110, 114–116, 124, 126, 131, 132, 134–137, 184–185, 191–192, 201, 277
Somalia and, 78–79
Svanidze and, 153
Ukraine-Russia war and, 222–223, 274–275, 286
Basayev, Shamil, 96, 97
Beaujolais Nouveau festival, 120
Belgrade, Serbia, 136, 252–253, 263–264
Beria, Lavrenty, 67, 68
Beslan terrorist incident, 108–115, 120–121
Biden, Joe, 251–252
bin Laden, Osama, 191–192
Black Hawk Down (movie), 82–83
Blant, Max, 150
Boender, Ary, 27
Bolsheviks, 17, 77
Borisov family, 119–120
Borogan, Irina, 5, 14, 22
   Agentura and, 41, 57–59, 85, 97–98, 138–140, 143, 167–168, 245, 281
   Akopov, Marina, and, 59–61, 79, 80, 124, 201
   Akopov, Petya, 59–62, 79, 80, 121, 201–204, 275–277, 281–284, 287–288
   Alekseenko and, 76, 82
   Babayeva and, 228
   Baranov, Zhenya, and, 80, 88, 93, 124–126, 131, 132, 134–137, 184–185, 191–192, 201, 277
   The Compatriots, 238–239, 245, 247, 274
   Duma club and, 60–62, 88
   Ej.ru and, 121, 123, 176
   exile from Russia, 246–249, 254, 273–274, 285
   family, 7, 126–127, 143, 257
   FSB and, 101–102, 120, 122, 174–178, 188, 260, 261, 264
   Gogolevsky Boulevard group, Ukraine-Russia war and, 275–278, 286
   Guardian Sochi surveillance story of, 214
   International Journalism Festival and, 233–234
   Izvestia and, 37, 44–48, 52, 83
   Kozlov and, 82–83, 274
   Kremlin and, 246
   lawsuit against, 274
   in London, 248–249, 264, 273–274
   Lyubimova and, 131, 278
   The New Nobility, 177, 178, 188, 203, 211, 265
   Novaya Gazeta and, 133–135, 140–144, 151, 166, 174–176
   Russian censorship of books by, 265
   Russian Interior Ministry charge against, 264
   Russian journalists and, 234
   Soldatov, Alexey, and, 212, 285
   Ukraine-Russia war and, 257, 260, 262, 274–275, 285
   Versia and, 84–85, 87, 91–99, 101–102
   Vzglyad and, 223
Borovik, Artyom, 85–86
Borovik, Genrikh (Artyom's father), 85–86
Borovik-Khilchevskaya, Veronika (Artyom's widow), 86–87, 104–105, 107
Bosnia, 255
Boston Marathon bombing, 214
Britain, Russia and, 145
British spies, 202–203
Browder, Bill, 177
Bulingua (arts club), 140
Burnt by the Sun (movie), 90
Bush, George W., 81
Bykov, Dmitry, 187

Catalonia, 240
censorship, Russian
   by KGB, 209
   by Kremlin, 250

censorship, Russian *(continued)*
    of movies/TV shows by Ministry of
        Culture, 250–251
    of online media, 218, 231, 244
    Putin and, 250, 251
    by Roskomnadzor agency, 244
    of social media, 261
    Ukraine-Russia war and, 261
Central Intelligence Agency (CIA), 68
Channel One (TV channel)
    Baranov, Zhenya, and, 130, 170–171,
        172, 181–183, 195, 222, 234, 241,
        251–252
    "Dreams of Russian" Sochi Olympics
        performance by, 215–216
    Ernst, Konstantin, and, 215
    interview with Medvedev on, 183
    Kremlin propaganda and, 222
    Lyubimova and, 195, 231, 234
    Myths About Russia documentary and,
        234–235
    Navalny poisoning story on, 252
    war with Georgia documentary on,
        170–171, 172
Chapman, Anna, 180–181
Chechen militants, 19, 96–99, 115
Chechnya, 144
    Novaya Gazeta and war with, 168
    war with Russia, 19, 48, 64, 74, 75,
        96–99, 142, 148, 168, 221
Chernomyrdin, Viktor, 96, 97
China, 287
Chinese, 221
the Church. *See* Russian Orthodox
    Church
CIA. *See* Central Intelligence Agency
Citizen Poet (TV show/play), 187–188,
    189–190
A City Girl, 133
CNN, 80–81
Cohen, Kenneth, 69
Cold War, 73
Committee of State Security
    (Komitet Gosudarstvennoy
    Bezopasnosti, KGB)
    Boroviks and, 85

censorship by, 209
Ej.ru and, 121, 123
FSB and, 122, 260
Izvestia and, 53
Komsomolskaya Pravda and, 64
Krutikov, Evgeny, and, 70, 71, 160
Krutikov, Felix (Evgeny's father), and,
    69, 70, 71
1991 putsch of, 29, 53
Putin and, 4, 26, 155–156, 180, 261
real estate of, 87–88
Russian liberal intelligentsia and, 119
Russian Orthodox Church and, 211
Serov and, 67, 68
Soviet Union and, 261
Communist Party, State Duma and, 18
Communist Party of the Soviet
    Union, 68
    Central Committee, 71
    Russian Orthodox Church and,
        128, 129
The Compatriots (Borogan and Soldatov),
    238–239, 245, 247, 274
COVID-19, 245, 246, 248–250
Crimea, 73
    Babayeva and, 227–228, 236, 269, 271
    Russian annexation of, 217–218, 223,
        224, 227, 228, 229

dacha, 5
The Death of Stalin (movie), 250–251
Demidov, Ivan, 192
demonstrations
    Kremlin and, 229
    March of Dissenters, 148–151, 223
    in Moscow, 148–151, 186, 190–191,
        196–200, 204, 229–230, 282
    Moscow police and, 149–151, 282
    Moscow protests (2011), 190–191,
        196–200, 204
    Navalny and, 282
    Putin and, 196–197
    Putin inauguration protest, 205
    Russia and, 147–151
    Russian intelligentsia and, 229, 230
    Russian media and, 147–151

INDEX

Soviet Union and, 146–147
Ukraine and, 229–230
Ukraine-Russia war and, 257–258
Doe, Marc, 202
Donbass, 224, 225
Donetsk, 268, 269
Dozhd (Rain) (TV station), 187
Dubrovka Theater terrorist incident, 92–99, 102–103
Duma club, 60–62, 88, 140

Eastern Ukraine, 225. *See also* Donbass
08.08.08: *The War on Air* (documentary), 170–171, 172
Ej.ru (*Yezhednevny Journal*) (Daily Journal), 117, 120, 231
   Borogan and, 121, 123, 176
   Gusinsky and, 118, 121
   KGB and, 121, 123
   Pavlova and, 123–124, 150, 151, 176, 196, 216, 218, 241–242
   Putin and, 118–119
   Soldatov, Andrei, and, 121, 123, 176
Ekho Moskvy (radio station), 95, 114, 121
Ernst, Konstantin, 215
Europe
   Gogolevsky Boulevard group and, 289
   Institute of Europe, 61
   Russia and, 215, 218, 246, 285–289

FAS. *See* Federation of American Scientists
Federal agency of government communications and information (Federalnoye Agentstvo Pravitelstvennoy Svyazi i Informatsii, FAPSI), 30, 31–32
Federal Security Service (Federalnaya Sluzhba Bezopasnosti, FSB), 4, 31
   Agentura and, 73, 76, 138
   Andropov and, 122
   Beslan terrorist incident and, 110–113, 120
   Borogan and, 101–102, 120, 122, 174–178, 188, 260, 261, 264
   Borovik-Khilchevskaya and, 87
   British spies and, 202
   Center of Public Communications, 32–33
   conspiracy theories and, 107
   Fifth Service department, 260, 261, 264
   independent media and, 254
   Izvestia and, 65, 70, 72, 81
   Kalinkin and, 64, 65, 72
   KGB and, 122, 260
   Khodorkovsky and, 105
   Krutikov, Evgeny, and, 65, 70, 72, 81, 160
   Lefortovo prison and, 99–102
   Litvinenko and, 144–145
   museum of, 76
   The New Nobility on, 177, 178, 188, 203, 211, 265
   Olympic Games security and, 214
   Politkovskaya's murder and, 174–176
   Putin and, 33, 121–122, 260, 261, 264
   Russian newspapers and, 35
   September 11th attack and, 81
   Soldatov, Andrei, and, 32–35, 98–99, 101–103, 120, 174–178, 188, 260, 261, 264
   terrorist incidents and, 96–99
   Versia and, 87–88, 98–104, 107
   West and, 77
Federation of American Scientists (FAS), 26–27, 28, 31
Franchetti, Mark, 94, 95
Freedom Street, 57–59
FSB. *See* Federal Security Service

Gaidar, Maria, 150
Gaidar, Yegor, 148, 150
gays, 194
Gazeta (online media organization), 227, 228
Georgia, 115, 221
   Channel One documentary on war with, 170–171, 172
   Medvedev and, 167
   Putin and war with, 167–168, 172–173

INDEX

Georgia (continued)
  Russian war with, 167–173
  South Ossetia conflicts with, 111, 112, 159, 161, 166–173
  Western media on Russian war with, 170, 171, 172
Germany/Germans, 127–128, 274
Gogol, Nikolai, 15
Gogolevsky Boulevard, 15
  Akopov's apartment on, 20–21, 42–43, 59, 117, 124, 131, 193–194, 234, 275, 277
Gogolevsky Boulevard group, 15–24, 41
  Europe and, 289
  Ukraine-Russia war and, 275–280, 284, 286, 289
Golden Mile, 89
Gorbachev, Mikhail, 86, 134, 147, 194
  pro-democracy perestroika of, 23, 108, 146, 190
Great Patriotic War (World War II), 76, 89, 127, 128, 230. See also World War II
Grozny, Chechnya, 74
GRU (military intelligence), 4
Gryzlov, Boris, 149
Guardian, 94, 214, 233
Gulag, 68
Gusinsky, Vladimir, 4, 12–14, 18, 118, 121

Harrison, Sarah, 233
Herzen, Alexander, 247
Hezbollah, 134, 137

independent media. *See also specific independent media outlets*
  FSB attack on, 254
  Kremlin attack against, 254–255
  online, 25, 231
  Roskomnadzor banning of, 261
Institute of Europe, 61
Institute of Foreign Trade, 66
International Journalism Festival (Perugia), 233–234
internet, Russia's, 242–244, 285. *See also* online Russian media

Investigative Committee, 212
Israel, 134–137
Ivanov, Sergei, 155–158, 178, 227–229
Izvestia (The News), x, 3–4
  Agentura and, 30–31
  Akopov, Petya, and, 16, 60, 78, 79, 108, 190
  Babayeva and, 38–40, 52, 60, 156, 227, 271
  Borogan and, 37, 44–48, 52, 83
  FSB and, 65, 70, 72, 81
  Kalinkin story in, 63–65, 72
  KGB and, 53
  Kovalchuk and, 194–195
  Krutikov, Evgeny, as columnist of, 58–59, 64–65, 70, 81, 83
  Krutikov, Evgeny, as political department head of, 5–6, 8, 10–14, 16, 31, 32, 36, 38, 40, 46–52, 58–59, 71, 278
  Kursk and, 39–40
  leadership of, 46–48, 51–52
  Lebedev and, 52–53
  MSU investigation, 44–47
  Muscovites' 2011 political awakening and, 188–190
  NTV and, 13, 14
  owners of, 8–9
  political department, 5, 6, 9, 36, 48, 51–52
  Putin and, 18, 39–40
  resignations from, 52, 57
  Russian security services and, 53
  September 11th attack and, 81
  Soldatov, Andrei, and, 32–35, 49, 51, 278
  Stalin and, 11, 12
  terrorist incidents and, 36–38, 48–50

Jean-Jacques (restaurant), 130, 151, 166, 184, 232
  backing and launch of, 119–120
  clientele, 120, 123–124, 140, 153, 191–192, 201, 205
  Putin inauguration police attack on, 206

310

INDEX

Kabardino-Balkaria, 141
Kachalov, Vasily, 88, 131
Kachmazov, Alan, 10, 59
Kadyrov, Ramzan, 144
Kalinkin, Vasily, 63–65, 72
Kasparov, Garry, 150
Kasyanov, Mikhail, 150
KGB. *See* Committee of State Security
Khodorkovsky, Mikhail, 32, 105–106, 108
Khrushchev, Nikita, 8, 68
King, Larry, 42–43
Kirill, 167–168
Kommersant (The Businessman), 23, 242
Komsomolskaya Pravda (tabloid), 63, 64
Kostina, Olga, 32, 35, 61, 105, 116
Kovalchuk, Yuri, 194–195
Kozhokin, Mikhail, 11–12, 18, 271
Kozlov, Sergei, 74
   Agentura and, 73, 75, 98
   Borogan and, 82–83, 274
   Soldatov, Andrei, and, 82–83, 274
Kremlin, 117
   Akopov, Petya, and, 192–193, 204
   assassinations of opponents of, 177
   attack on independent media by, 254–255
   Borogan and, 246
   censorship by, 250
   demonstrations and, 229
   infighting in 1954 Soviet Union, 68–70
   liberal journalists and, 280
   Moscow protests and, 196–197
   NTV and, 12–14, 25
   Olympic Games and surveillance by, 213
   Rossotrudnichestvo, 252, 253
   Russian journalists and, 228
   Russian media and, 95, 195, 254
   Russian Orthodox Church and, 127
   Russia's internet and, 242, 243
   Shpioni (The Spies) and, 202, 203
   signal sending of, 246
   social media and, 213
   Soldatov, Alexey, and, 242–243, 285
   Soldatov, Andrei, and, 246
   Ukraine-Russia war and, 259, 260, 275
Kremlin propaganda
   Babayeva and, 269, 270, 272
   Baranov, Zhenya, and, 116, 136, 252, 253–254
   Channel One and, 222
   Chechen war and, 75
   NTV and, 13
   Ukraine and, 222, 229
   Ukraine-Russia war and, 259, 260, 275
   West and, 229
   about World War II, 231
Kremlin secret police. *See* Federal Security Service
Krutikov, Alexei D. (Evgeny's grandfather), 65–68
Krutikov, Evgeny, 123
   Agentura and, 83
   Akopov, Petya, and, 16, 199
   Baranov, Zhenya, and, 19
   Beslan terrorist incident and, 111–113
   Donbass and, 225
   family of, 7, 65–70
   FSB and, 65, 70, 72, 81, 160
   as *Izvestia* columnist, 58–59, 64–65, 70, 81, 83
   as *Izvestia* political department head, 5–6, 8, 10–14, 16, 31, 32, 36, 38, 40, 46–52, 58–59, 71, 278
   KGB and, 70, 71, 160
   Krutikov, Felix (Evgeny's father), and, 7, 65–71
   Medoyev and, 10, 160–161, 167, 240
   Putin's press pool and, 65
   on Russian breakup with West, 288–289
   Russian journalists and, 279–280
   Russian military intelligence and, x, 7, 71, 160
   September 11th attack and, 81
   Soldatov, Andrei, and, 65, 70, 111, 116, 225, 278–280, 288
   South Ossetia and, 111–112, 116, 159, 160, 161, 167, 169

INDEX

Krutikov, Evgeny *(continued)*
  on Soviet Union, 226
  spy thriller fiction of, 159–160
  Telegram channel of, 259
  Ukraine-Russia war and, 224–226, 259, 280, 286
  Versia and, 87, 97–99, 108
  Vzglyad and, 224, 225, 259
Kudrin, Alexey, 198
Kukly (puppet show), 13, 216
Kurchatov Institute, 29, 30, 139
Kursk (submarine), 38–40, 42–43

Latysheva, Marina, 28, 41, 84, 92, 212
Lebanon, 134
Lebedev, Alexander, 133–134, 198
Lebedev, Andrei, 52–53
Lefortovo Palace, 211
Lefortovo prison, 99–102, 212
Lenin, Vladimir, 247
Limonka (newspaper), 17
Limonov, Eduard, 17, 100
Lipov, Andrei, 243, 244
Litvinenko, Alexander, 144–145
LiveJournal (social networking site), 135, 183–185, 190, 251
London
  Borogan and Soldatov, Andrei, in, 248–249, 264, 273–274
  police counterterrorism branch, 273–274
Lubyanka prison, 67
Luhansk, 268, 269
Lukoil (Russian oil company), 265
Lyubimova, Olga
  Akopov, Marina, and, 194, 201
  Akopov, Petya, 194, 199, 201, 269
  on antiwar Russian artists, 267–268, 303n14
  Baranov, Zhenya, and, x, 88–89, 90, 123, 131–132, 135, 169–170, 184–185, 191, 201, 234, 240, 241, 251
  Borogan and, 131, 278
  Channel One and, 195, 231, 234
  as documentarian, 231, 234, 235

EU sanctions against, 269, 286
family and early life, 88, 131–132
LiveJournal and, 183–185, 251
Medinsky and, 231, 235
Mikhalkov, Nikita, and, x, 106, 132, 216, 250, 251
as minister of culture, 237, 250–251, 267–269, 278
Ministry of Culture and, 231, 234, 235, 237, 250–251, 267–269, 278
on Muscovites' 2011 political awakening, 190–191
Orthodox news agency and, 132–133
Putin and, 268
social media and, 183–185, 251
Ukraine-Russia war and, 268, 269, 286
urinal post about Medvedev's Ostankino visit by, 183–185, 251
World War II documentary series and, 231

MacAskill, Ewen, 233–234
MacFarquhar, Neil, 239
Magnitsky, Sergei, 177
Maidan Revolution (2013-2014), 217, 222–223
Malaysia Airlines Flight MH17, 225
Manezhnaya Square, 167–168
March of Dissenters, 148–151, 223
Marines, US, 75
Masterskaya (club/theater), 188, 189, 200–201, 231
Medinsky, Vladimir, 231, 235
Medoyev, Dmitry
  Krutikov, Evgeny, and, 10, 160–161, 167, 240
  as prime minister, 195, 196
  South Ossetia and, 10, 160–161, 166, 167, 169, 240
Meduza (news website), 243
Medvedev (Svanidze), 153, 168–169
Medvedev, Dmitry, 271
  Akopov, Petya, and, 194, 196
  assassinations of Kremlin opponents and, 177

Channel One interview with, 183
Citizen Poet parody of, 187–188
Georgia and, 167
Lyubimova's urinal post about Ostankino visit of, 183–185, 251
Novaya Gazeta and, 176
Obama and, 178, 179
Putin and, 152–154, 159, 167, 180, 195, 196
Russian 2012 presidential election and, 189, 195
as Russian president, 152–155, 158, 159
South Ossetia and, 169
Svanidze and, 152–154, 168–169
Melton, Keith, 76
Mikhalkov, Nikita, 89
Lyubimova and, x, 106, 132, 216, 250, 251
Putin and, 90, 251
Mikhalkov, Sergey, 89
Mikhalkov clan, 89, 90
Mikoyan, Anastas I., 65–68
Ministry of Culture
censorship of movies/TV shows by, 250–251
Lyubimova and, 231, 234, 235, 237, 250–251, 267–269, 278
Myths About Russia documentary and, 234–235
Misha (documentary), 115–116
Mogadishu, Somalia, 77, 78, 79, 82–83
Montenegro, 136, 240–241, 261, 263
Moscow, 3, 84, 117, 286
demonstrations in, 148–151, 186, 190–191, 196–200, 204, 229–230, 282
opportunities in 1990s in, 248–249
prosperity of mid-2000s, 165–166
Russian liberals and, 231
Western embassy parties, 228
Moscow clubs, 231–232. *See also specific Moscow clubs*
Moscow News, 108–115, 120
Moscow police
demonstrations and, 149–151, 282

March of Dissenters and, 149–151
Putin inauguration and, 206
Moscow protests (2011), 190–191, 196–200, 204
Moscow State University (MSU)
Izvestia investigation into, 44–47
journalism department, 22, 23
Soldatov, Alexey, and, 185, 212–213
Moskovia (TV channel), 95, 98
MSU. *See* Moscow State University
Muscovites (Moscow residents)
Moscow protests and, 190–191, 196–200, 204
political awakening and demonstrating in 2011, 188–191, 199
prosperity in 2000s of, 165–166
Putin and, 167, 189
Myths About Russia (documentary), 234–235

Nalchik, 141–142, 159
National Bolshevik Party, 17
NATO. *See* North Atlantic Treaty Organization
Navalny, Alexei, 168, 190, 197, 200, 218
Akopov, Petya, and, 198–199, 283–284
death of, 281, 283
demonstrations and, 282
poisoning of, 252, 284
Soldatov, Andrei, and, 278
Nazis, Ukrainian, 230
Nemetskaya Sloboda (German Quarters), 211
Nemtsov, Boris, 197, 205–206, 229–230
The New Nobility (Borogan and Soldatov), 177, 178, 188, 203, 211, 265
New York Times, 58, 59, 67, 86, 239
NGOs. *See* nongovernmental organizations
Nikitsky Boulevard, 117
Nikolina Gora, 89
nongovernmental organizations (NGOs), 202

INDEX

Nord-Ost (play), 92, 93, 99, 102
North Atlantic Treaty Organization (NATO), 171, 241, 252–253
North Caucasus, 141–142, 159, 214, 221
North Ossetia, Russia, 111
Novaya Gazeta (New Newspaper), 23
  Borogan and, 133–135, 140–144, 151, 166, 174–176
  Medvedev and, 176
  Nalchik terrorist attack and, 141–142
  Politkovskaya and, 111, 142–144, 174–176
  Russian security services and, 141, 175
  Soldatov, Andrei, and, 133–135, 140–144, 151, 154, 174–176, 233
  war with Chechnya and, 168
Novy Arbat (street), 117, 204–205
NTV, 115–116
  Izvestia and, 13, 14
  Kremlin and, 12–14, 25

Obama, Barack, 178, 179
Old Believers, 126
Olympic Games (Nazi Germany, 1936), 217
Olympic Games (Sochi, 2014), 213–217
online Russian media, 139–140. *See also specific online Russian media outlets*
  censorship of, 218, 231, 244
  independent, 25, 231
  Russian exiled journalists and, 262
Orthodox (TV show), 132
Orthodox Church. *See* Russian Orthodox Church
Ostankino, Russia, 183–185
Ozernoy, Ilana, 177

Palestinians, 135, 137
Panama Papers, 232–234
Pan-Slavism, 171
Papernys family, 119, 188, 231
Patriarch of Moscow, 127
Patrushev, Nikolai, 87
Pavlova, Anna (pseudonym)
  Akopov, Petya, and, 241, 242
  Baranov, Zhenya, and, 22, 23–24, 123–125, 153, 176, 191–192, 197, 240, 241, 242, 254
  Ej.ru and, 123–124, 150, 151, 176, 196, 216, 218, 241–242
  Moscow protests and, 196, 197
  Svanidze and, 152, 153
perestroika (reform program of 1980s), 23, 44, 108, 118, 129, 146, 190
Political Journal, 121, 141, 192, 201
Politizdat (Soviet publisher), 124–125, 154
Politkovskaya, Anna, 95
  murder of, 143–144, 148, 160, 174–176
  Novaya Gazeta and, 111, 142–144, 174–176
Potanin, Vladimir, 9, 267
Powell, Jonathan, 203
Pravda (Truth), 22
Primakov, Evgeny, Jr., 252–253
Project on Government Secrecy website, Federation of American Scientists, 26–27, 28, 31
Prokhorov, Mikhail, 198
Pushkin, Alexander, 3, 149, 222
Pushkin Square, 194, 195
  March of Dissenters demonstration in, 149–151, 223
  terrorist attack, 37–38
Putin, Vladimir, 89, 272
  approval ratings, 173
  authoritarianism and, 141
  Beslan terrorist incident and, 114–115
  censorship and, 250, 251
  Citizen Poet parody of, 187–188
  Ej.ru and, 118–119
  FSB and, 33, 121–122, 260, 261, 264
  inauguration of, 205–206
  Ivanov and, 155–156, 158, 227, 228–229
  Izvestia and, 18, 39–40
  KGB and, 4, 26, 155–156, 180, 261
  King and, 42–43
  Kursk and, 39–40, 42–43
  Lyubimova and, 268

314

INDEX

Medvedev and, 152–154, 159, 167, 180, 195, 196
Mikhalkov, Nikita, and, 90, 251
Moscow protests and, 196–197, 198, 204
Muscovites and, 167, 189
Navalny and, 281, 283
Olympic Games and, 213, 215–217
Ostankino visit of, 183
Panama Papers and, 232, 233
Politkovskaya's murder and, 144
as prime minister, 154, 155
Russian 2012 presidential election and, 189, 195, 196, 199–201, 204
Russian annexation of Crimea and, 217–218, 224, 229
Russian constitution and, 236–237
Russian journalists and, 144, 279, 280
Russian liberals and, 118–119, 280
Russian media and, 118, 121
Russian NGOs and, 202
Russian wars and, 173
secret police of, 212
September 11th attack and, 81
Soviet Union and, 216, 261
SVR and, 180
terrorism and, 37–38, 96, 97, 114, 168
traditional values of, 157
Ukraine and, 229
Ukraine-Russia war and, 257, 259, 268, 286
US visit of, 41–43
war with Chechnya and, 168
war with Georgia and, 167–168, 172–173
West and, 172–173
World War II and, 230
Yeltsin and, 25, 38, 96, 153
"Putin and a Girl on Skates" (Shenderovich), 217
Putin's press pool
Babayeva in, x, 10, 18, 39, 40, 52, 60, 156, 279
Krutikov, Evgeny, in, 65

al-Qaddafi, Muammar, 197
al-Qaeda, 81

Red Star (Russian army newspaper), 157
RELCOM, 29–30
religion, in Russia, 126–129. *See also* Russian Orthodox Church
restaurants, Russian, 119
RIA Novosti (government news agency), 227, 253
    Akopov, Petya, op-ed on Ukraine war, 258–259, 275
    Babayeva and, 157, 158–159, 178, 180, 226, 228, 236
Roldugin, Sergei, 232
Roskomnadzor (government media agency), 244, 245, 246, 254, 256, 261
Rossotrudnichestvo (Kremlin agency), 252, 253
Rublyovka, 79–80, 89, 90, 117
Russia. *See also specific topics*
    Britain and, 145
    constitution, 236–237
    demonstrations and, 147–151
    isolation from West of, ix–x, 215, 286–289
    signal sending of bureaucracy of, 245–246
    Somalia and, 79
    in 2000s, xi
    US and, 41–43, 81, 285, 286
Russia Today (media agency), 229, 269
Russian artists, antiwar, 267–268, 303n14
Russian elites, 25, 77, 80, 90
Russian emigrants, 238–239, 252
Russian exiled journalists
    Borogan and Soldatov, Andrei, as, 246–249, 254, 273–274, 285
    Montenegro meetings of, 261, 263
    online Russian media and, 262
    Russian spies and, 273–274
    Russians trusting, 262
    Sarajevo meeting of, 255–256
    Ukraine-Russia war and, 262
Russian House (Belgrade), 252, 253–254, 264

INDEX

Russian intelligentsia
  demonstrations and, 229, 230
  liberal, 119, 120, 145, 231
  Ukraine and, 229, 230
Russian Interior Ministry, 262–263, 264
Russian journalists, 22. *See also specific Russian journalists*
  Borogan and, 234
  exodus from Russia by, 254–255
  Kremlin and, 228
  Krutikov, Evgeny, and, 279–280
  liberal, 140–141, 147, 279–280
  Panama Papers and, 232–234
  Putin and, 144, 279, 280
  Soldatov and, 234
Russian liberals
  attacks on, 280
  intelligentsia, 119, 120, 145, 231
  journalist, 140–141, 147, 279–280
  liberal media, 282–283
  Moscow and, 231
  Putin and, 118–119, 280
Russian media. *See also online Russian media*
  demonstrations and, 147–151
  Dubrovka Theater terrorist incident and, 93–99, 102–103
  Kovalchuk and, 194–195
  Kremlin and, 95, 195, 254
  liberal, 282–283
  Medoyev and, 161
  Putin and, 118, 121
  Roskomnadzor, 244, 245, 246, 254, 256, 261
Russian military, Eastern Ukraine and, 225
Russian military intelligence, 4
  Baranov, Zhenya, and, 240, 241
  Krutikov, Evgeny, and, x, 7, 71, 160
Russian Ministry of Justice, 265
Russian nationalism, 131
Russian newspapers. *See also specific Russian Newspapers*
  FSB and, 35
  Russian security services and, 28
Russian NGOs, 202

Russian oil company deaths, 265–266
Russian oligarchs, sanctions on, 266, 267
Russian Orthodox Church (Orthodox Church, the Church), 60, 211
  Akopov, Petya, and, 129–130
  Baranov, Zhenya, and, 124–126, 129–131, 135–136
  Communists and, 128, 129
  Lyubimova and, 132–133
  news agency of, 132–133
  Russia and, 127–130
  Stalin and, 127, 128
Russian parliament, 105, 118
Russian presidential election (2012), 188, 195, 196, 199–201, 204
Russian propaganda. *See also Kremlin propaganda*
  Akopov, Petya, and, 269
  about Ukraine-Russia war, 230–231, 236, 259, 260, 268, 275
Russian security services, 4, 74. *See also Federal Security Service; specific security services*
  Agentura and, 26, 28–31, 40–41, 85, 138
  Beslan terrorist incident and, 110–113, 120
  conspiracy theories and, 107
  infighting after Stalin's death, 66–67
  Izvestia and, 53
  Litvinenko on, 144–145
  Novaya Gazeta and, 141, 175
  real estate and, 87–88
  Russian newspapers and, 28
  terrorist incidents and, 96–103
  Versia and, 107
Russian spies, 263–264, 273–274
Russian television, 133, 153–154. *See also specific Russian TV channels*
The Russian View (TV show), 133
Russian wars, 170, 171, 172, 173. *See also specific Russian war topics*
Russians
  Americans and, 81
  trust in Russian exiled journalists by, 262

INDEX

Ukraine-Russia war and, 257
Ukrainians and xenophobic, 221–222, 225–226
Russian-Turkish war, 171

Saakashvili, Mikheil, 115–116, 171
Sakharov, Andrei, 197
Sakharov Prospekt, 197, 199
sanctions on Russia/Russians, 232
    on Akopov, Petya, 269, 286
    on Lyubimova, 269, 286
    on Russian oligarchs, 266, 267
    Ukraine-Russia war and, 266, 267, 269
    by West, 217
Sarajevo, Bosnia, 255
Schwartz, Harry, 67
scientific atheism, 124–125
Secret Intelligence Service (SIS), 69
secret police
    of Bolsheviks, 77
    of Putin, 212
    of Stalin, 66, 68, 70, 76
Segodnya (Today), 4, 5, 12, 13, 22, 123, 280
Semyonov, Yulian, 85, 86
September 11th attack, 80–81
Serbia, 136, 170, 223, 241, 263–264
    NATO and, 171, 252–253
Sergey of Radonezh, 128
Serov, Ivan, 66, 67, 68
Seventeen Moments of Spring (TV series), 85
Shchekochikhin, Yuri, 22–23, 105, 133, 145
Shenderovich, Viktor, 13, 216–217
Shevkunov, Tikhon, 60, 130
Shpioni (The Spies) (documentary), 202–203
Simferopol, Crimea, 236
Simonov, Konstantin, 127–128
SIS. *See* Secret Intelligence Service
Slav people, 171
Snowden, Edward, 214, 233
Sochi hotel terrorist incident, 48–50
Sochi Olympic Games (2014), 213–217

social media. *See also specific social media websites*
    activists, journalists, opposition and, 213
    Kremlin and, 213
    Lyubimova and, 183–185, 251
    Russian censorship of, 261
Soldatov, Alexey (Andrei's father)
    Agentura and, 29, 30, 73, 138–139, 155
    arrest of, 243–245
    Borogan and, 212, 285
    as deputy minister of communications, 154–155, 178, 185
    Kommersant accusation against, 242
    Kremlin and, 242–243, 285
    MSU and, 185, 212–213
    Russia's internet and, 242–244, 285
    Soldatov, Andrei, and, 29, 30, 73, 138–139, 154–155, 178, 185, 207, 212–213, 242–244, 285
    trial and imprisonment of, 285
Soldatov, Andrei, 5, 8
    Agentura and, 26–31, 40, 41, 57–59, 73, 85, 97–98, 138–140, 143, 167–168, 245, 281
    Akopov, Marina, and, 59–61, 79, 80, 124, 201
    Akopov, Petya, and, 59–62, 79, 80, 121, 201–204, 275–277
    Alekseenko and, 76, 82
    Babayeva and, 228
    Baranov, Zhenya, and, 88, 93, 109–110, 114–116, 124, 126, 131, 132, 134–137, 184–185, 191–192, 201, 277
    Beslan terrorist incident and, 109–115, 121
    book collection of, 208, 210–211, 265
    The Compatriots, 238–239, 245, 247, 274
    Duma club and, 60–62, 88
    Ej.ru and, 121, 123, 176
    Ekho Moskvy and, 121
    exile from Russia, 246–249, 254, 273–274, 285

317

INDEX

Soldatov, Andrei *(continued)*
  family, 257
  foreign agent designation, 265
  Freedom Street apartment of, 57–59
  FSB and, 32–35, 98–99, 101–103, 120, 174–178, 188, 260, 261, 264
  Gogolevsky Boulevard group, Ukraine-Russia war and, 275–280, 286
  Guardian Sochi surveillance story of, 214
  International Journalism Festival and, 233–234
  Izvestia and, 32–35, 49, 51, 83, 278
  Kozlov and, 82–83, 274
  Kremlin and, 246
  Krutikov, Evgeny, and, 65, 70, 111, 116, 225, 278–280, 288
  lawsuit against, 274
  in London, 248–249, 264, 273–274
  Moscow News and, 108–115, 120
  mother of, 128–129, 177
  Navalny and, 278
  new Moscow apartment and neighborhood of, 207–211
  The New Nobility, 177, 178, 188, 203, 211, 265
  Novaya Gazeta and, 133–135, 140–144, 151, 154, 174–176, 233
  Russian censorship of books by, 265
  Russian Interior Ministry charge against, 262–263, 264
  Russian journalists and, 234
  Soldatov, Alexey, and, 29, 30, 73, 138–139, 154–155, 178, 185, 207, 212–213, 242–244, 285
  Ukraine-Russia war and, 257–258, 260, 262, 274–275, 285
  Versia and, 84–85, 87, 91–99, 101–104, 107
  Vzglyad and, 223
Soldier of Fortune (magazine), 74–75
Solzhenitsyn, Alexander, 85, 120
Somalia, 77–79, 82–83

Soros, George, 115
South Ossetia
  foreign intelligence agency, 111–112, 116
  Georgia conflicts with, 111, 112, 159, 161, 166–173
  Krutikov, Evgeny, and, 111–112, 116, 159, 160, 161, 167, 169
  Medoyev and, 10, 160–161, 166, 167, 169, 240
  Medvedev and, 169
Sovershenno Sekretno (Top Secret, media holding company), 85, 86, 104, 116
Soviet Union. *See also specific topics*
  Afghanistan and, 86
  Africa, 77–78, 83
  army of, 63
  collapse of, 22, 71, 74, 77, 86, 129, 168, 216
  demonstrations and, 146–147
  elites of, 7, 8, 22, 68, 70, 71
  as isolated country, 77, 287
  KGB and, 261
  Kremlin infighting in 1954, 68–70
  Krutikov, Evgeny, on, 226
  Putin and, 216, 261
  Russian liberal intelligentsia and, 119, 120
  secularism and, 126
  Somalia and, 77, 78
  World War II and, ix, 115, 127–128, 230
spetsnaz (special forces), 73, 75
  Babayeva's training for, 270
  Dubrovka Theater terrorist incident and, 95–98
  March of Dissenters and, 149, 150
Spooks (amateur radio group), 27–28
Spy Game (movie), 81–82
Stalin, Joseph, 65, 67, 115, 226
  death of, 66, 68, 69, 70, 89, 250–251
  Izvestia and, 11, 12
  Russian Orthodox Church and, 127, 128
  secret police of, 66, 68, 70, 76

318

INDEX

World War II and, 115, 127–128, 231
Yefimov and, 11, 12
Stanislavski, Konstantin, 88
State Duma, 17–18, 61, 118
Sunday Times (newspaper), 94
surveillance, mass, 213, 214
Sutyagin, Igor, 181, 182
Svanidze, Nikolai, 152–154, 168–169
SVR (foreign intelligence agency), 4, 53
    Komsomolskaya Pravda and, 64
    Sovershenno Sekretno and, 116
    US and undercover agents of, 179–183

TASS (state news agency), 250
Telegram (social media website), 259, 276–278, 281
terrorism
    Boston Marathon bombing, 214
    September 11th attack, 80–81
terrorism, in Russia
    Beslan hostage incident, 108–115
    Chechen militants and, 96–99
    Dubrovka Theater terrorist incident, 92–99, 102–103
    FSB and, 96–99
    Izvestia and, 36–38, 48–50
    Nalchik attack, 141–142
    Pushkin Square, 37–38
    Putin and, 37–38, 96, 97, 114, 168
    Russian security services and, 96–103
    Sochi hotel, 48–50
    US and, 64
de Thou, Jacques-Auguste, 208
Tokhtakhunov, Alimzhan (Taiwanchik), 90–91
Tolstoy, Leo, 130
Tolstoy, Petr, 130
Tretyakov, Sergey, 182
Turkey, 171

Ukraine, 74
    elites, 260–261
    Kremlin propaganda and, 222, 229
    Moscow demonstrations and, 229–230
    Russian intelligentsia and, 229, 230

Ukraine-Russia war, ix. *See also* Donbass; Eastern Ukraine
    Akopov, Petya, and, 258–259, 269, 275, 286
    Babayeva and, 271, 272
    Baranov, Zhenya, and, 222–223, 274–275, 286
    Borogan and, 257, 260, 262, 274–275, 285
    changes to Russian society by, 286–287
    demonstrations and, 257–258
    Donbass separatists and, 224
    Gogolevsky Boulevard group and, 275–280, 284, 286, 289
    Kremlin and, 259, 260, 275
    Krutikov, Evgeny, and, 224–226, 259, 280, 286
    Lyubimova and, 268, 269, 286
    Maidan Revolution, 217, 222–223
    Putin and, 257, 259, 268, 286
    Russian artists against, 267–268, 303n14
    Russian censorship and, 261
    Russian exiled journalists and, 262
    Russian oil/gas funds for, 265–266
    Russian propaganda about, 230–231, 236, 259, 260, 268, 275
    Russians and, 257
    sanctions on Russia/Russians and, 266, 267, 269
    Soldatov, Andrei, and, 257–258, 260, 262, 274–275, 285
Ukrainians, 221–222, 225–226, 230
Union of Journalists, 118
United Russia party, 149, 158
United States (US)
    Babayeva and diplomats of, 179
    mass surveillance by, 214
    Olympic Games security and, 214
    Panama Papers and, 232–233
    Putin visit to, 41–43
    Russia and, 41–43, 81, 285, 286
    Somalia and, 82–83
    spy swap with Russia, 181–183
    SVR undercover agents in, 179–183
    terrorism in Russia and, 64

INDEX

Venediktov, Alexey, 121
Versia (newspaper), 86, 106, 116
   Borogan, Irina, and, 84–85, 87, 91–99, 101–102
   Dubrovka Theater terrorist incident and, 92–99, 102–103
   FSB and, 87–88, 98–104, 107
   Krutikov, Evgeny, and, 87, 97–99, 108
   Russian security services and, 107
   Soldatov, Andrei, and, 84–85, 87, 91–99, 101–104, 107
Volodin, Vyacheslav, 227
Voskresnoye Vremya (Times on Sunday) (TV show), 130
Vyshinsky, Andrei, 69
Vzglyad (View) (news website), 148–149, 223–225, 259

Walsh, Nick Paton, 94
The War and the Myths (documentary series), 231
West
   Kremlin propaganda and, 229
   Moscow-based embassy parties of, 228
   Putin and, 172–173
   Russia's isolation from, ix–x, 215, 286–289
   sanctions on Russia by, 217
   spy agencies of, 76–77
Western media, on Russian wars, 170, 171, 172
Westernization, of Russia, 218
WikiLeaks, 232–233
World War II, 69
   as Great Patriotic War, 76, 89, 127, 128, 230
   Kremlin propaganda about, 231
   Soviet Union and, ix, 115, 127–128, 230
   Stalin and, 115, 127–128, 231
   Ukraine and, 230

Yefimov, Boris, 10–12
Yefremov, Mikhail, 187
Yeltsin, Boris, 22, 74, 97, 147, 148, 168
   Putin and, 25, 38, 96, 153
   Russian Orthodox Church and, 129
Yesenin, Sergei, 131
Yezhednevny Journal (Daily Journal), 117. *See also* Ej.ru
Yugoslav wars, 136, 171, 253
Yumashev, Valentin, 22
Yushenkov, Sergei, 105

Zagoryanka, 5
Zakharov, Viktor, 33–34

Courtesy of the author

Andrei Soldatov is an investigative journalist and cofounder and editor of Agentura.ru, a watchdog of the Russian secret services' activities. He has been covering security services and terrorism issues since 1999, and his work has been featured in the *New York Times*, the *Moscow Times*, the *Washington Post*, *Le Monde*, the *Christian Science Monitor*, Online Journalism Review, CNN, and the BBC. He is coauthor with Irina Borogan of *The New Nobility: The Restoration of Russia's Security State and the Enduring Legacy of the KGB* (2010), *The Red Web: The Struggle Between Russia's Digital Dictators and the New Online Revolutionaries* (2015), and *The Compatriots: The Brutal and Chaotic History of Russia's Exiles, Émigrés, and Agents Abroad* (2019), all published by PublicAffairs. He lives in London.

Courtesy of the author

Irina Borogan is an investigative journalist and cofounder and deputy editor of Agentura.ru, a watchdog of the Russian secret services' activities. She has reported on the NATO bombing in Yugoslavia and tensions in the West Bank and Gaza Strip, among other topics, and has extensively chronicled the Kremlin's campaign to gain greater control of civil society. She is coauthor with Andrei Soldatov of *The New Nobility: The Restoration of Russia's Security State and the Enduring Legacy of the KGB* (2010), *The Red Web: The Struggle Between Russia's Digital Dictators and the New Online Revolutionaries* (2015), and *The Compatriots: The Brutal and Chaotic History of Russia's Exiles, Émigrés, and Agents Abroad* (2019), all published by PublicAffairs. Her reporting has also been featured in the *New York Times*, the *Moscow Times*, the *Washington Post, Le Monde*, the *Christian Science Monitor*, Online Journalism Review, CNN, and the BBC. She lives in London.